IMAGES
of America

Albuquerque's Parks and Open Space

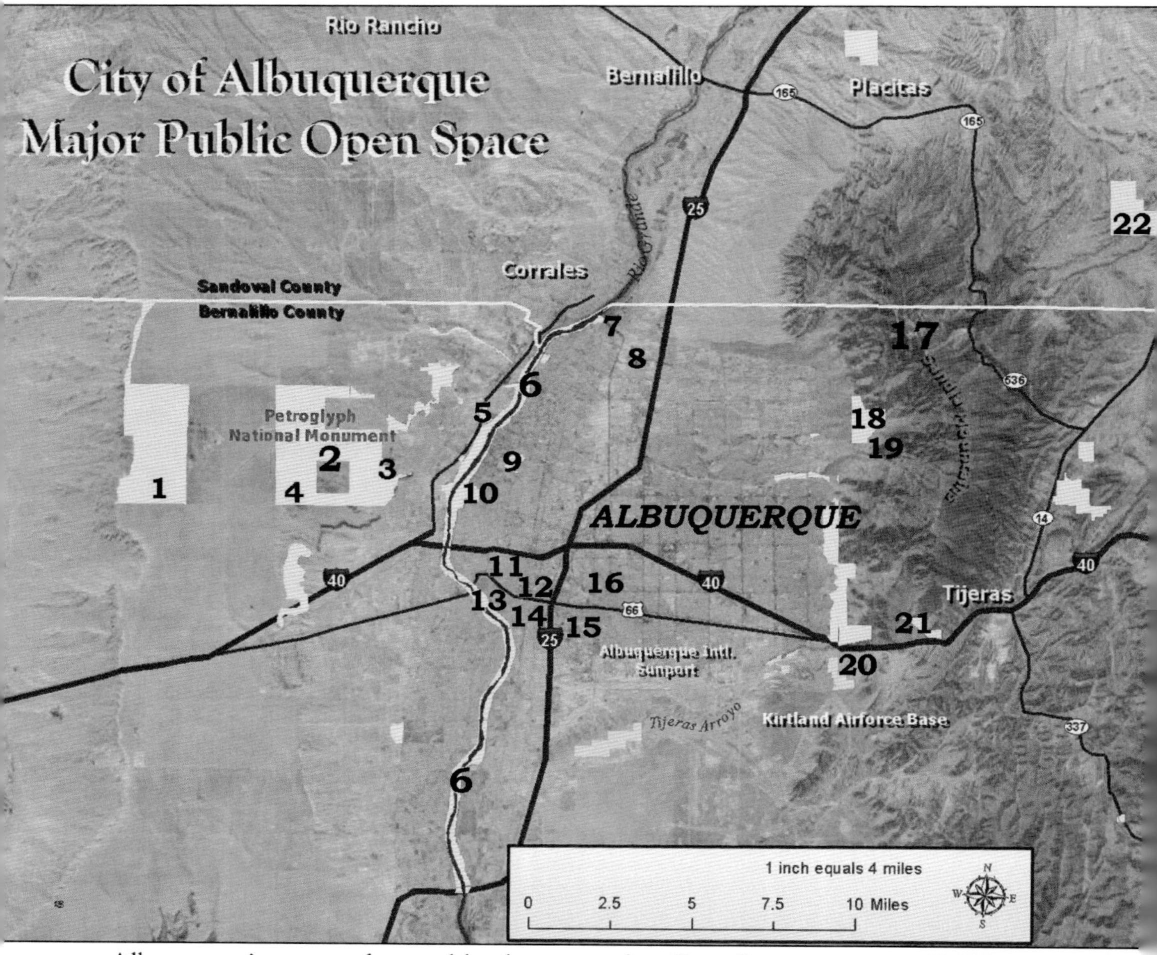

Albuquerque's system of natural lands preserved as Open Space comprises 29,000 acres in the greater metropolitan area. Larger Open Space parcels are shown in white on the above map. Numbered locations are mentioned in the text of this book: 1.) Shooting Range State Park, 2.) Petroglyph National Monument, 3.) West Mesa, 4.) Volcanoes, 5.) Open Space Visitor Center, 6.) Rio Grande Valley State Park, 7.) Alameda, 8.) Balloon Fiesta Park, 9.) Poblanos (Anderson) Field, 10.) Rio Grande Nature Center, 11.) Old Town, 12.) Robinson Park, 13.) Tingley Beach, 14.) Highland Park, 15.) Roosevelt (Terrace) Park, 16.) Bataan Memorial Park/McDuffie Park, 17.) Sandia Mountains, 18.) Elena Gallegos Picnic Area, 19.) Bear Canyon, 20.) Little Beavertown, 21.) Tres Pistolas, and 22.) Golden. (Author's collection.)

ON THE COVER: Albuquerque's wonderful system of formal parks and its spectacular holdings of natural lands called "open space" are exemplified in this fun-filled image from 1929. Children gather around a maypole for a birthday party on a fine spring day at Highland Park, near the city's downtown. (Museum of Albuquerque Photographic Archives, 1978-152-435.)

IMAGES
of America

Albuquerque's Parks and Open Space

Matt Schmader

ARCADIA
PUBLISHING

ISBN 978-0-7385-8470-6

Published by Arcadia Publishing
Charleston, South Carolina

Printed in the United States of America

Library of Congress Control Number: 2011924547

For all general information, please contact Arcadia Publishing:
Telephone 843-853-2070
Fax 843-853-0044
E-mail sales@arcadiapublishing.com
For customer service and orders:
Toll-Free 1-888-313-2665

Visit us on the Internet at www.arcadiapublishing.com

This book is dedicated to the citizens of Albuquerque, without whom the Open Space Program would not be possible, and to my wife, Bonnie, who makes all things possible.

Contents

ACKNOWLEDGMENTS

No undertaking this complex can succeed without the help of many people. Certainly books, which rely heavily on the power of historic images, are squarely in the realm of the photo archivist. Without their knowledge or the care for their craft to preserve our communities' photographic heritage, much would be lost. I was most fortunate to have the great assistance of Glenn Fye, photo archivist at the Albuquerque Museum. In many ways, I regard him as this book's coauthor. The support of Deb Slaney, Albuquerque Museum curator of history, was also critical. I received excellent help from staff at the University of New Mexico's Center for Southwest Research: director Mike Kelly, Clare Daniels, and Kathlene Ferris. Mary Wyant at the university's Map and Geographic Information Center was especially gracious with her help in scanning historic maps.

Except where noted, all photographs were taken by the author. Images otherwise used are from the Albuquerque Museum photographic archive (AMPA), the University of New Mexico Center for Southwest Research (CSWR), and the City of Albuquerque Open Space Division slide archive (OSD).

I make no claim to be the first person to write a book with great early photographs of Albuquerque. I humbly follow in the footsteps of several excellent earlier books, whose authors had already found many of the best images reproduced here. They include Byron Johnson and Bob Dauner's *Early Albuquerque: A Photographic History*; Charles Biebel's *Making the Most of It*; Mo Palmer's *Albuquerque Then and Now*; and Sandra Fye's *Historic Photos of Albuquerque*.

I have benefited from much encouragement given by colleagues, friends, and loved ones. The idea for this book grew out of a series of slide shows, including one suggested by Janet Saiers of the Albuquerque Historical Society. At the City of Albuquerque Parks and Recreation Department, my thanks go to director Barbara Baca, Jeff Hart, David Flores, and Judith Wong. At my own Open Space Division, many encouraged me along the way, but my greatest appreciation is reserved for James Lewis, who patiently scanned the many slides used in chapter five. I enjoyed the many talks I had with my children Ivan and Liana and the enthusiasm of friends. But my deepest gratitude will always be reserved for my wonderful wife, Bonnie, who told me I could do this and who inspired me through every moment of doubt and elation.

Introduction

Many have tried to describe the natural setting of the city of Albuquerque. Words like *breathtaking, enchanting, dramatic,* and *spectacular* only scratch the surface. Add *diverse, dynamic, living, interrelated,* and *complex,* and you begin to understand more deeply. The latter words also apply to the cultural—and even the political—landscape that permeates Albuquerque. More than a few people have been profoundly affected by the mountains, river, and volcanic landscape and the diversity of cultures that have occupied this area. It is ironic that often those who have had the most influence on parks and open space came here from elsewhere. They had seen other cities bulldoze and pave their natural settings and were determined not to let that happen to such a magnificent and rich landscape. My first experience with Albuquerque came when I accepted a position as a biology teacher at West Mesa High School in 1969. I soon joined a small group of people who were working to protect the Rio Grande in the heart of the city. This began a 25-year career as an advocate, planner, and open-space administrator for the city. As you will learn from reading this comprehensive history, my story is not unique.

This book documents the history of the city's parks and open space. More than that, it tells how a few people were changed by the place and how these people changed broader public perceptions of the place and moved their leaders to preserve and enhance it for others to enjoy. It is fair to say that Albuquerque citizens have taken their parks and open space to heart. They are both supportive (through bond issues, sales tax referendums, fees, etc.) and protective of these resources.

Part of Albuquerque's history is a story of equilibrium between the built environment and the natural setting. At times, human activities have threatened natural diversity and richness. Draining thousands of acres of wetlands along the Rio Grande made room for development but banished the wildlife that called them home. Today, remnants of these diverse habitats are preserved and enhanced within Rio Grande Valley State Park in the heart of the city. While many cities have stood idly by as builders of mansions played "king of the mountain," Albuquerque drew a "blue line" in the spectacular Sandia Foothills and refused to provide water or services above it. Today, these areas have been acquired as part of the Open Space network for thousands of mountain bikers and hikers to enjoy. Rather than allow vandals to destroy antiquities such as the petroglyphs and archaeological sites, citizens fought to protect them as parks, open space, and national monuments.

Albuquerque has always been an outdoor town. The climate, clear air, and a health-conscious culture are conducive to outdoor recreation. Sometimes, recreation takes the form of organized sports leagues for youth or adults, golf, swimming, or tennis. Thanks to park and recreation advocates, there are neighborhood and regional parks and sports complexes with facilities for these activities all over town. The many trails attract hikers, bikers, skaters, and equestrians. Bird-watchers and nature lovers find fulfillment here, too, as do groups and families using the many picnic areas and interpretive sites. In short, the people like to get outside and play. And what a place to play! With nearly 300 neighborhood and regional parks, four golf courses, and over 200 miles of paved and natural trails, there is something for everyone here.

Recreation is a primary benefit of both parks and open space. I can remember stressful times when I sought the quiet order of the natural landscape. Looking down at the city from the Elena Gallegos Picnic Area, I began to see the world in perspective. Suddenly, my problems did not seem so overwhelming, and the city was reduced to a more realistic proportion. Floating on a raft slowly along the Rio Grande, the verdant Bosque enfolded me and the city disappeared for a while, along with my stress and problems. It was during these times that I came to appreciate one of the best reasons for preserving parks and open space: recreation.

It is appropriate to say a few words about the author of this compelling story. I have known Matt Schmader for over 30 years. While working for the city, I contracted with Matt to perform archaeological surveys of Open Space lands. I quickly grew to appreciate him not only as a competent professional but also as an advocate and ambassador for cultural resource and open space preservation. Later, Matt and I contributed to a project called *Albuquerque's Environmental Story: A Guidebook for Teachers*. He was active on the Open Space Task Force and other groups supportive of these efforts. In the early 1990s, it was my pleasure to hire Matt as a supervisor of the newly formed interpretive section in the Open Space Division. From there he rose to become assistant superintendent and finally superintendent, a position he occupies at this writing. Matt has not merely observed the story of Albuquerque's parks and open space, he has lived it and contributed to it. He is, thus, uniquely qualified to tell it. He is a multidimensional, multitalented, and accomplished human being. A scholar, archaeologist, administrator, and leader, his vision continues to infuse the city's Open Space Program.

As Matt guides you through the remarkable history of Albuquerque's parks and open space, think of the possibilities. Albuquerque's experience teaches us that while "you can't stop progress," you can redefine it, and progress to citizens of Albuquerque is indistinguishable from quality of life. This account demonstrates that there is no end to what a few determined people can accomplish in establishing and protecting a legacy. I was often asked if open space would be there permanently. I would always answer, "The price of democracy is eternal vigilance." A legacy is only as good as the citizens who value and protect it.

—Rex Funk
Tucson, Arizona
January 2011

One

Roots and Early Beginnings

Albuquerque is almost entirely a product of its geographic setting and its cultural history. No other location in the country has a comparable geography—with mountains rising 5,000 above it to the east, one of the longest rivers on the continent running through its heart, and a string of volcanoes framing its western horizon. Each of these features, which remind Albuquerqueans where they live each day, is preserved as part of its Open Space system. Flying into the city, one sees a panoramic landscape that can only exist in one place called Albuquerque.

The same is true of the area's deep cultural legacy. Native people have lived here for well over 10,000 years, from a time when glaciers were found on Sandia Crest and when extinct creatures such as mastodons and camels drank from shallow lakes near the volcanic peaks. Inhabitants of villages built along the banks of the Rio Grande left thousands of petroglyphs—images marked on stone—in reverence of their surroundings. The first European and Mexican nonnatives to enter the Southwest, in the expedition of Francisco Vázquez de Coronado, passed right through the future site of Albuquerque from 1540 to 1542. The official founding of the Villa de Alburquerque by Francisco Cuervo y Valdes in 1706 established a plaza on the east bank of the Rio del Norte. Later, lands would be divided and held in pueblo or Spanish grants with the intent of providing access to the river, grazing lands, and timber. Portions of several community land grants—Alameda, Elena Gallegos, Atrisco, Pajarito, San Pedro, and Cañon de Carñuel—are framed on the north and south by the pueblo grants of Sandia and Isleta. Eventually, the coming of the railroad in 1880 and contributing factors such as health-seekers and the military industry resulted in several growth spurts.

As its park system tried to keep apace, the growing, modern city developed. This cultural history is also contained within Open Space lands now managed by the city, and these roots have helped shape not only the way Albuquerque began but also the way it evolved in its unique context.

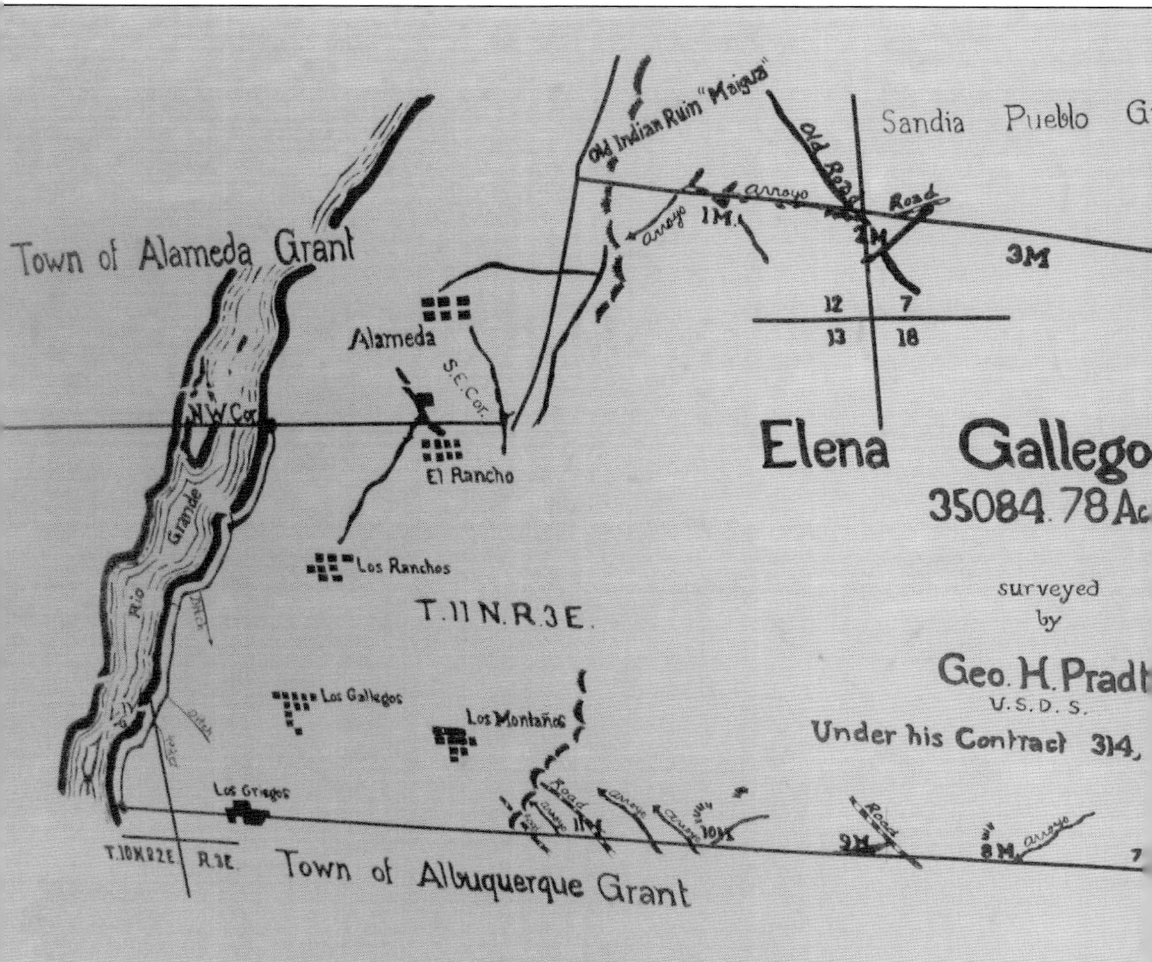

Capt. Diego Montoya was awarded a 35,000-acre grant stretching from the Rio Grande to the crest of the Sandia Mountains in 1694, following the Pueblo Revolt. Grants to militia were common as a means to keep guard over the newly reclaimed colony. Although he had direct descendants, Montoya bequeathed the entire grant to his niece Elena Gallegos in 1712. In 1699, Elena Gallegos married Santiago Gurule (Hispanicized from Jacques Grolet), one of two cabin

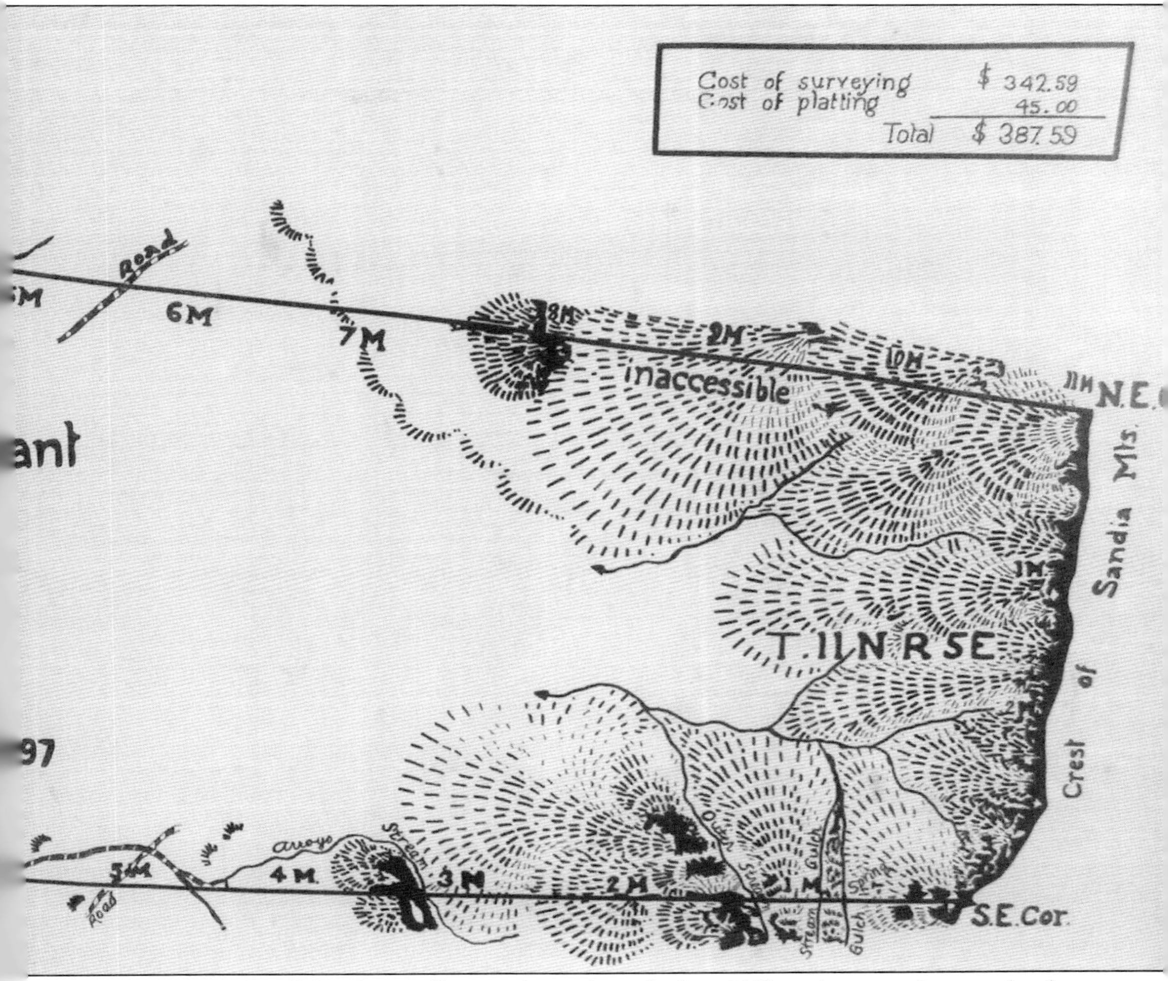

boys who survived the ill-fated La Salle expedition launched in 1687 to discover the mouth of the Mississippi. When rescued by Spanish priests, the cabin boys were "tattooed in the manner of their captors," the Karankawa tribe of the Texas Gulf Coast. The other surviving cabin boy, Juan Archibeque, stood in as witness to the marriage ceremony. (Map redrawn by Bonnie Schmader from 1859 original.)

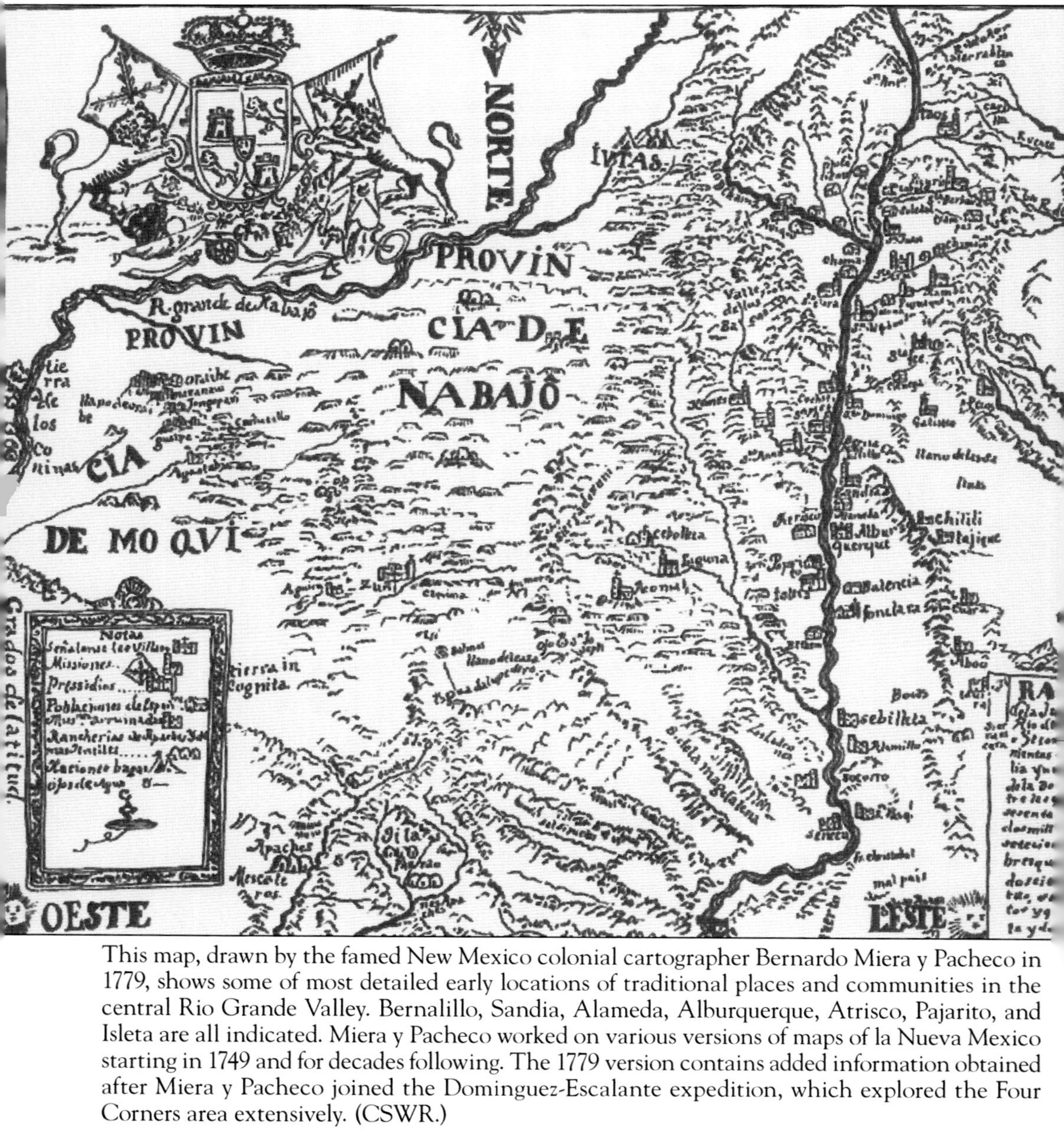

This map, drawn by the famed New Mexico colonial cartographer Bernardo Miera y Pacheco in 1779, shows some of most detailed early locations of traditional places and communities in the central Rio Grande Valley. Bernalillo, Sandia, Alameda, Alburquerque, Atrisco, Pajarito, and Isleta are all indicated. Miera y Pacheco worked on various versions of maps of la Nueva Mexico starting in 1749 and for decades following. The 1779 version contains added information obtained after Miera y Pacheco joined the Dominguez-Escalante expedition, which explored the Four Corners area extensively. (CSWR.)

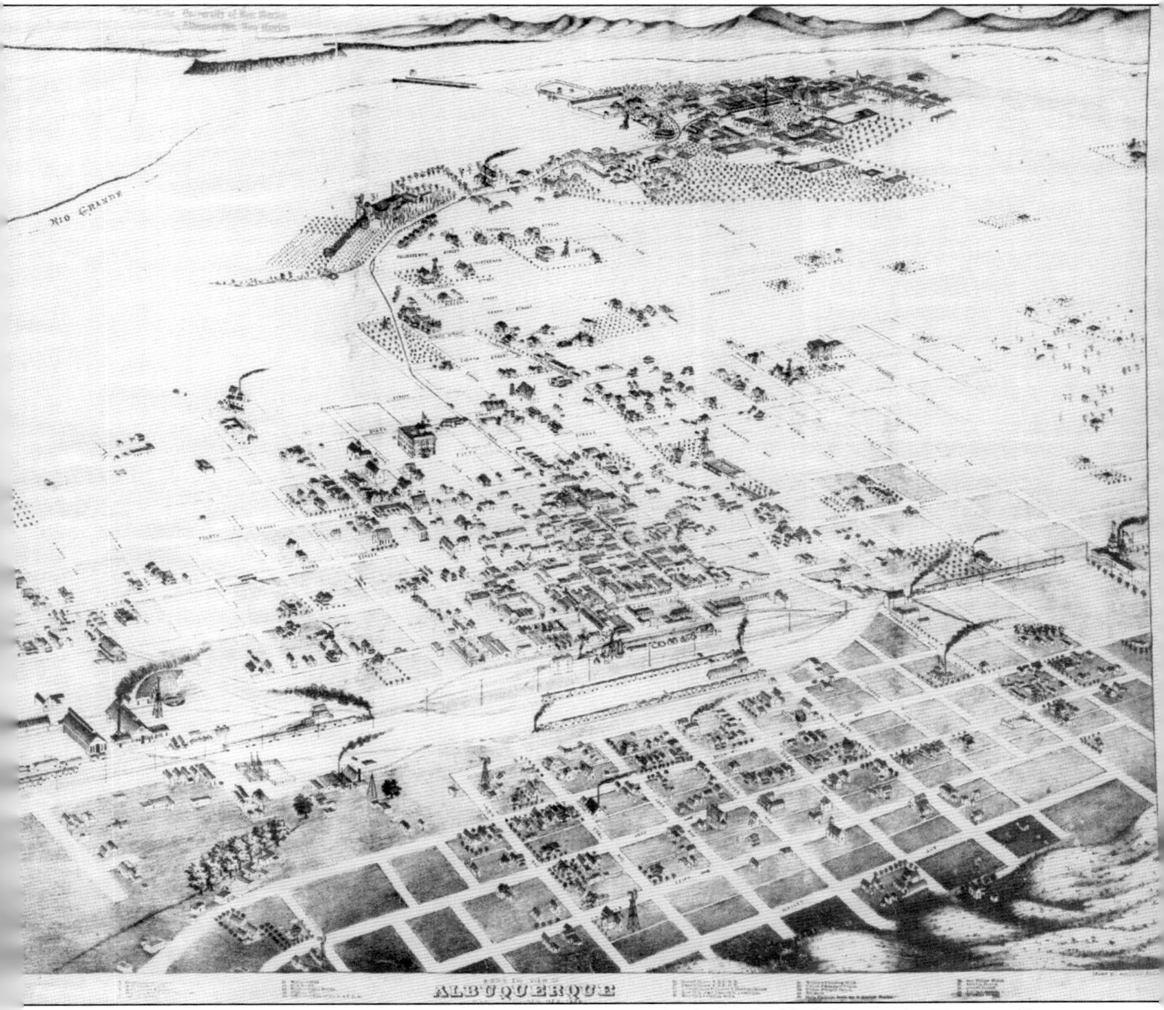

Panoramic, or bird's-eye view, maps of towns were popular in the latter half of the 1800s. Eventually, over 1,700 such maps were made of Canadian and American cities. This bird's-eye view of Albuquerque was done by Augustus Koch in 1886. It shows the Territorial Fairgrounds, one of the most prominent recreational centers at the time, at the western edge of Old Town at the top center of the map (depicted by a racing oval). It also shows a remarkably accurate profile of the West Mesa, the volcanic escarpment, and the Rio Grande, although the size, number, and extent of the volcanoes are greatly exaggerated. (Valliant Printing Company.)

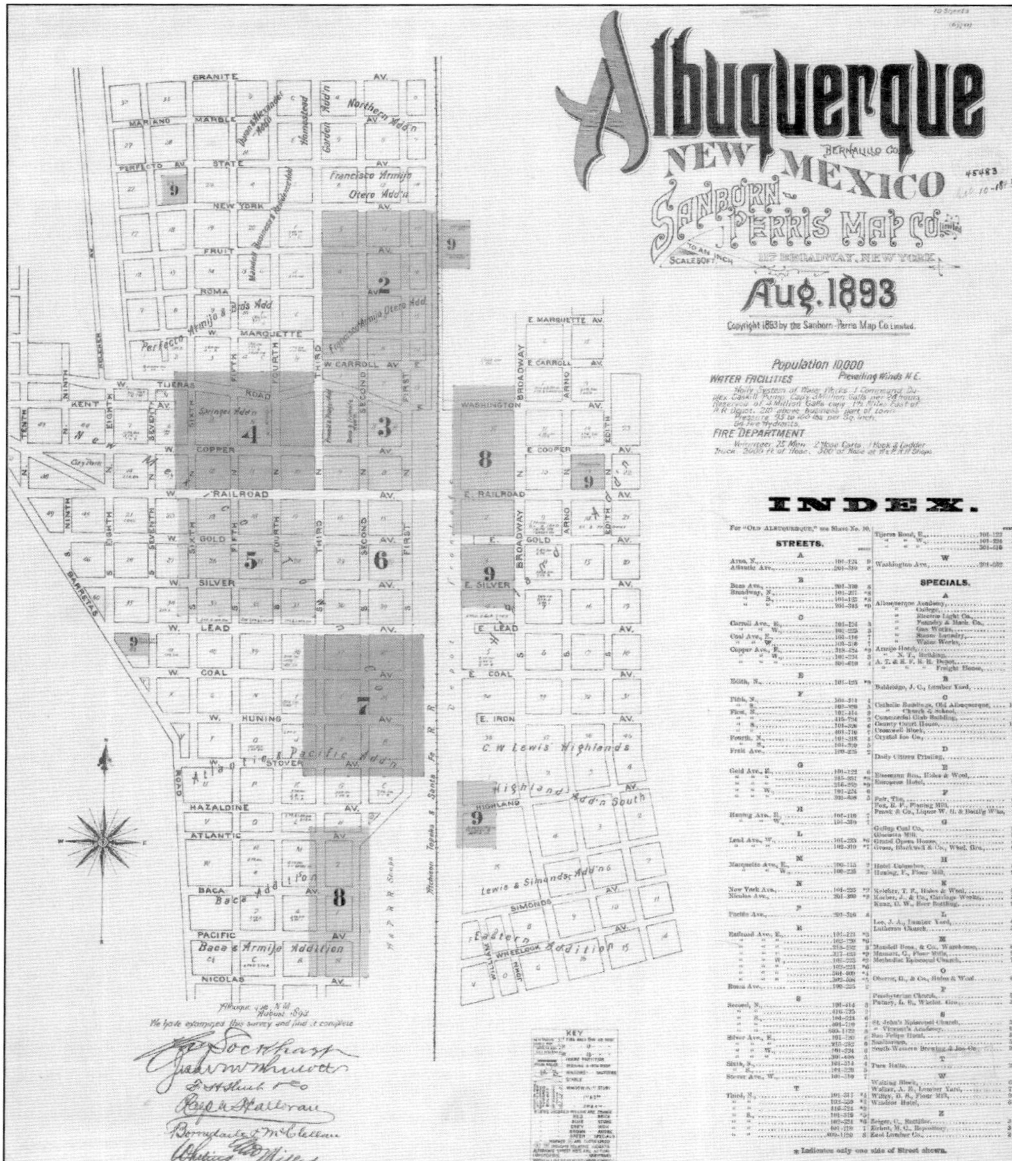

The Sanborn Map Company created detailed insurance maps of many cities in the United States. Started in 1867, the Sanborn Company would produce fine, lithographed color maps of 12,000 cities over the next 100 years. This 1893 Sanborn map of Albuquerque gives a population of 10,000, with a volunteer fire department of 75 men with access to 2,000 feet of water hose. The main east-west road is still called Railroad Avenue, before the name was changed to Central. The insurance rating maps were focused on the newer part of town, and they did not include Old Town in the beginning. (University of New Mexico, Map and Geographic Information Center.)

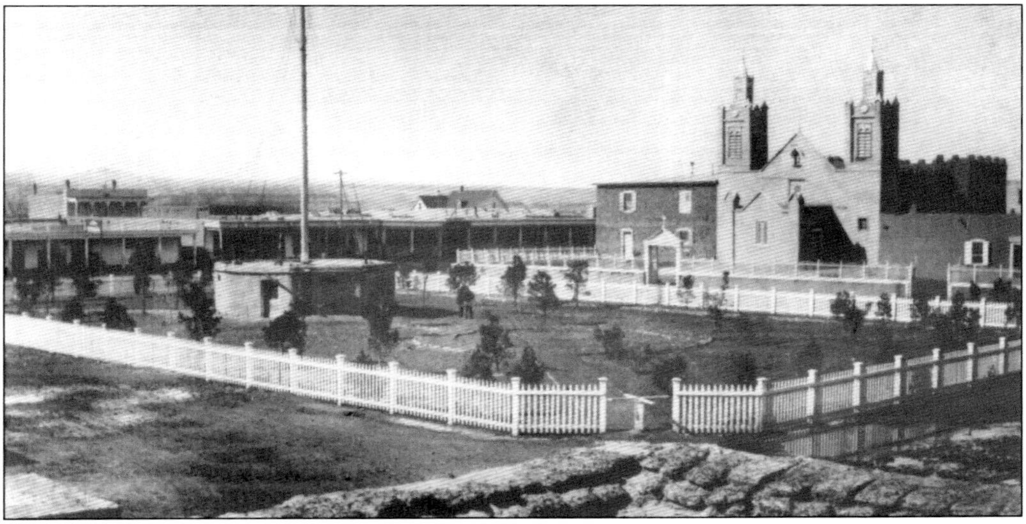

Civic spaces forming the *centro,* or plaza, of each royally decreed colonial villa were prescribed by Spanish conventions of urban planning. The *cuadrícula* town form established a more or less orderly grid of streets around the plaza. This 1880 view to the northwest shows the familiar appearance of San Felipe de Neri Church fronted by a sparse, formal plaza. The building at the center was an armory and stockade. (AMPA.)

Albuquerque's New Town grew almost overnight with the coming of the railroad in 1881. A shantytown of canvas-sided tents was quickly replaced by stores, hotels, and saloons, but a rough-hewn edge lingered over the boomtown. This 1880s Cobb studio photograph looking toward the corner of First Street and Railroad (later Central) Avenue shows longhorn steers lying in the dusty street while a horse-drawn trolley passes in the background. (CSWR.)

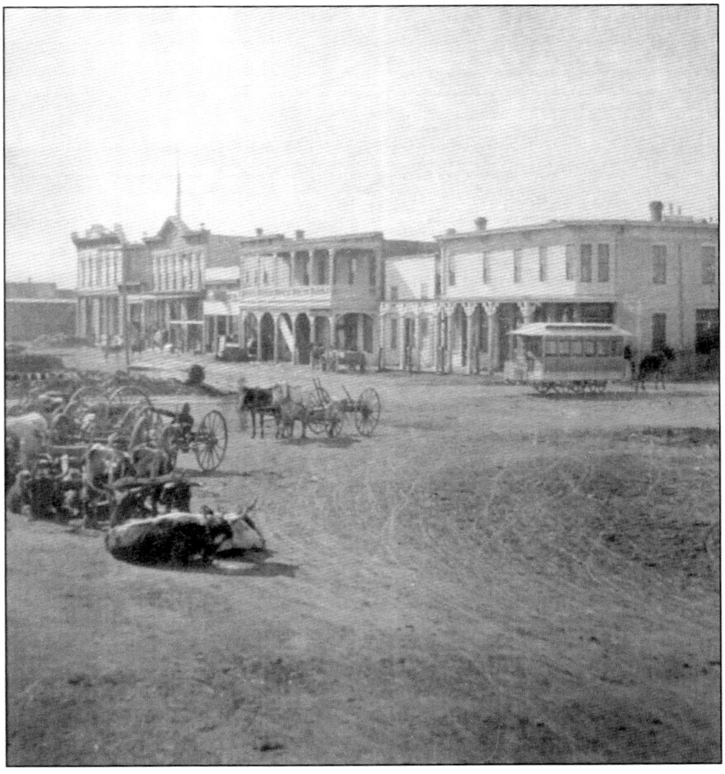

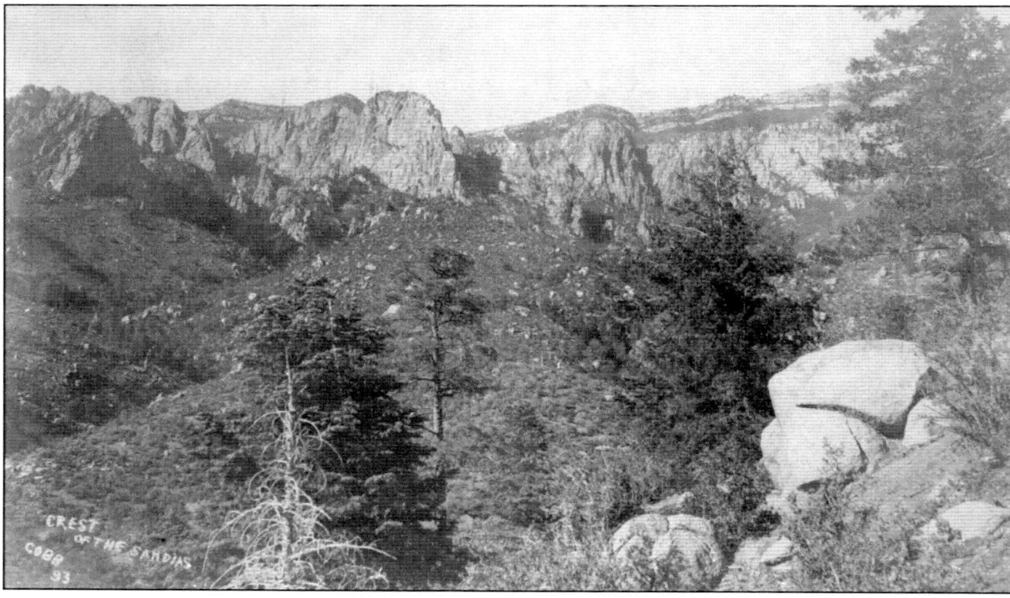

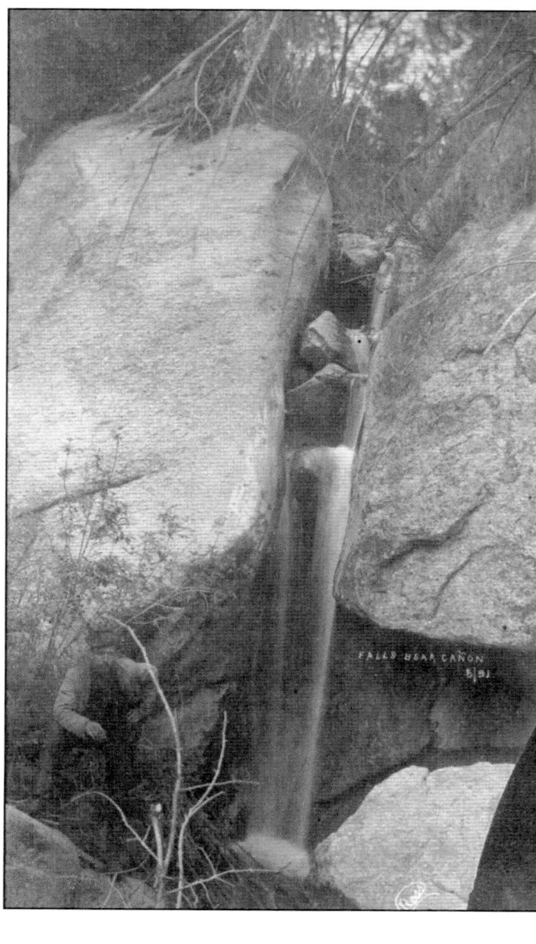

Albuquerque's iconic and majestic eastern backdrop is formed by the rugged Sandia Mountains, the southernmost chain in the Rocky Mountains. Pueblo people regard the Sandias as one of their sacred peaks, referred to as the Turtle Mountain by some. The enduring appearance and allure of the mountains was captured in this 1893 Cobb studio photograph titled *Crest of the Sandias.* (CSWR.)

Venturing into the foothill canyons of the Sandias was popular even 100 years ago. While the journey was more difficult than today, the outdoor experience was no less appealing or rewarding. In this 1891 image, renowned local photographer William Henry Cobb was captured by his wife, Edwinna "Eddie," beside a Bear Canyon waterfall. William died in 1909, aged just 49, but Eddie continued the Cobb studio until the 1940s. (CSWR.)

A view along the east bank of the Rio Grande looking northwest toward the silhouette of the Albuquerque volcanoes was shot about 1910 by photographer William Walton. At the time, the unaltered floodplain of the river was broad and shallow with considerable areas of flats and sandbars. Levees and dams built in the mid-1900s would later confine the river to a narrower floodplain and cause it to downcut. (AMPA.)

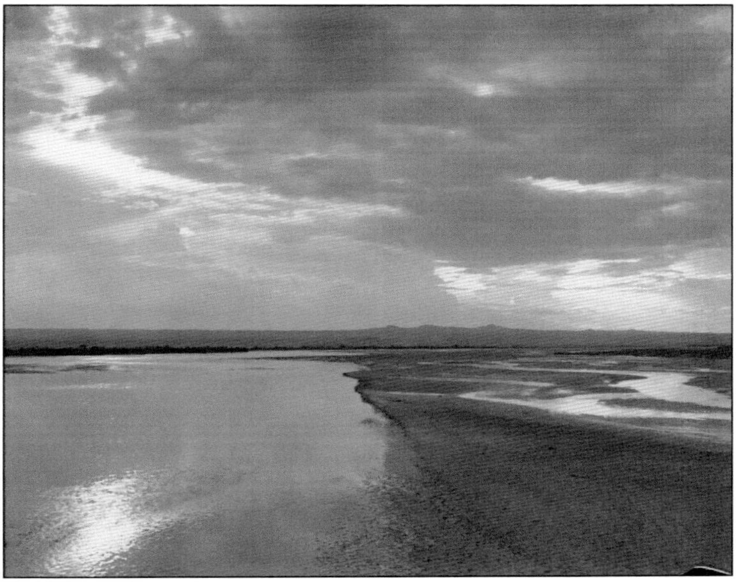

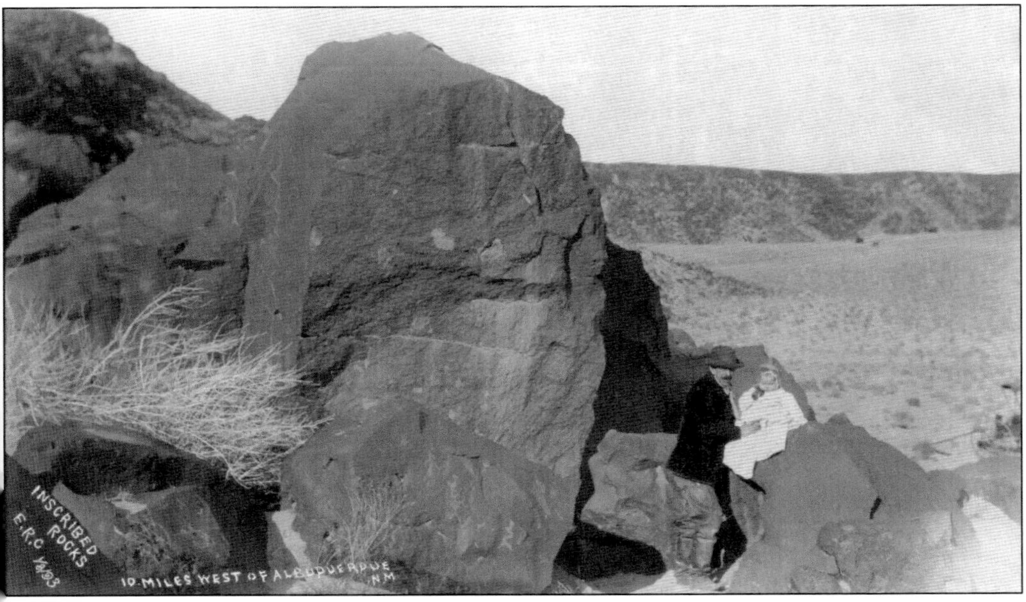

Even as early as the 1890s, Albuquerqueans were aware that thousands of ancient petroglyphs existed on the cliffs outside the town. In this January 1893 image by Edwinna Cobb, titled *Inscribed Rocks 10 Miles West of Albuquerque*, local photographer William Cobb is seen holding their young daughter Daphne, with a horse-drawn carriage barely visible in the background. Nearby petroglyphs include birds, a footprint, and a serpent or lightning bolt. (CSWR.)

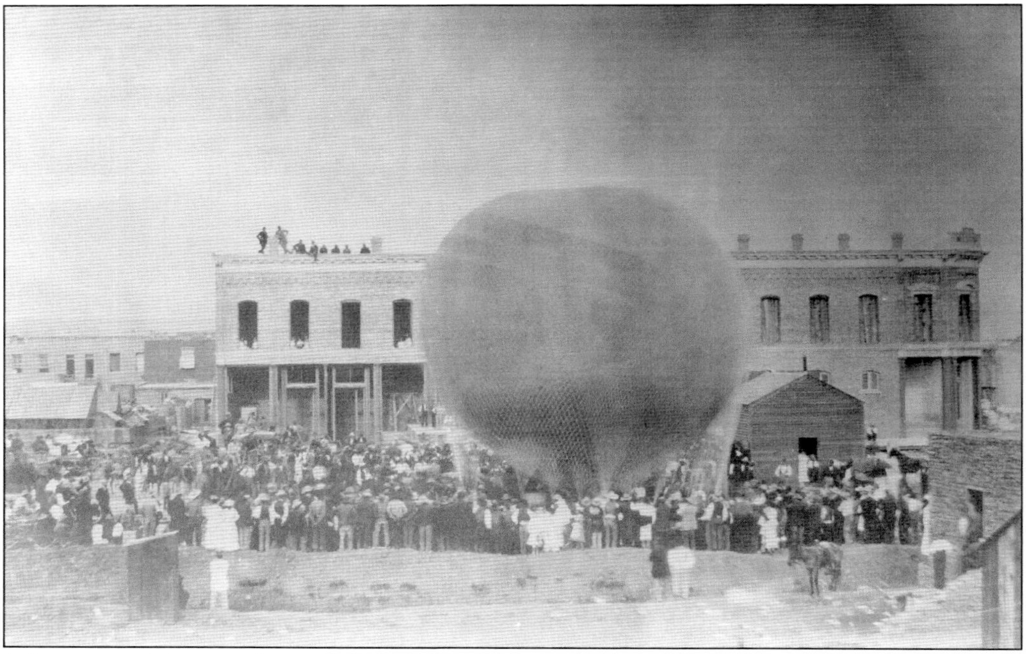

Albuquerque's long and proud association with aviation and hot-air ballooning was literally launched by a single act performed by "Professor" Arthur van Tassel on July 4, 1882. His coal gas–filled balloon took off from Railroad Avenue in New Town and landed in a cornfield near the Territorial Fairgrounds west of Old Town. This photograph is another of the Cobb studio's series of indelible images chronicling early Albuquerque. (CSWR.)

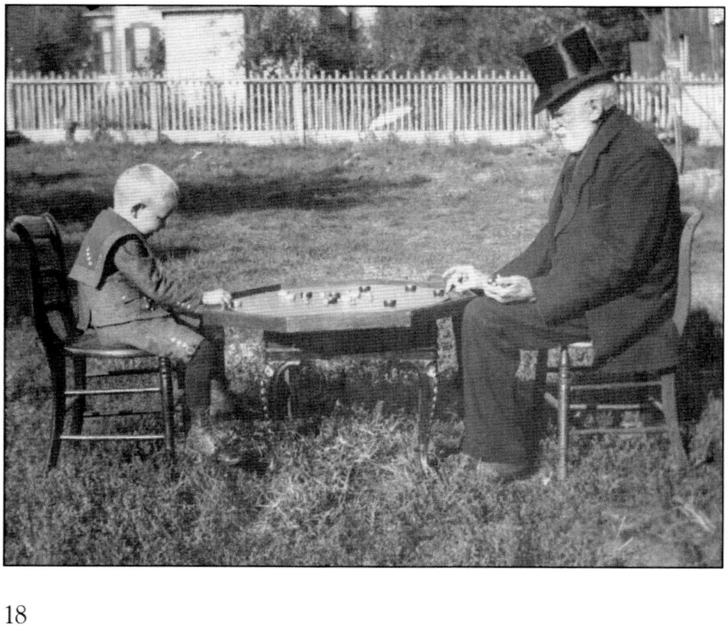

With a general lack of formally developed public places within which to recreate at the turn of the past century, families often resorted to the simple pleasures of backyard play. In this Cobb studio image from about 1900, a top-hatted Sen. George Coffin of Kansas plays a board game called crokinole with his great-grandson Percy Gillette Cornish while visiting the family's home on Walter Avenue in the Huning Highlands. (CSWR.)

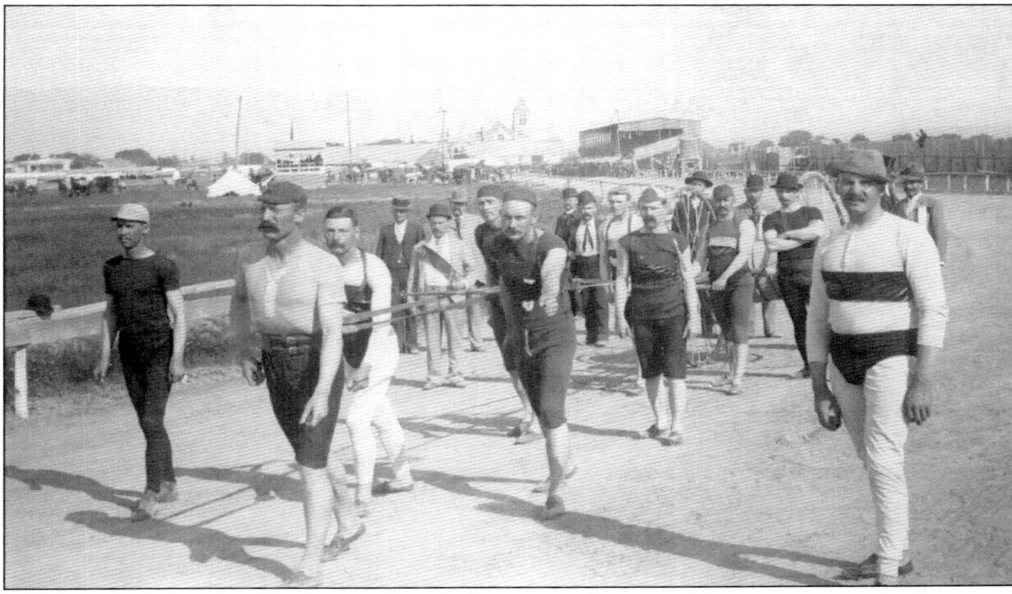

One of the most important recreational focal points at the turn of the century was the Territorial Fairgrounds, built west of Old Town plaza. In addition to the many exhibitions held there, the fairgrounds had a racing oval where track-and-field events took place. The first fair was held in October 1881. Members of the volunteer fire company are shown in a Cobb studio image, engaged in a tug-of-war. (CSWR.)

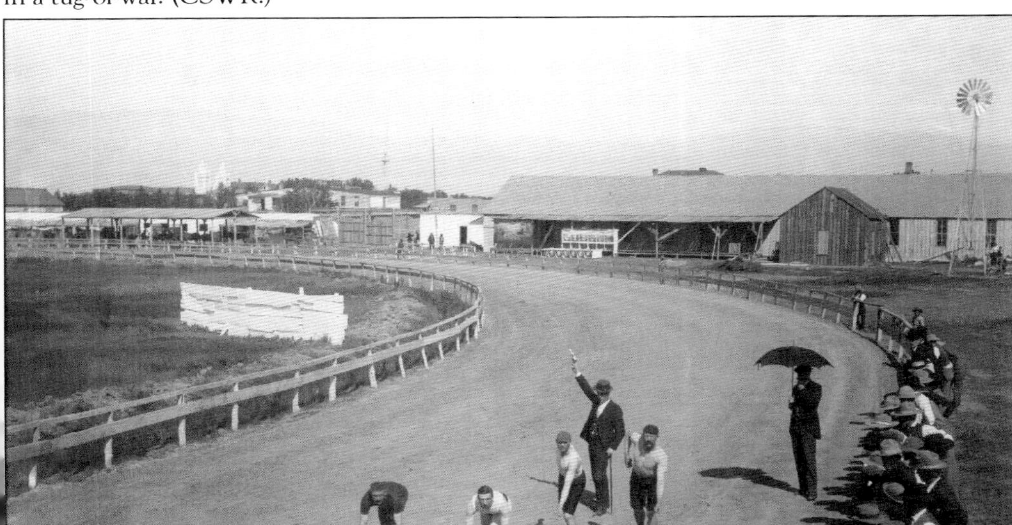

Footraces were also held at the Territorial Fairgrounds, although some were apparently less competitive than others. Here, just four runners from the volunteer fire company line up in anticipation of the starter's gun in a Cobb studio photograph from the 1880s. (CSWR.)

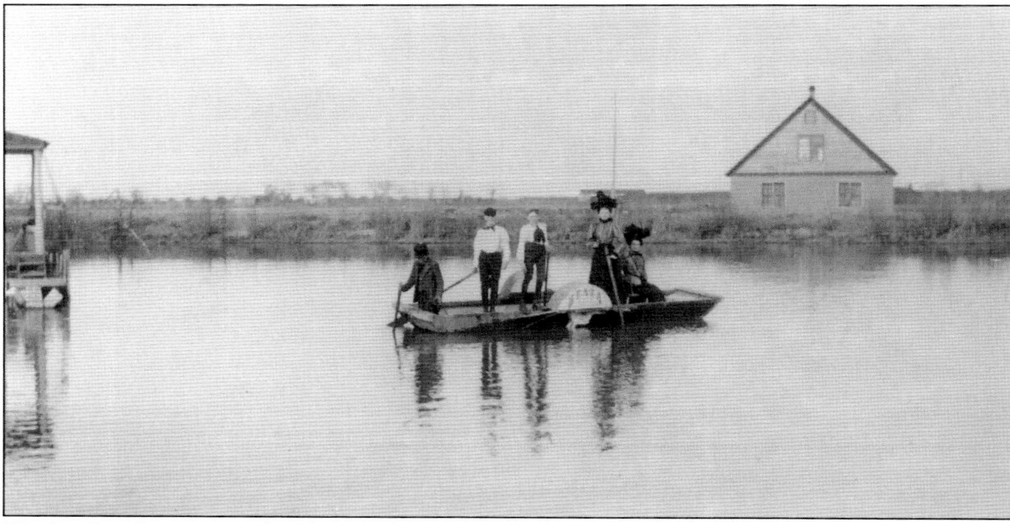

Blueher Pond was a popular place for boating and swimming near Old Town around 1895. Present-day Tiguex/TriCentennial Park now covers the spot. Herman Blueher was a merchant who dealt in farm equipment, and the family owned gardens along Mountain Road (formerly called Blueher Road). Herman Blueher also built a fabulous Italianate mansion at the southeast corner of Old Town, now the site of the Hacienda Restaurant. (AMPA.)

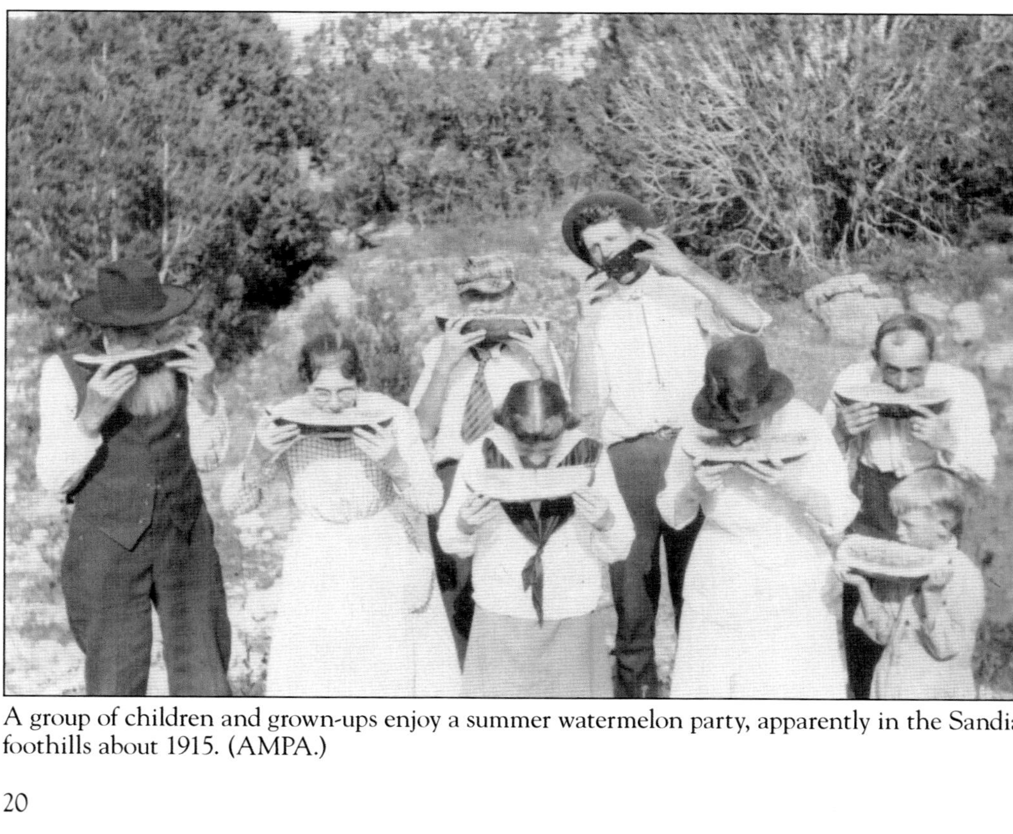

A group of children and grown-ups enjoy a summer watermelon party, apparently in the Sandia foothills about 1915. (AMPA.)

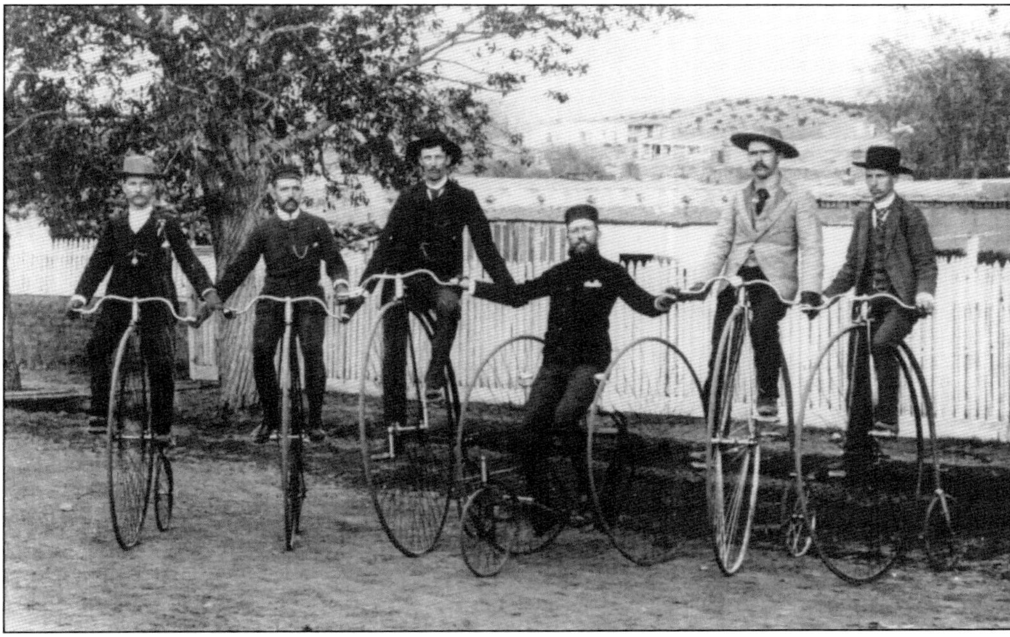

As a mile-high western city with clean air, Albuquerque has always boasted a great love of bicycling. Bicycle racing and riding organizations were popular even when the sport was in its relative infancy. This photograph, taken about 1885, shows members of an Albuquerque bicycling club posing with their high-wheelers in front of a house southwest of the sandhills at the edge of Martineztown. (CSWR.)

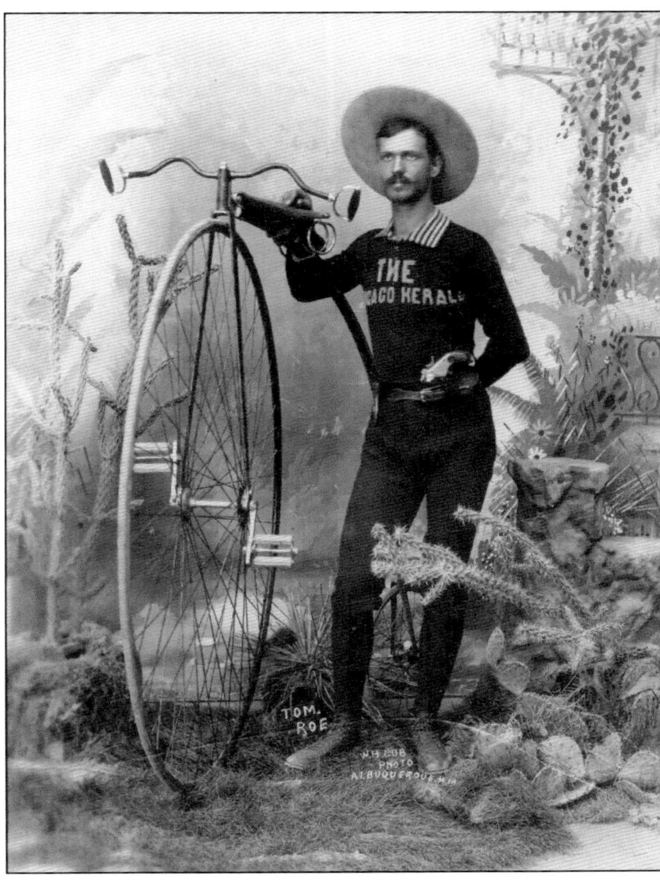

Competitive bicycle racing also drew contestants to Albuquerque. This c. 1890 image shows a confident Tom Roe, evidently sponsored in a race by the *Chicago Herald*, with a pistol stuffed in his belt as he posed aside his high-wheeled, or penny-farthing, bicycle. The Cobb studio interior included rock piles, yucca, fake grass, and cholla cacti. (CSWR.)

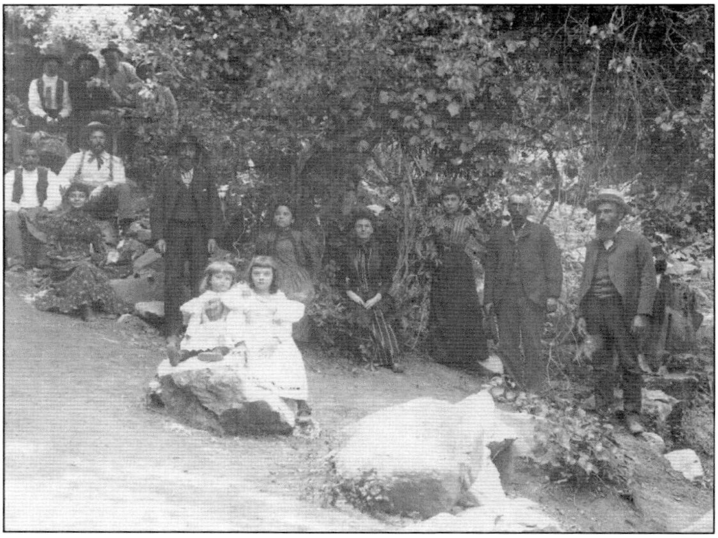

Affluent families could afford to dress up and take carriages for picnics in the Sandias. Among those pictured are alderman and Bernalillo County assessor Perfecto Armijo (seated, far left in vest), Anita Armijo and Mrs. Hall (center), and Dr. John S. Easterday with R.P. Hall, owner of the Albuquerque Foundry and Machine Works (far right, with hat). This c. 1890 Cobb studio image is identified as taken in Bear Canyon. (CSWR.)

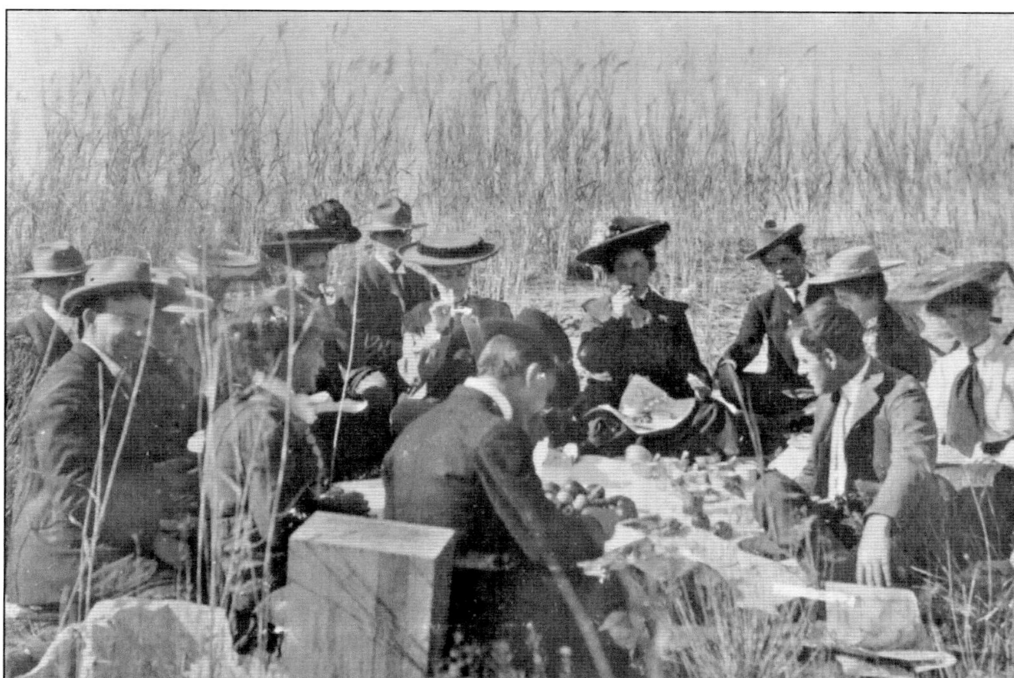

This photograph taken around 1895 shows a picnic with an unidentified group dressed in their Sunday best and dining on fruit somewhere in the Sandia foothills. (AMPA.)

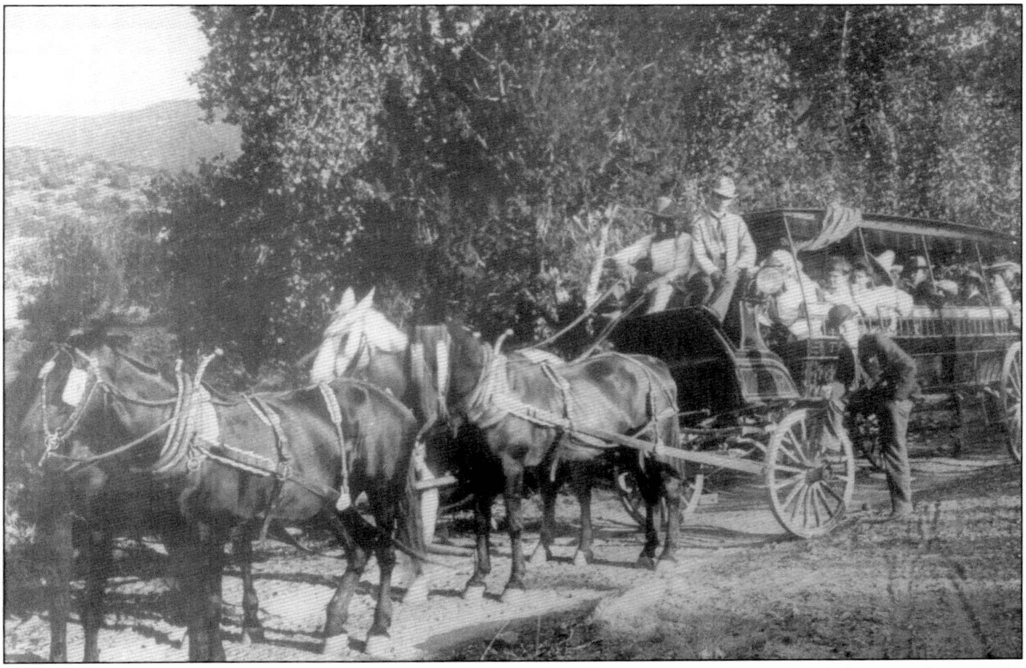

Carriage rides to the mountains were also available to those who could afford them. This 1890s photograph appears to have been taken in the East Mountains, possibly in Tijeras Canyon. The tour operator may have been William Trimble, who also ran the horse-drawn trolleys in Albuquerque. (AMPA.)

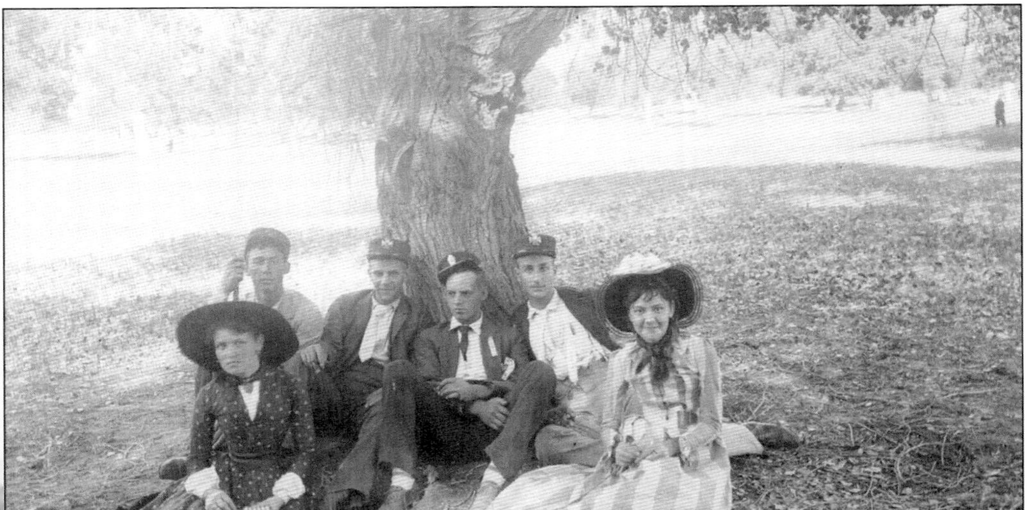

Picnics along the Rio Grande were also popular at the turn of the century. This image of an informal group of four men in firefighter uniforms and their accompanying lady friends was taken around 1890 at Alameda Grove, presumably on the east side of the river in the far North Valley area. (CSWR.)

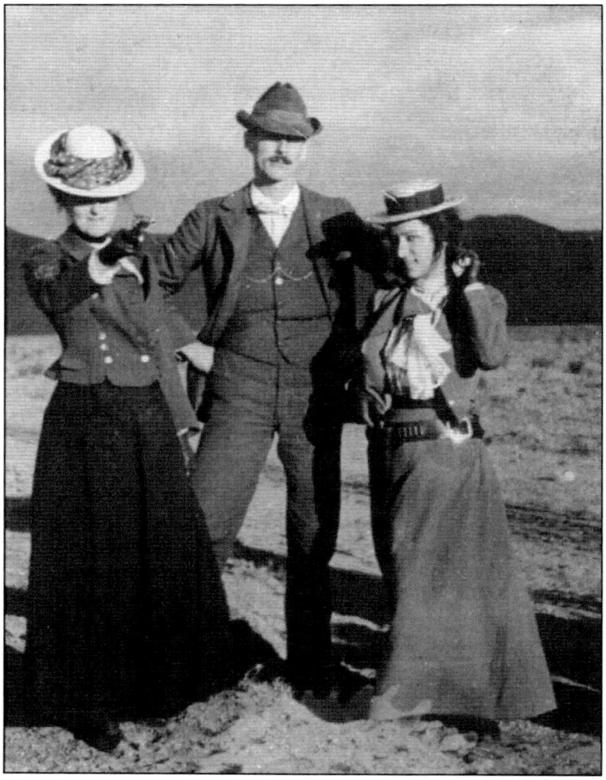

Albuquerque's roots as a western town were in full display when it came to the sport of shooting. Not to be contended with, these two gun-toting women in formal dress enjoy target practice on the East Mesa around 1895 as an unarmed man looks on. (AMPA.)

A group portrait of the Albuquerque Gun Club was taken about 1891, most likely in the environs southwest of town. The photograph may have been taken in the vicinity of today's Gun Club Road in the South Valley. (CSWR.)

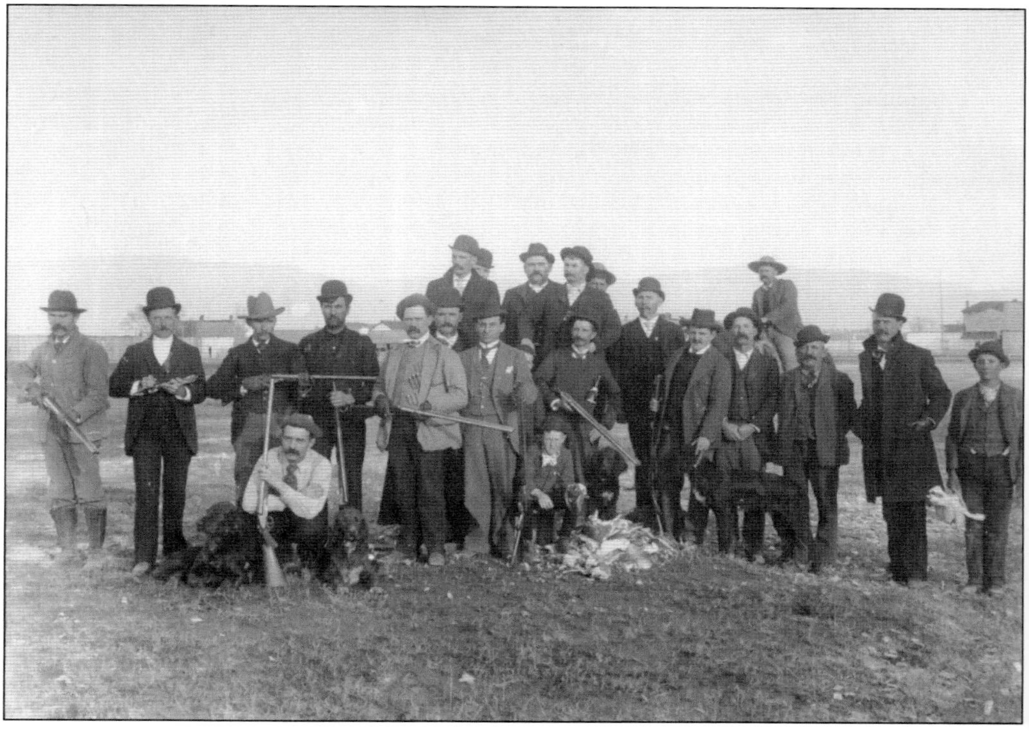

A more formal portrait of two unidentified men holding shotguns and in full hunting gear was taken in this Cobb studio cyanotype from the 1890s. (CSWR.)

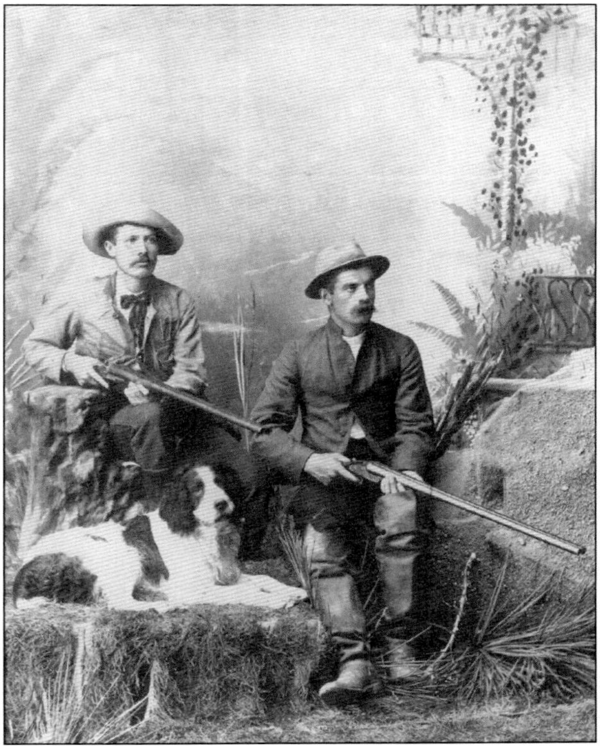

The Albuquerque Maroons were dubbed the "Champion Baseball Team of the Southwest, 1891." Some of the team members identified in the Cobb studio portrait include Knight (right field), McCann (left field), Lockhart (umpire), Shannon (mascot), H.A. McCreight (field manager), Riegke (scorer), Rudolph (second base), Hagel (first base), Murry (shortstop), and Timmons (third base). (CSWR.)

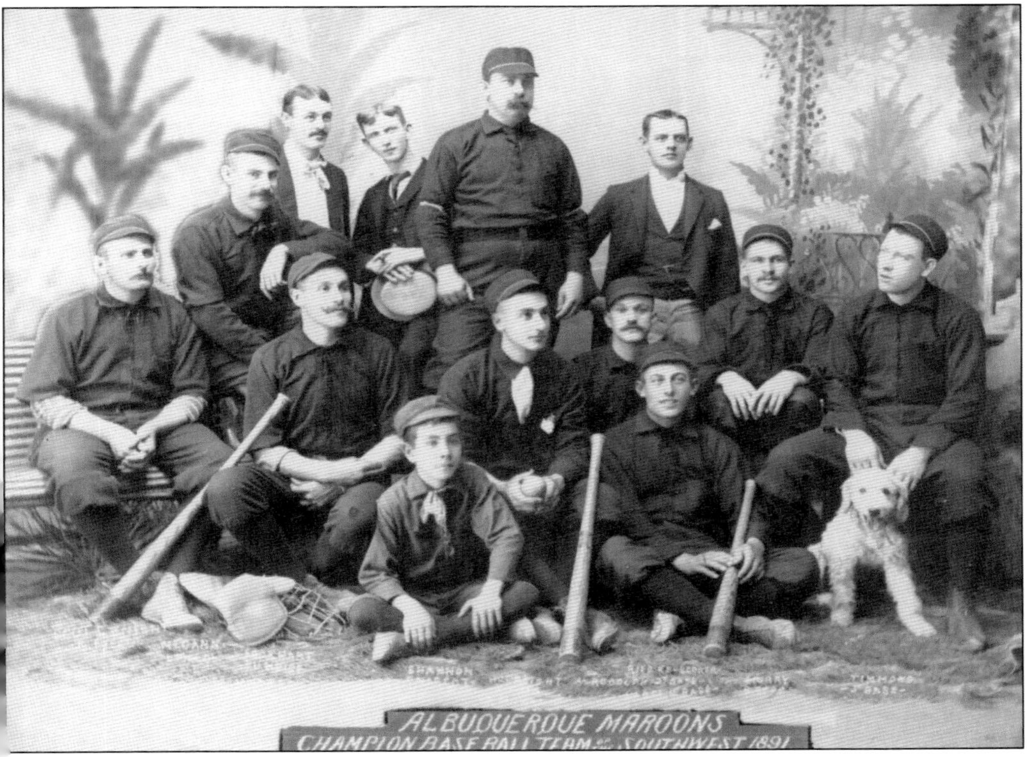

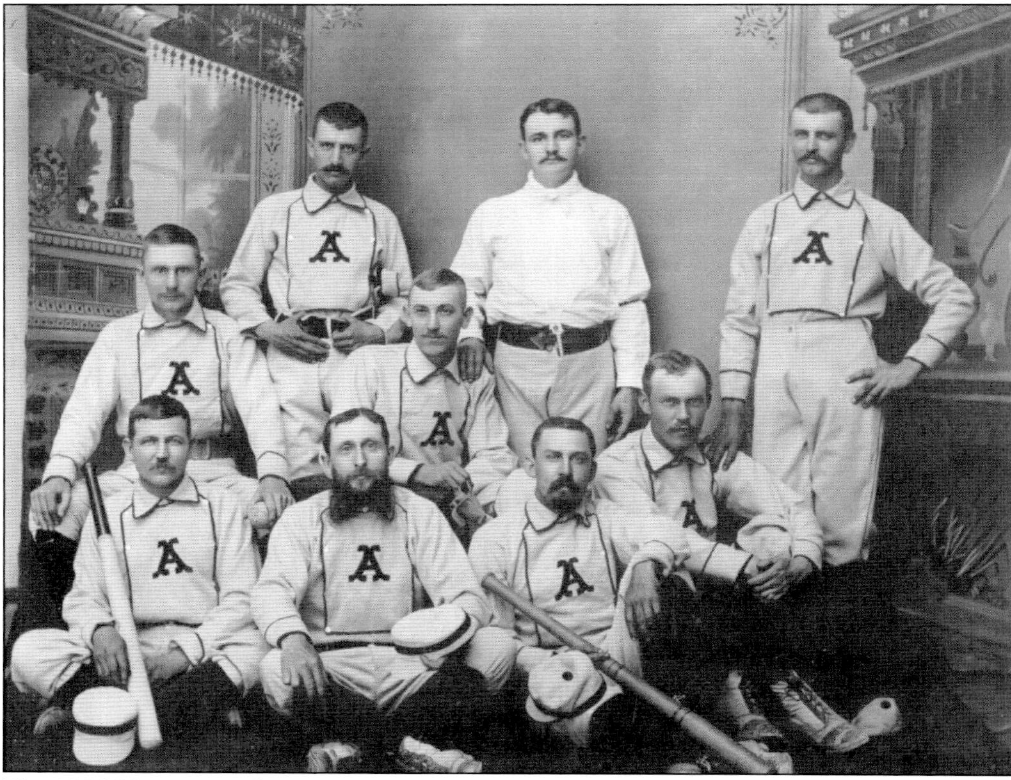

The 1906 University of New Mexico baseball team was coached by Martin Angell (standing, center), as seen in this Cobb studio portrait. The team won five of seven games, including a victory over the semiprofessional Albuquerque Browns. (CSWR.)

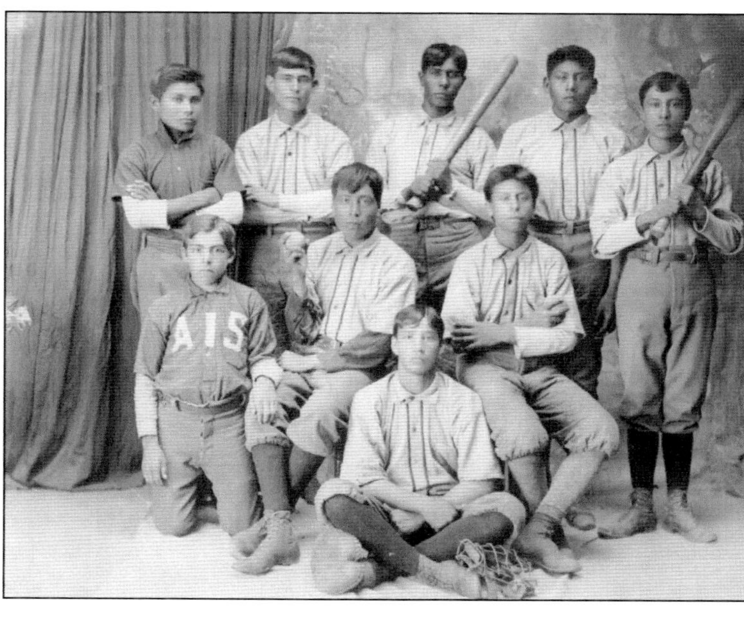

The Albuquerque Indian School baseball team poses for a formal portrait about 1900, but the names of the players are unknown. The cultural disruption of being taken from their native communities, housed in boarding school, given haircuts and unfamiliar clothing, and taught strange games is clearly seen in these boys' faces. (CSWR.)

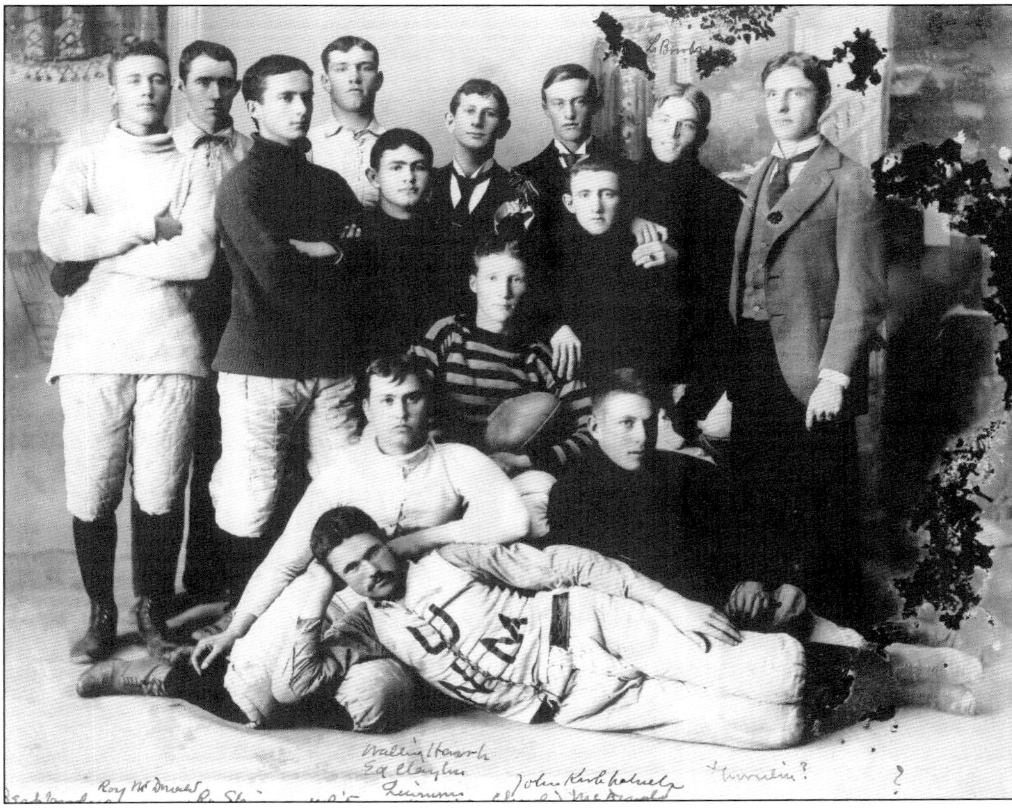

This 1894 team picture of the University of New Mexico football team may have today's Lobos fans dreaming of past glory. Some of the identified players pictured are, from left to right, (reclining) Lloyd Gibbons; (seated) Fred Whiteman, Seymour Lewinson, and Charles McDonald; (standing) Bert Vorhees, Roy McDonald, Roy Stamm, Stark Ames, Wally Harsch, Edmund Clayton, Johnnie Kirkpatrick, Lewis Brooks, and two unidentified men. (CSWR.)

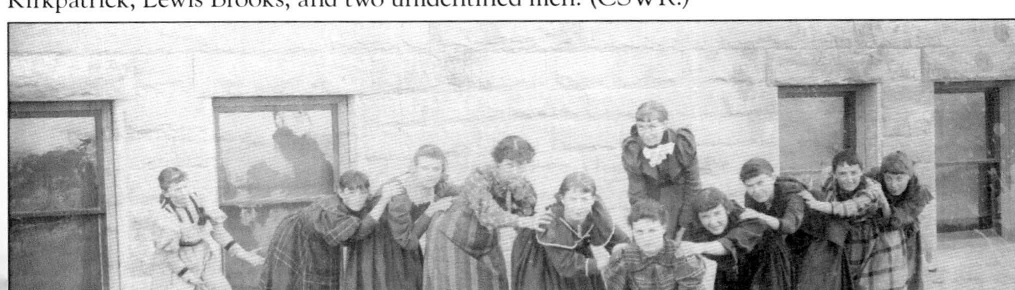

Remarkably, the University of New Mexico also fielded a women's football team, shown in this portrait likely taken outside of Hodgin Hall sometime between 1894 and 1898. The names of the team members are not known. One wonders why women's football was ultimately dropped by universities across the country. (CSWR.)

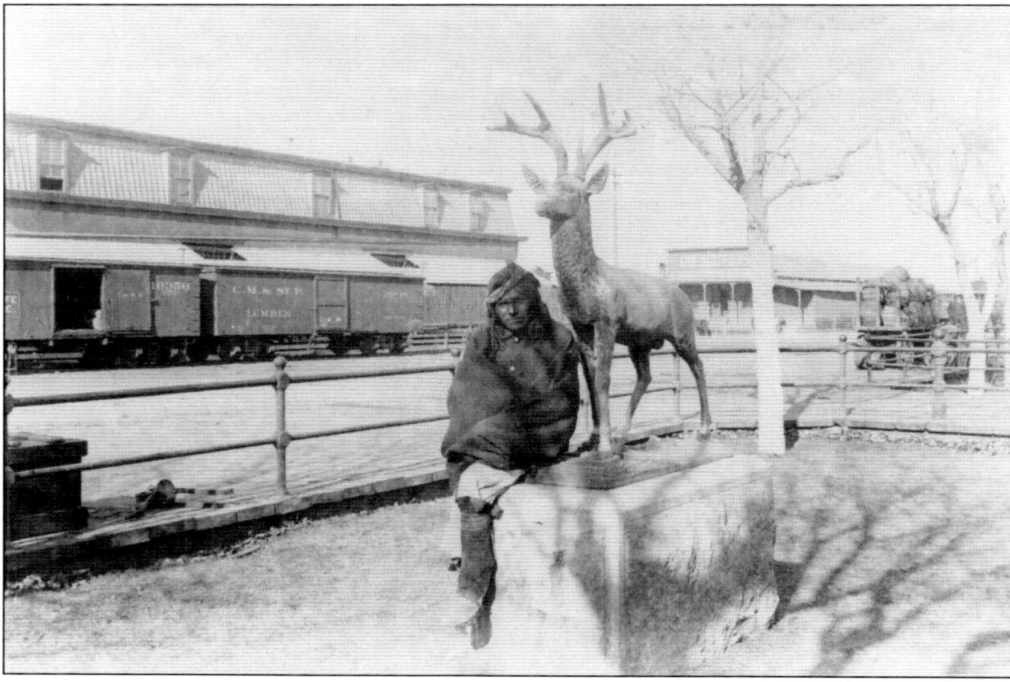

The existence of some small early parks has been completely lost. A 1880s winter scene at Depot Park shows a native man sitting by a deer statue within an iron railing enclosure. Depot Park was near the southeast corner of First Street and Railroad (later Central) Avenue, where the Alvarado Hotel would be built. Lyman Putney's store (background) was a known place where Indian traders could stay overnight. (CSWR.)

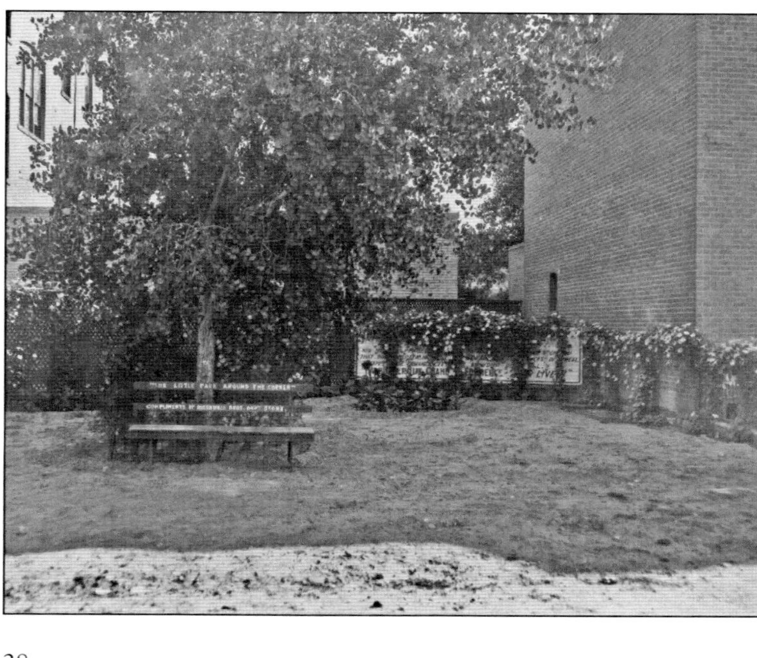

Another of the now-lost small early park spots, the bench here reads, "The Little Park Around the Corner, Compliments of Rosenwald Bros. Dept. Store." Rosenwald's was on the corner of Third Street and Central Avenue. This little park was presumably on the south side of the building as pictured around 1920. (AMPA.)

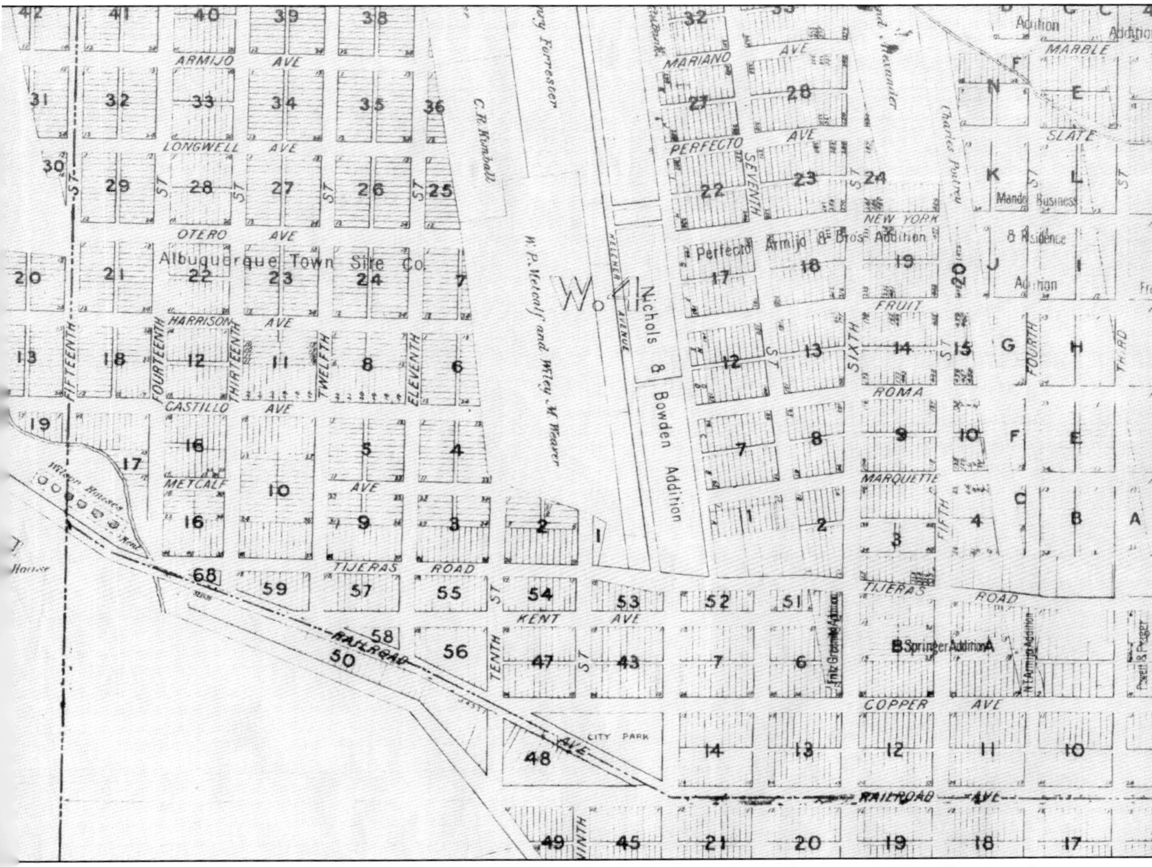

This 1889 Real Estate Title Insurance Company map shows the triangular tract of land set aside by the Albuquerque Townsite company as a "city park" along Railroad Avenue. The Albuquerque Townsite company was headed up by Elias Stover, William Hazeldine, Franz Huning, and F.H. Kent. Built around 1880 at the time of the railroad's arrival, the park is situated halfway between Old Town and New Town between Eighth and Tenth Streets. Development of the park was spearheaded by civic-minded women who raised funds to beautify it. A contest to name the space was won by Lena Robinson, whose father bought her the most votes. (University of New Mexico, Map and Geographic Information Center.)

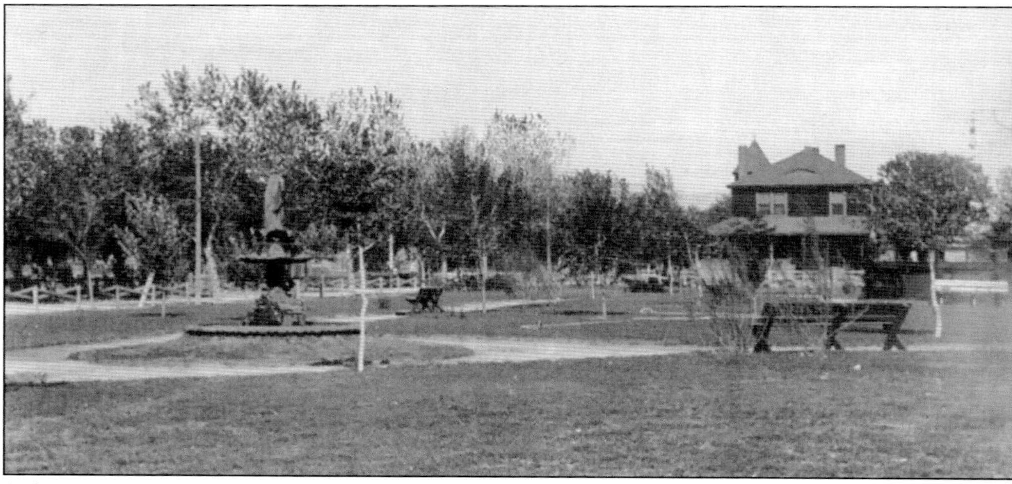

Robinson Park is considered to be the oldest surviving park in Albuquerque. This photograph, taken around 1900, shows the sparse open design of the young park just after it was being improved. A statue honoring John Braden, a heroic firefighter who died in 1896 when he drove a flaming wagon full of fireworks from a parade to the park, can be seen. The statue still stands at the park. (AMPA.)

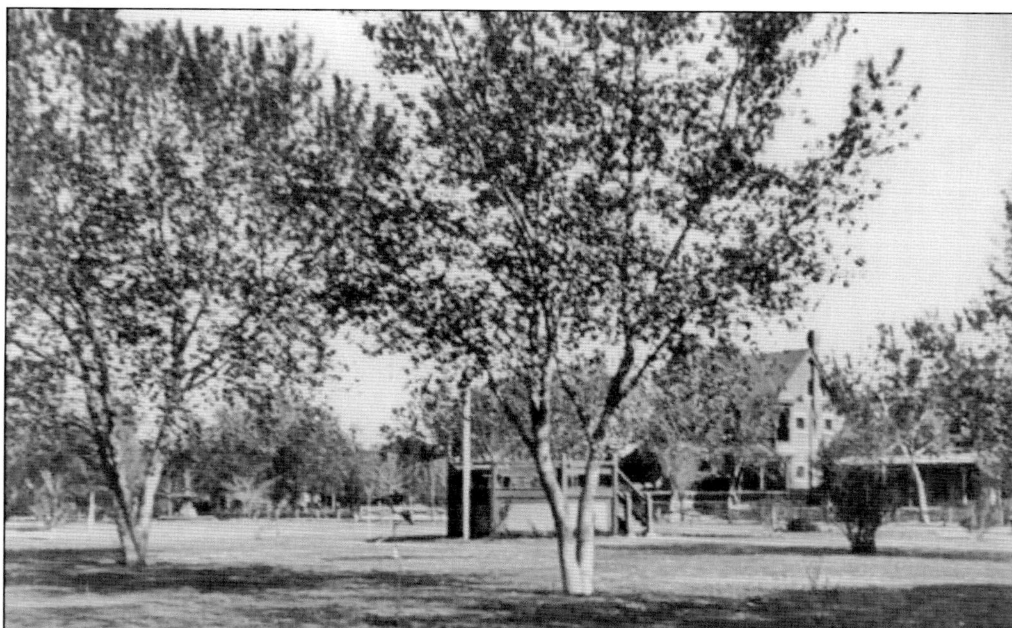

In a photograph taken from about the same vantage point around 1910, the now maturing trees begin to obscure the mansion in the background known as the Sisk House. About 150 trees planted in an 1885 Arbor Day event have grown to maturity. A bandstand, which would figure prominently in the park's history, has also been added. (CSWR.)

Two

"The Boys Go to the River"

Like many western American cities, Albuquerque began modernizing during the first decades of the 20th century. By 1900, the small town had come out of the railroad years with a population of about 8,000. But Albuquerque was still the largest town in New Mexico, and it attracted commerce, industry, education, and health services along with a growing wave of immigrants. Within two generations, New Town had joined with Old Town and a pre–World War I American city had emerged. By 1930, the population had reached 26,570. Along with prosperity came growth pains: there was no organized sanitation, the fire department was made up of volunteers, and a red-light district thrived in the downtown. Due to the general lack of sewer and water, many basics of life were still unavailable. This also meant that the city had few developed parks.

One person who symbolized Albuquerque's can-do spirit of the time was Aldo Leopold. He moved to Albuquerque in 1915 as a man in his late 20s, raising a young family and starting a career with the newly formed US Forest Service. Although he would only live in Albuquerque for five years, his mark was profound. His energies poured over into civic duties and boosterism. As secretary of the chamber of commerce, Leopold lobbied tirelessly for his new hometown to improve itself. He urged urban planning to avoid having the city "grow like topsy." He encouraged that swampy areas of the valley be drained so that land could be put into production, which led to the establishment of the Middle Rio Grande Conservancy District in 1925. But above all, Leopold was an outdoorsman. He would go on to champion the creation of the nation's first wilderness area—southwestern New Mexico's Gila Wilderness—and to become the father of modern ecology. The personal legacy he left for Albuquerque was protection of the Rio Grande. He was shocked at how the river had become a trash dump but was inspired how, in spite of that, people still wanted to connect with the river without a formally designated park.

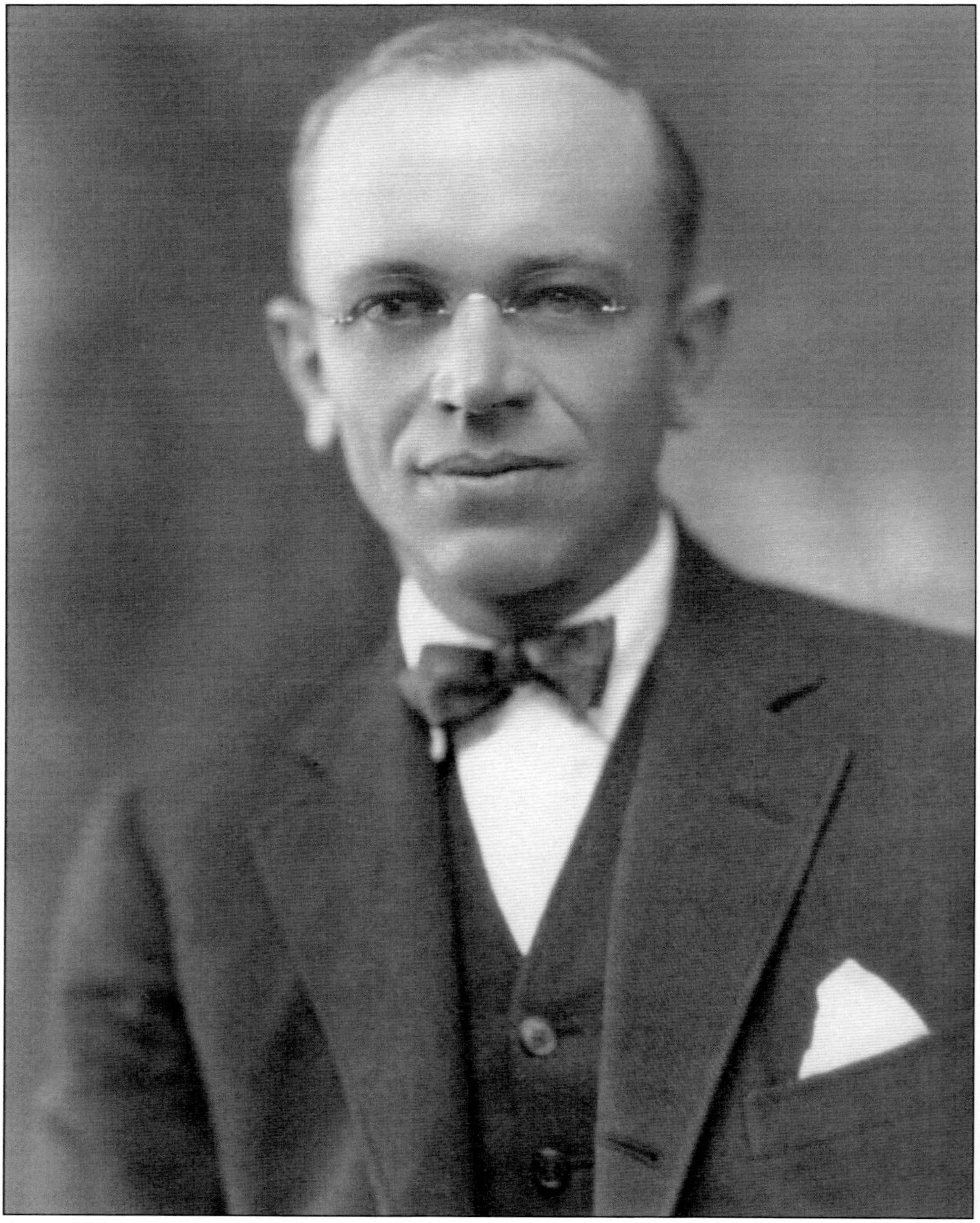

Arguing that no great city can exist without them, the young forester Aldo Leopold began to tout the need for parks just before World War I. Leopold went on to become the father of the American wilderness movement and one of the preeminent ecologists of the modern era. During his short five-year stay in Albuquerque, he advocated for the creation of a Rio Grande park. Asking why so few children were seen in the city's parks, he provided the simple answer, "The boys go to the river." Always a visionary, his idea for a riverside park in the city would take 65 years to be fully realized. Some land he did secure was eventually used for the zoo, and one feature he did encourage—a lake—would be built in the early 1930s. (Aldo Leopold Foundation.)

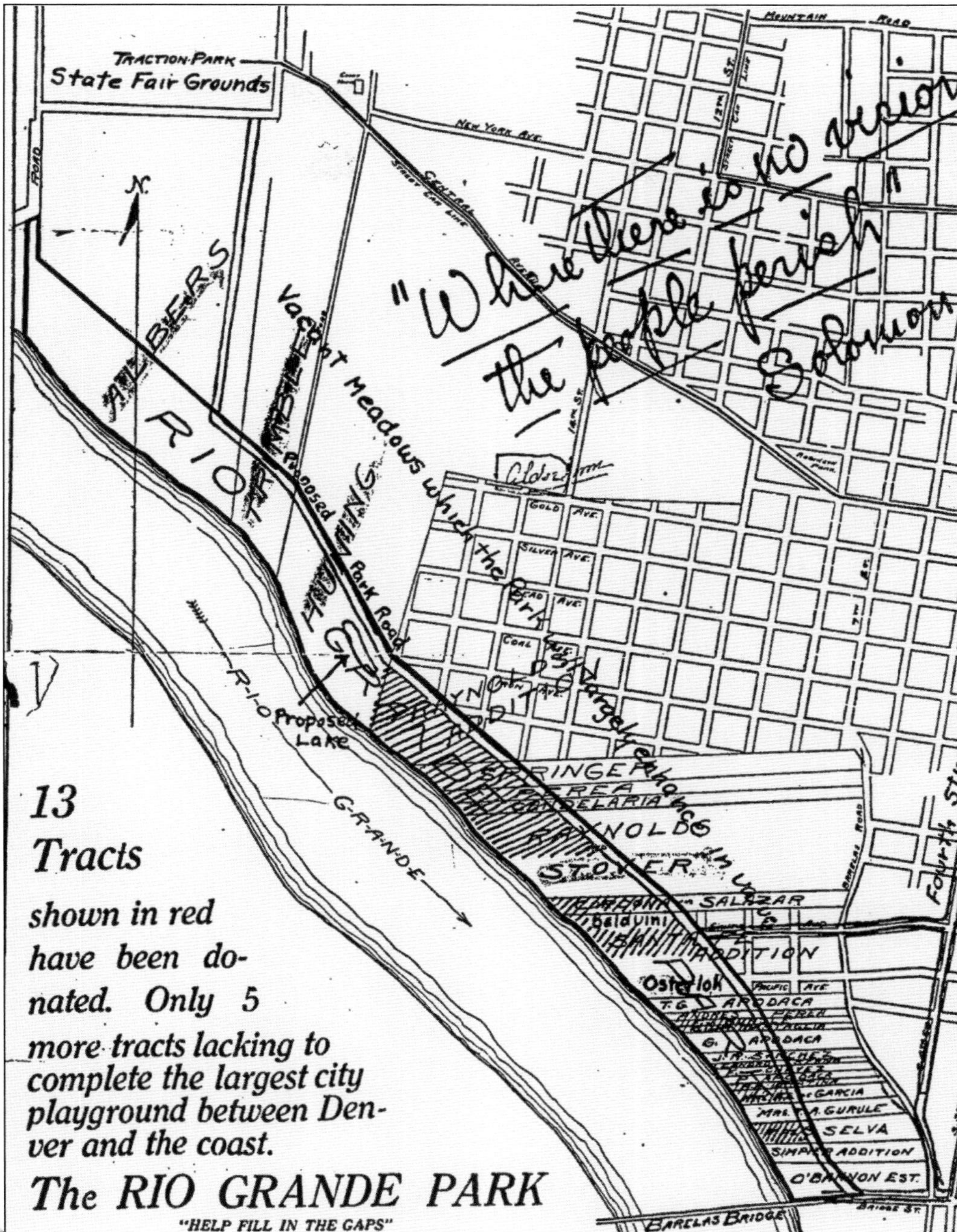

As the Albuquerque Chamber of Commerce secretary, Leopold waged dual battles to promote Rio Grande Park and to secure land for the project. Editorializing across the top of a park map in his own hand, he quoted Solomon while exhorting owners to donate land. His successes with ordinary folk were encouraging, but the park idea stalled when wealthy landowners resisted. The five tracts needed "to complete the largest city playground between Denver and the coast" did not materialize. (Albuquerque Chamber of Commerce.)

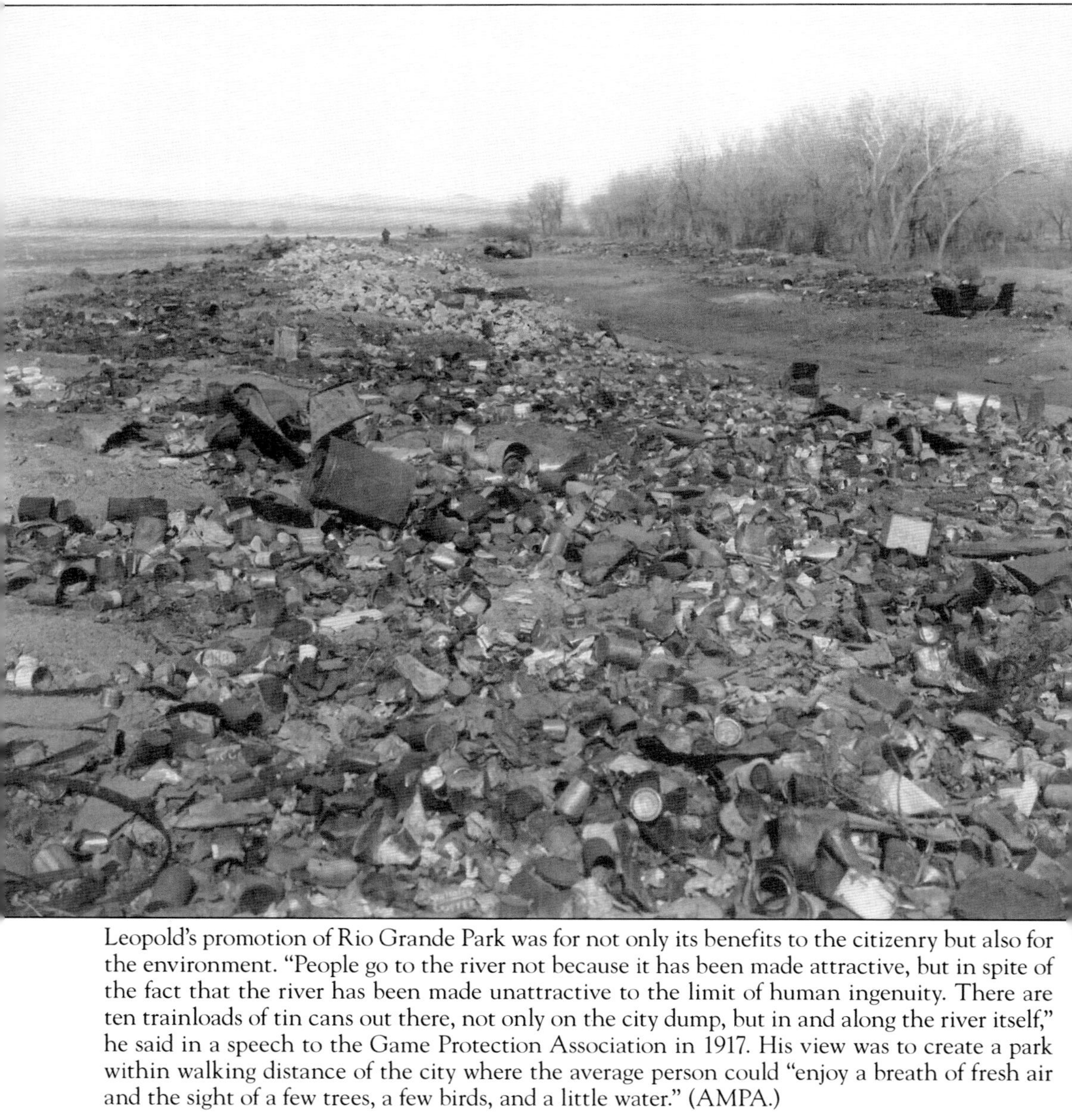

Leopold's promotion of Rio Grande Park was for not only its benefits to the citizenry but also for the environment. "People go to the river not because it has been made attractive, but in spite of the fact that the river has been made unattractive to the limit of human ingenuity. There are ten trainloads of tin cans out there, not only on the city dump, but in and along the river itself," he said in a speech to the Game Protection Association in 1917. His view was to create a park within walking distance of the city where the average person could "enjoy a breath of fresh air and the sight of a few trees, a few birds, and a little water." (AMPA.)

Aldo Leopold was an avid hunter and fisherman. Realizing that wilderness areas served to protect species while creating a need for game management, he carefully balanced conservation with sport. This c. 1915 photograph shows a characteristic Leopold pose: fishing for carp on the Rio Grande in Albuquerque with a bamboo rod and his trademark pipe at one corner of his mouth. (University of Wisconsin.)

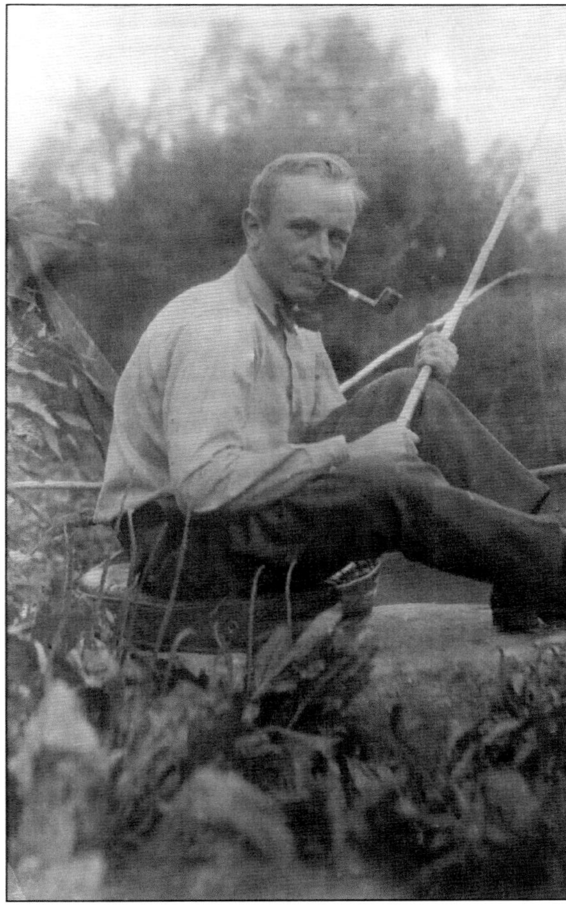

Leopold was also physically vigorous in answering the call of the outdoors despite nearly dying as a young man. Here, he is seen hauling his skiff, called the *Binnacle Bat II*, across the mudflats of the Rio Grande outside Albuquerque in 1918. (Aldo Leopold Foundation.)

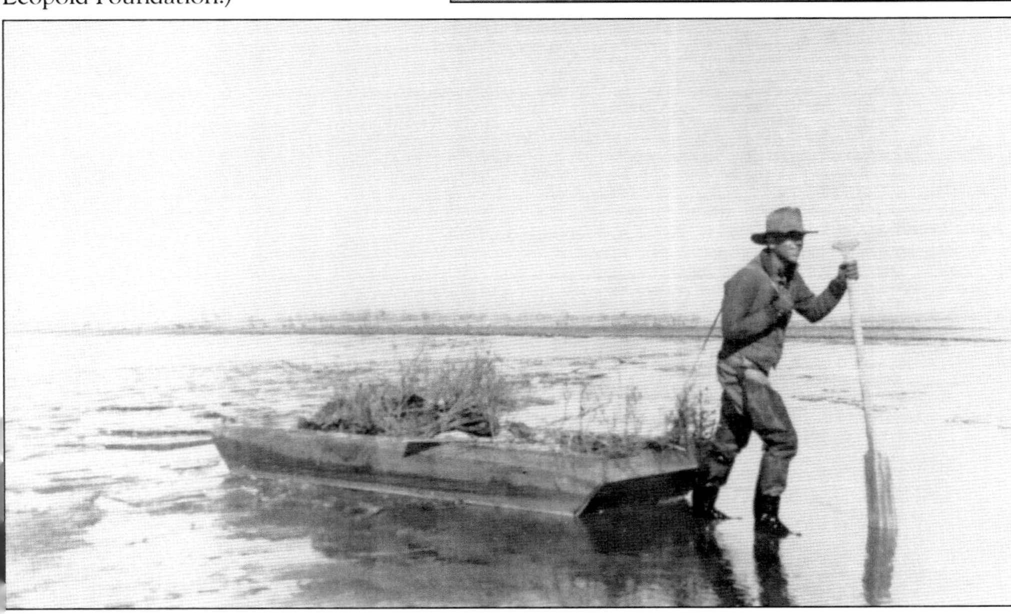

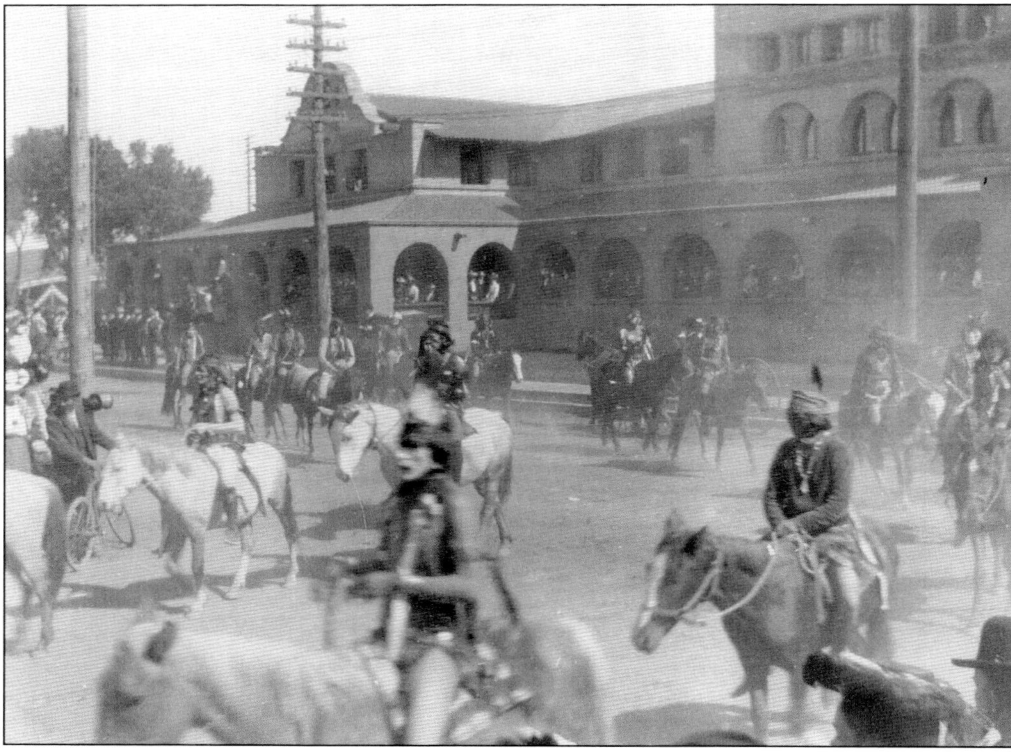

Outdoor amusements in Albuquerque took on many forms, including promoters' views of what should pass as interesting (or exotic) displays of culture to a new crop of tourists arriving by train. This photograph of Native Americans on horseback participating in the Montezuma Ball was taken in front of the Alvarado Hotel in 1915. (AMPA.)

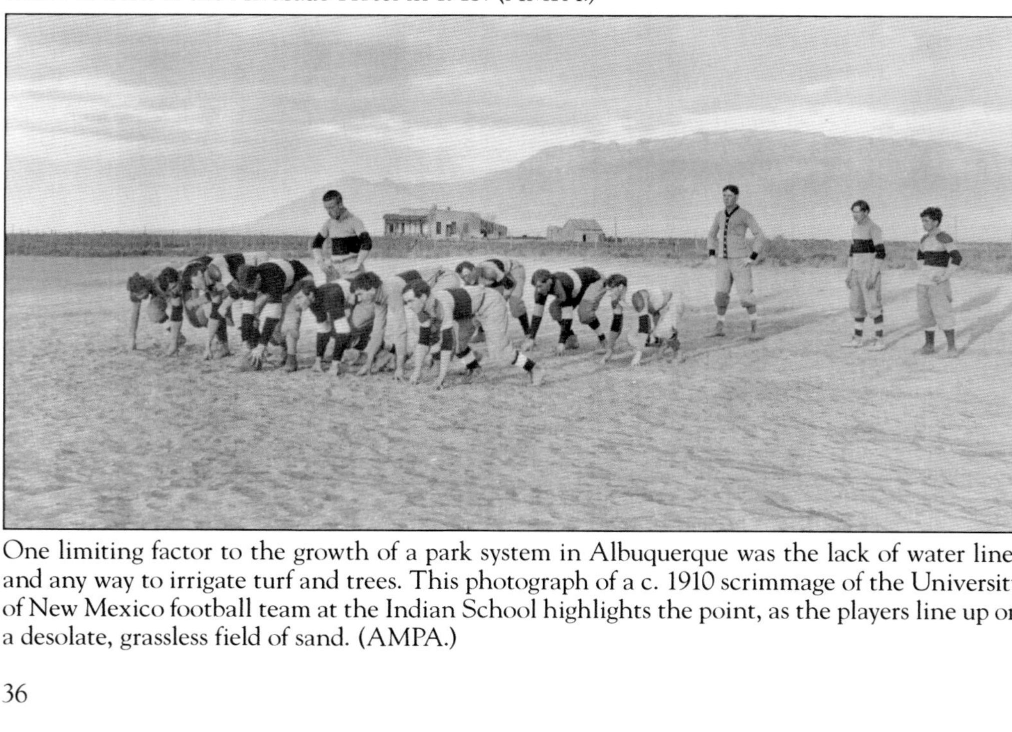

One limiting factor to the growth of a park system in Albuquerque was the lack of water lines and any way to irrigate turf and trees. This photograph of a c. 1910 scrimmage of the University of New Mexico football team at the Indian School highlights the point, as the players line up on a desolate, grassless field of sand. (AMPA.)

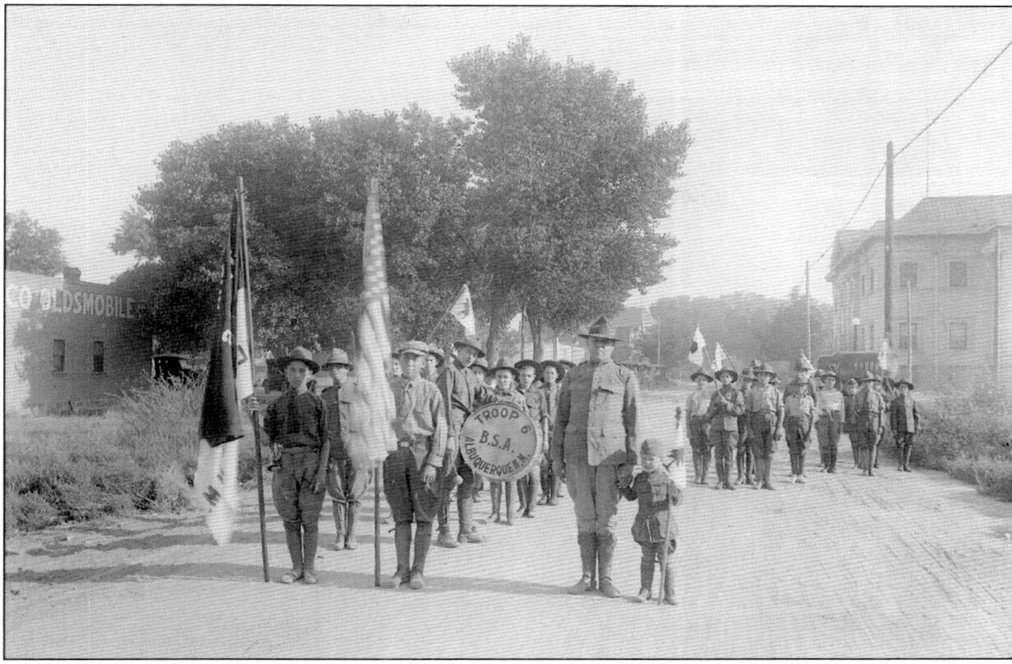

The role of the Scouts was all the more important to youngsters growing up early in the last century. In this 1920s image, boys of varying ages from Boy Scout Troop 6 form parade lines on a dirt roadway near Seventh Street and Central Avenue. (CSWR .)

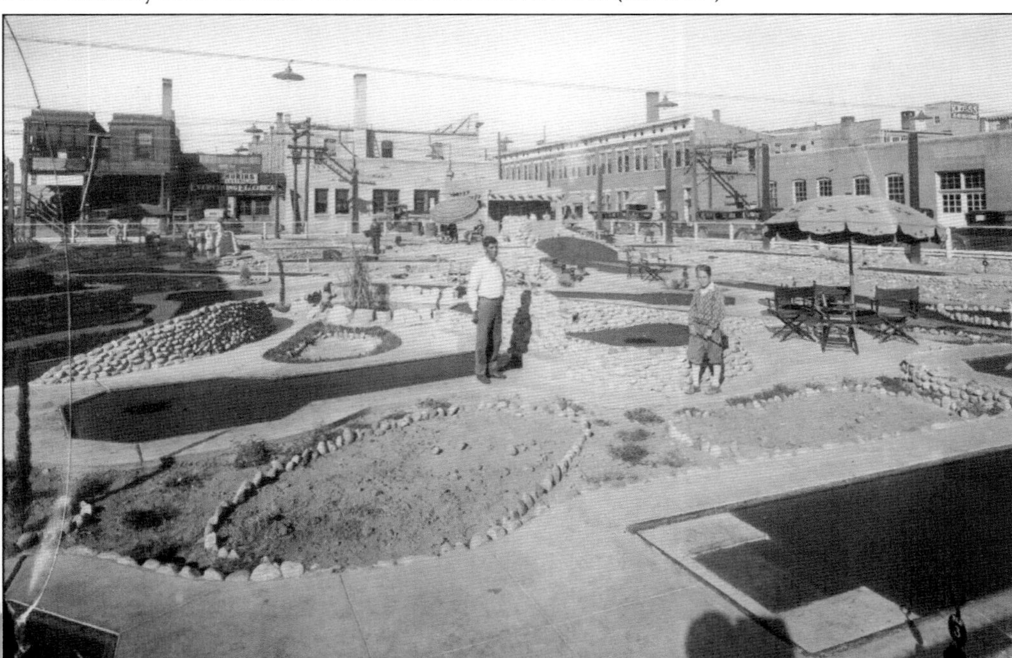

Another way for children to enjoy the outdoors was to play miniature golf. This layout, called the Tom Thumb Golf Course, was built at 501 West Gold Avenue (across from the old post office). The photograph was taken in the fall of 1930. (AMPA.)

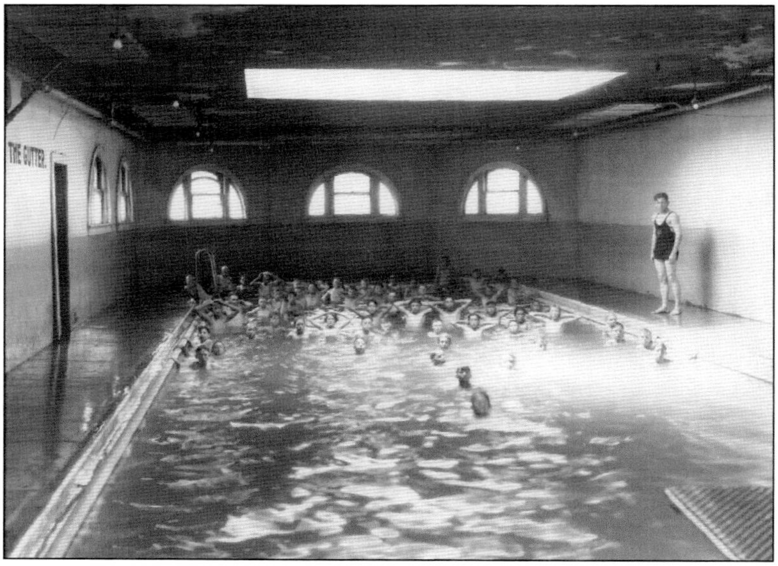

The first known public swimming pool in Albuquerque was at the YMCA, which was built in 1915 at the corner of First Street and Central Avenue. This c. 1917 interior view shows a group of children under the eye of a swimming instructor. (AMPA.)

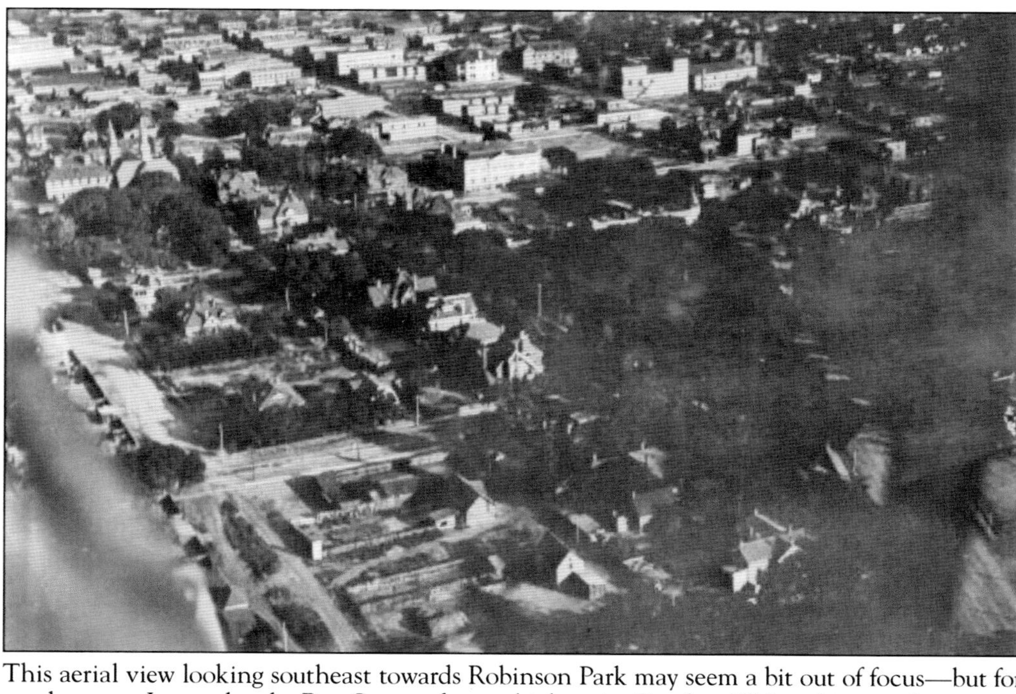

This aerial view looking southeast towards Robinson Park may seem a bit out of focus—but for good reason. It was shot by Roy Stamm from a biplane in October 1913 and is noted as one of the earliest aerial photographs taken in Albuquerque. (CSWR.)

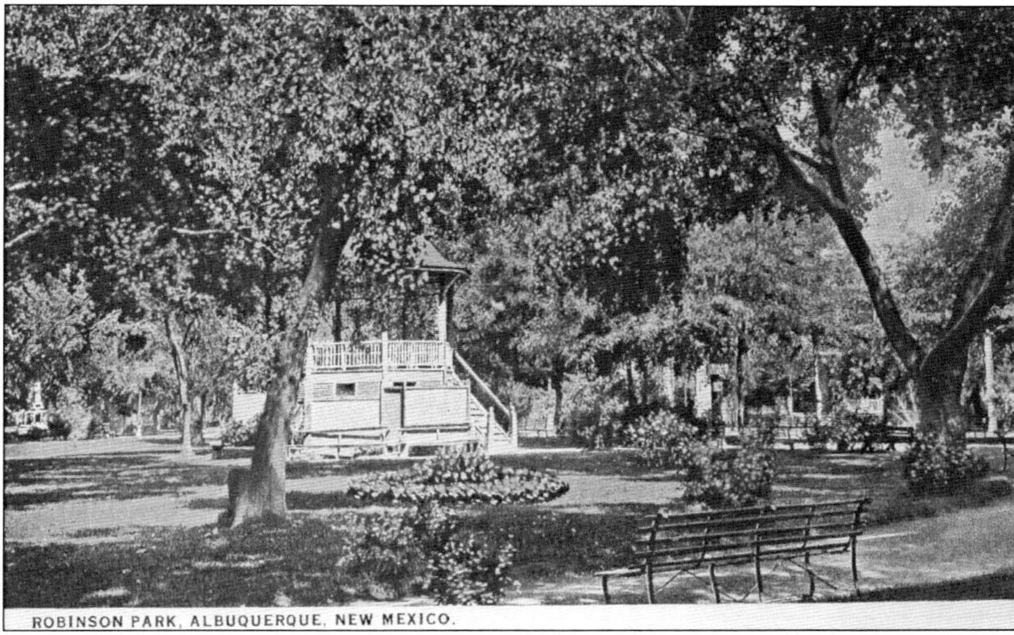

This 1920s postcard view shows a tranquil Robinson Park setting with a bandstand, long since removed. In his book *A Boy's Albuquerque*, author Kenneth Balcomb describes Sunday afternoon concerts played at the bandstand while families relaxed in the park. (Albuquerque Library Special Collections.)

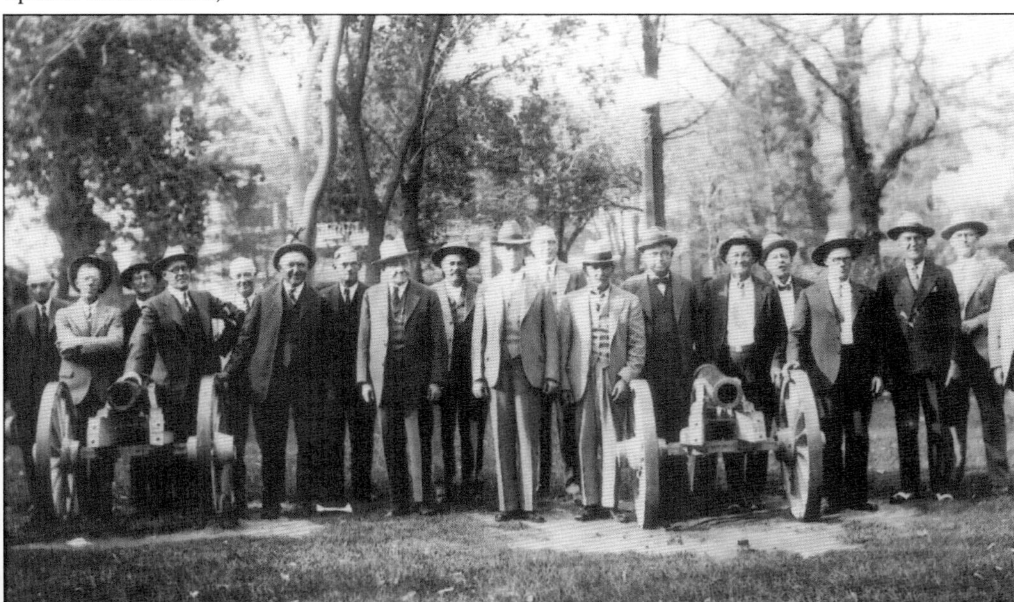

A group of Spanish-American War veterans poses at Robinson Park in 1926 behind two Civil War–era cannons unearthed near Old Town. Confederate major Trevanian Teel buried the cannons in 1862 when the Army was in retreat and returned in 1889 to dig them back up. The cannons were periodically displayed at ceremonies such as this before being permanently retired to the Albuquerque Museum. (AMPA.)

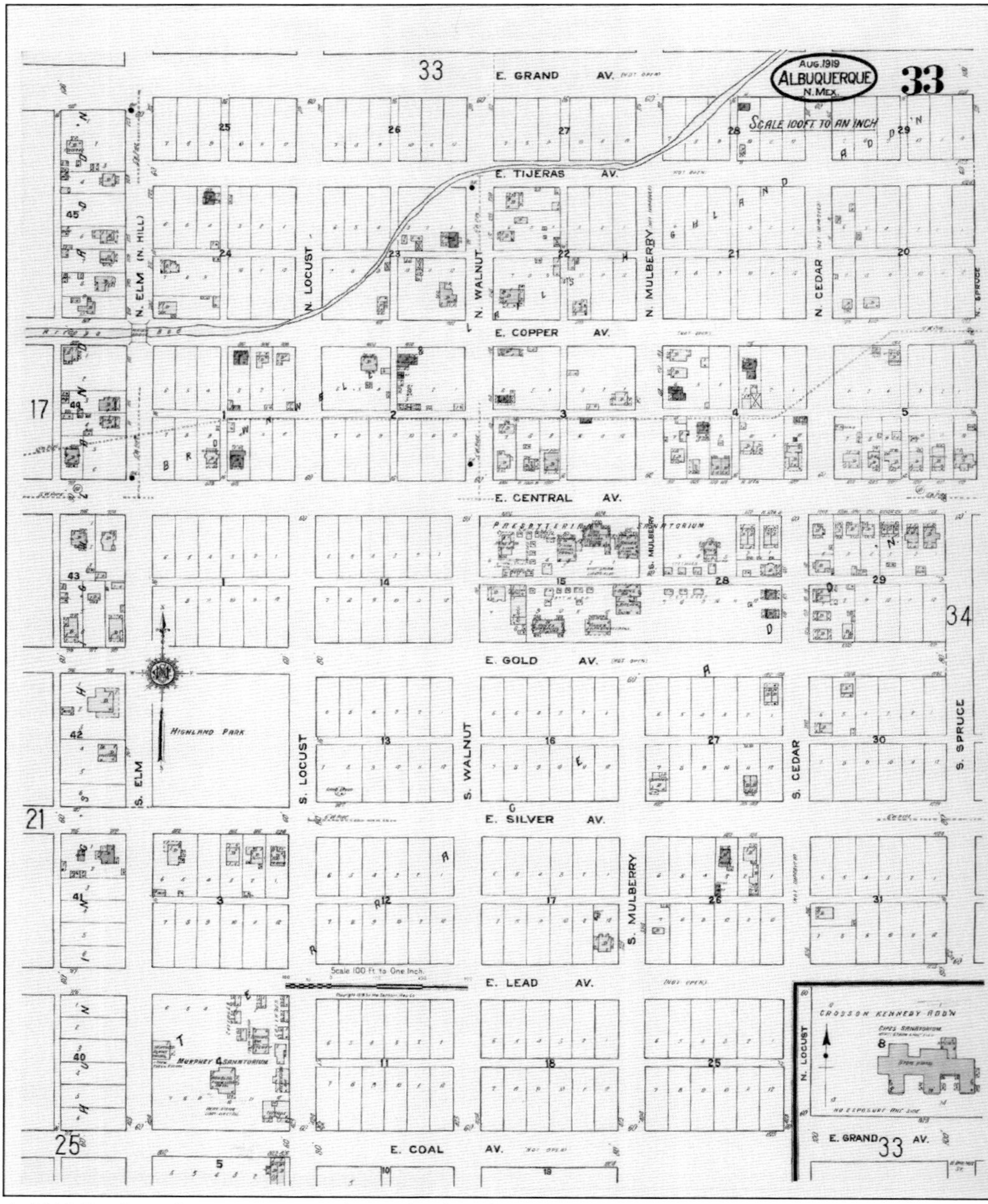

A 1919 Sanborn Insurance Map shows the first formal designation of Highland Park at the corner of Elm Street and Gold Avenue. The park was named due to its location at the eastern edge of Huning Highlands, a well-to-do early suburb of New Town. Franz Huning was a successful merchant whose mansion stood from 1883 until 1955 as an architectural icon on Central Avenue near Old Town. (University of New Mexico, Map and Geographic Information Center.)

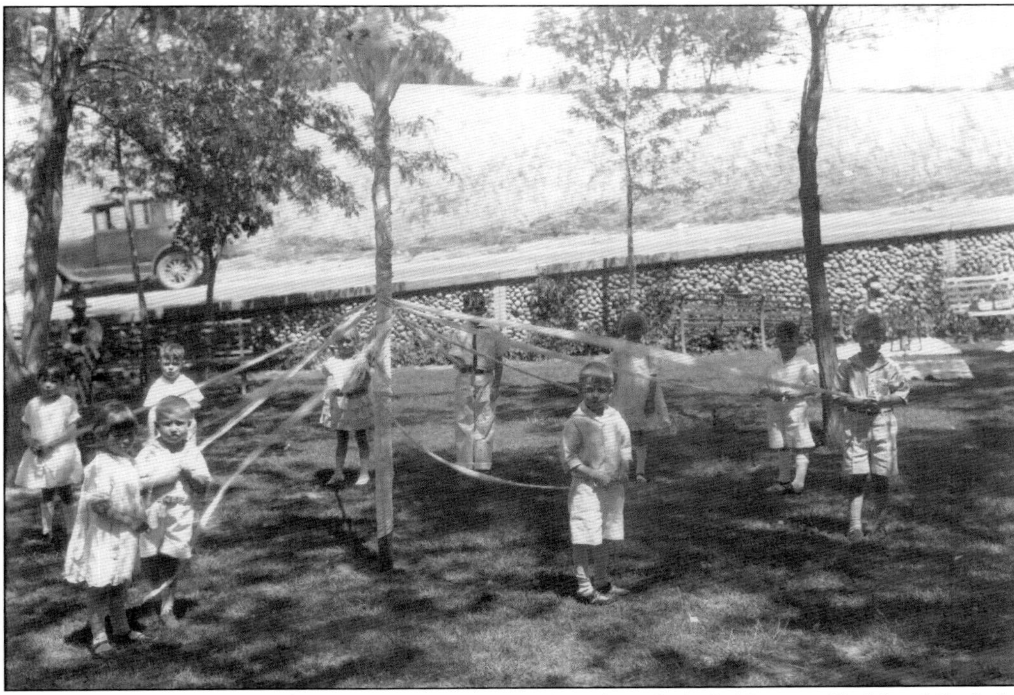

A perfect spring day in 1929 brought this group of unidentified children to Highland Park for birthday fun around the maypole, shown in this Brooks Studio photograph. Highland was one of only three developed parks in Albuquerque built before World War I; the other two were Robinson and Soldiers and Sailors. The cobble-walled driveway to the Whittlesey house, which would later become the Albuquerque Press Club, is in the background. (AMPA.)

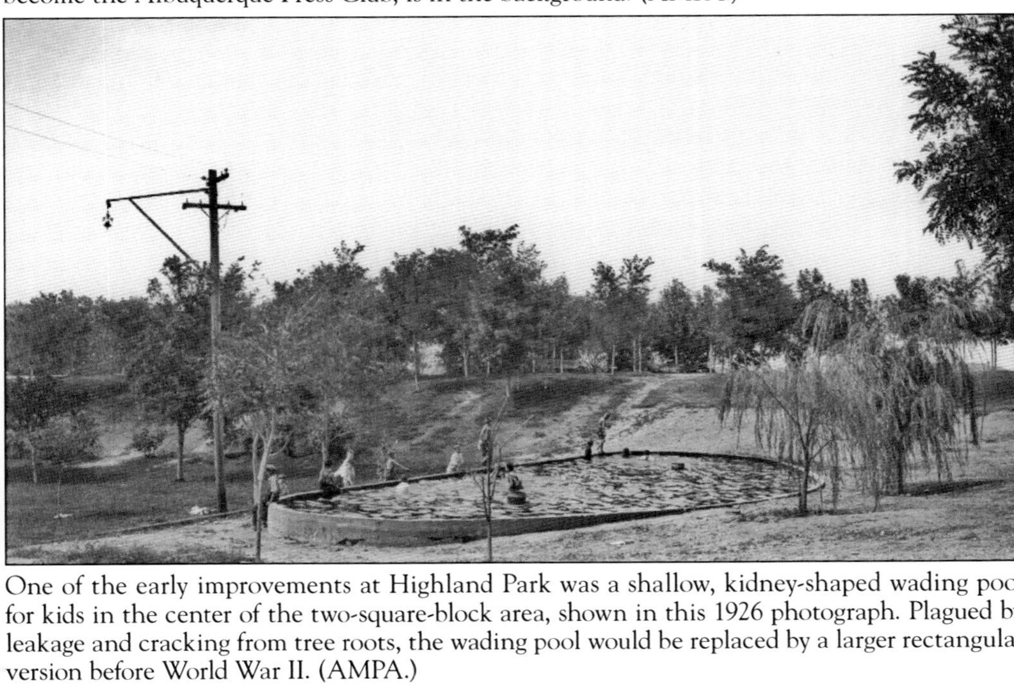

One of the early improvements at Highland Park was a shallow, kidney-shaped wading pool for kids in the center of the two-square-block area, shown in this 1926 photograph. Plagued by leakage and cracking from tree roots, the wading pool would be replaced by a larger rectangular version before World War II. (AMPA.)

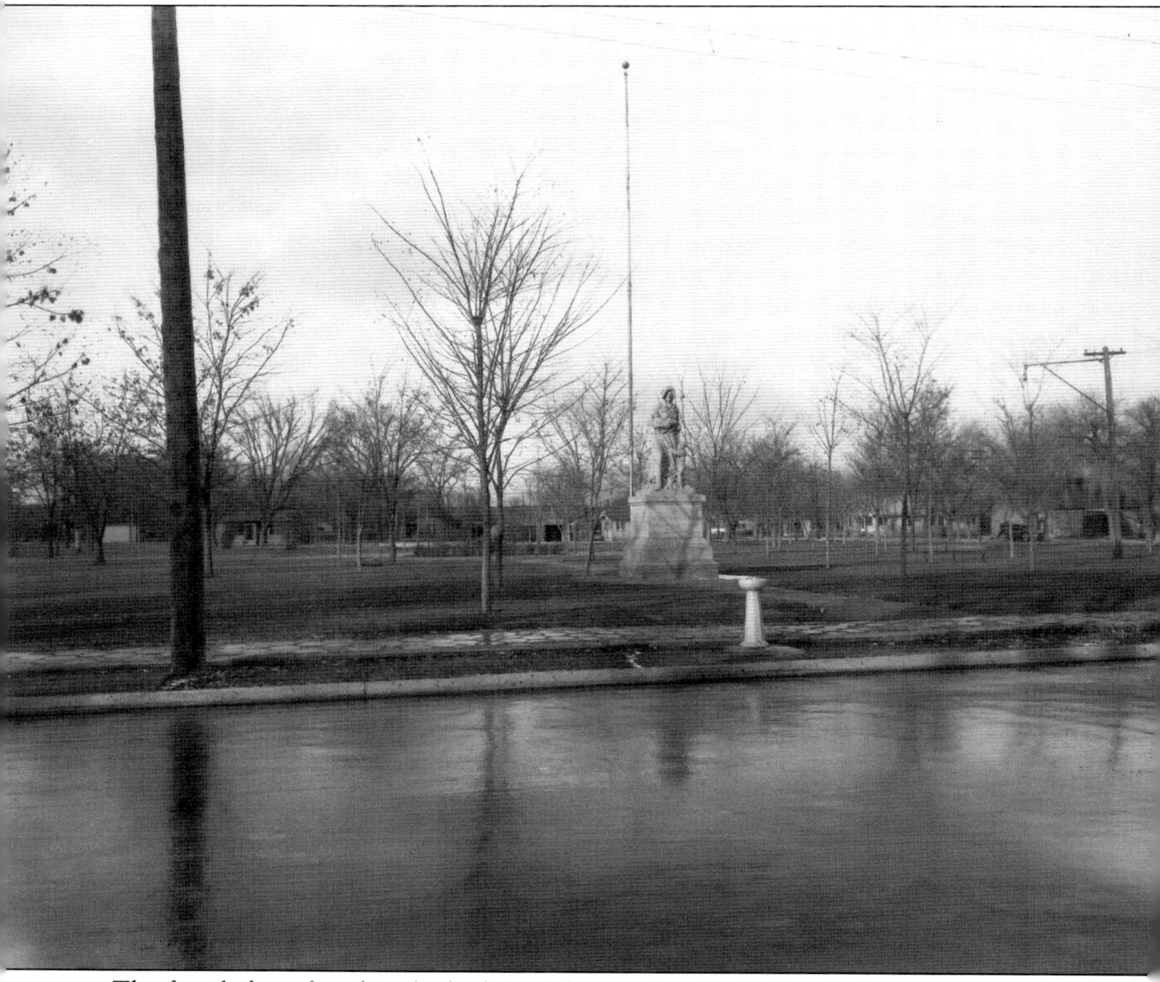

The fourth formal park to be built in Albuquerque, McClellan Park happened as the result of private fundraising and enterprise. In 1919, part of an orchard was cleared north of Lomas Boulevard between Fifth and Sixth Streets, and the means to start watering a green space was found. A 16-foot-high statue, one of 12 created in the 1920s by the Daughters of the American Revolution to commemorate old trails and promote new roads, was placed in McClellan Park in 1928 after Santa Fe rejected New Mexico's gift from the organization. The *Madonna of the Trail* remained near its original place near Lomas Boulevard and Fourth Street at the behest of the DAR even though the park itself was lost in the late 1990s to make way for a new federal courthouse. (AMPA.)

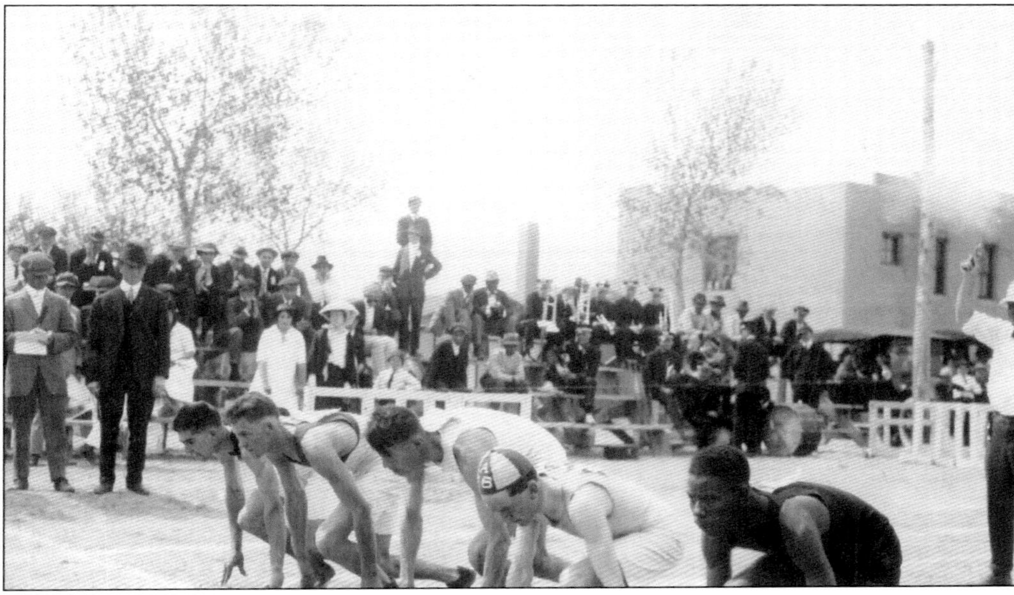

A remarkable series of stop-action photographs taken by the Cobb studios in the 1920s captures the flavor of a track-and-field meet likely held at the University of New Mexico. Above, runners are at the starting line at the precise moment that the starter's gun is fired. Below, with grandstands in the background, racers in mid-stride clear hurdles. (Both, CSWR.)

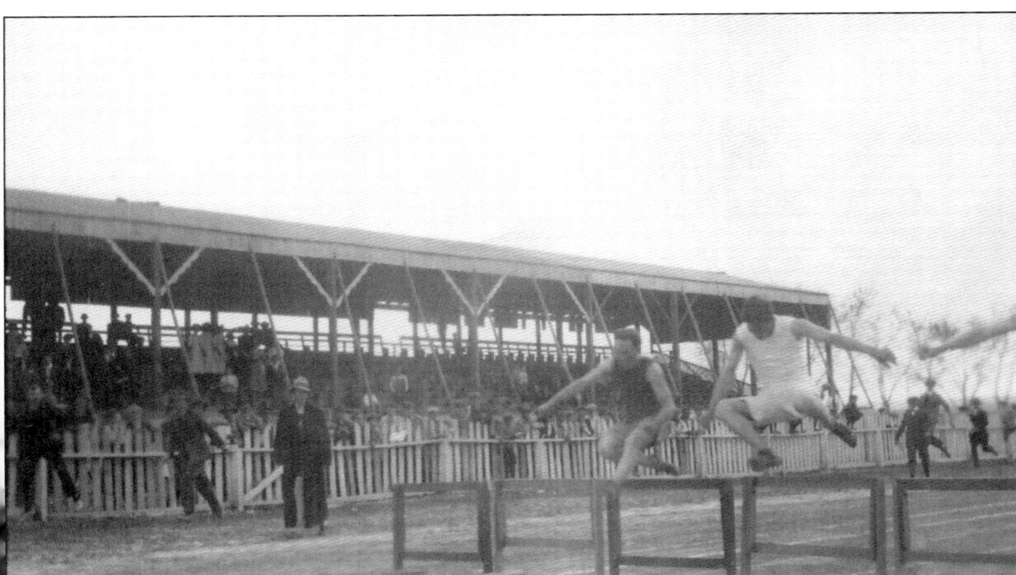

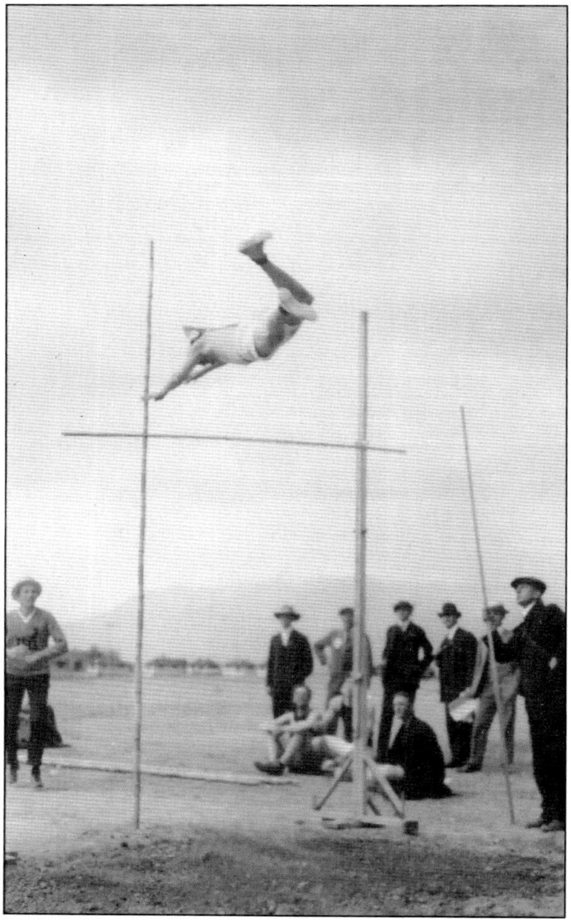

At left, a pole-vaulter photographed in midair easily clears the bar as a small crowd looks on. Note the lack of any cushioning and the use of a bamboo pole. Below, the shot put has just left the hand of this competitor. (Both, CSWR.)

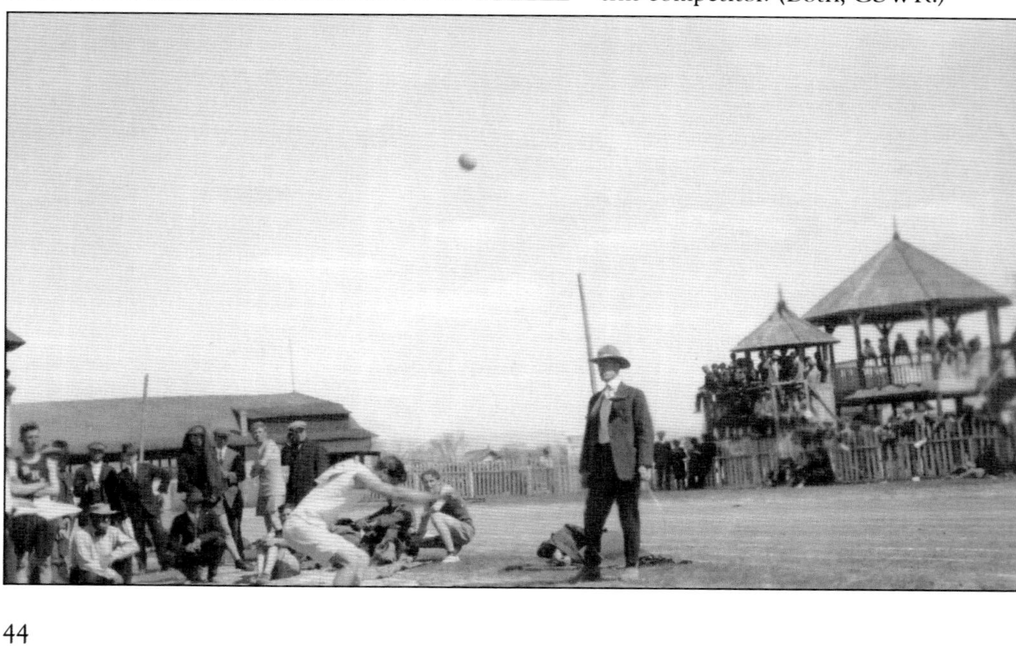

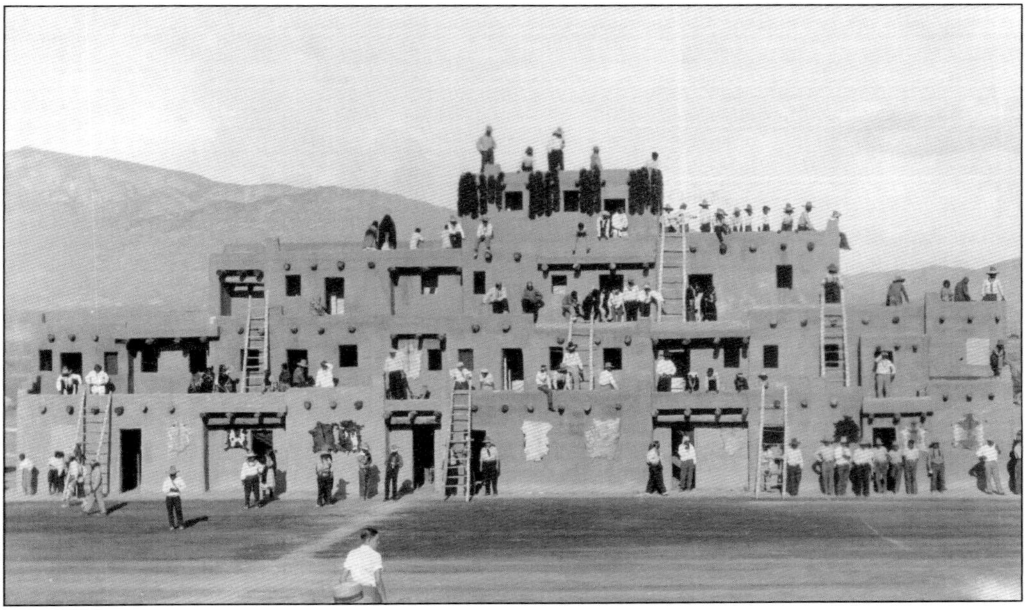

During the Great Depression, Albuquerque Chamber of Commerce members Arthur Praeger, Clinton Anderson, Clyde Oden, Sol Benjamin, and Ward Hicks put together a four-day-long exhibition to promote the area's multicultural heritage called the First American Pageant. Dances, parades, and crafts shows took place in the early fall from 1928 through 1931. A full-scale false-fronted replica of a pueblo was constructed for the occasion. (AMPA.)

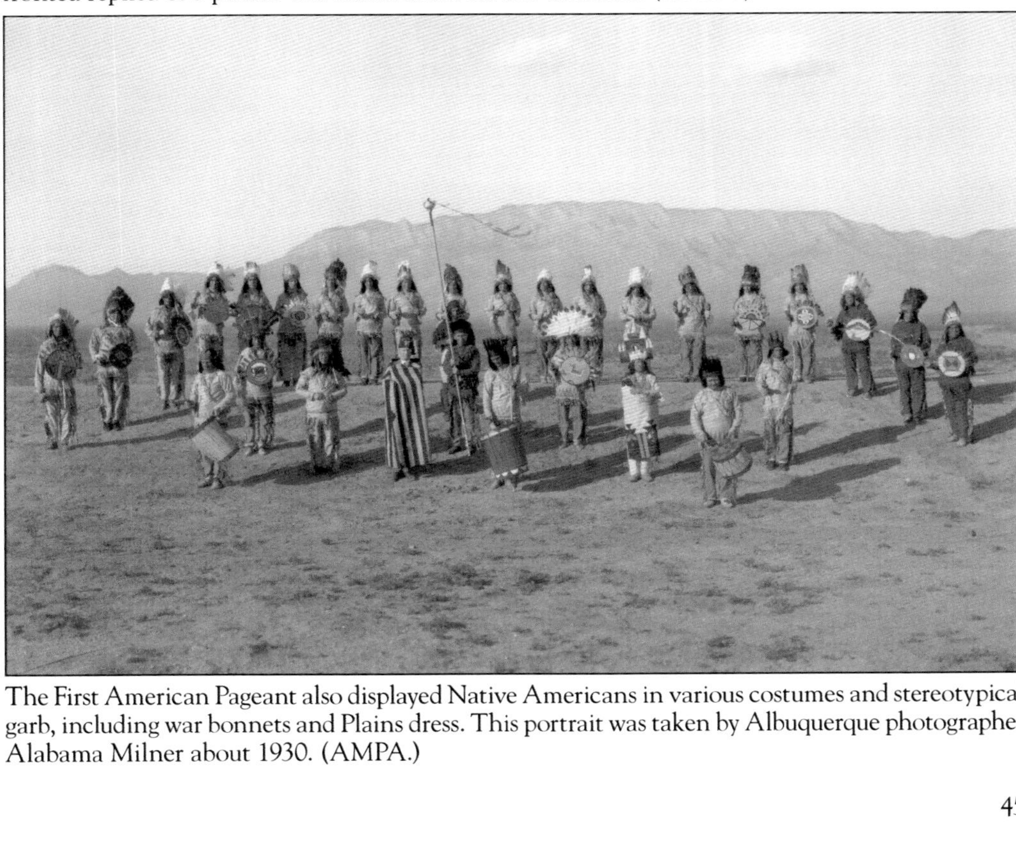

The First American Pageant also displayed Native Americans in various costumes and stereotypical garb, including war bonnets and Plains dress. This portrait was taken by Albuquerque photographer Alabama Milner about 1930. (AMPA.)

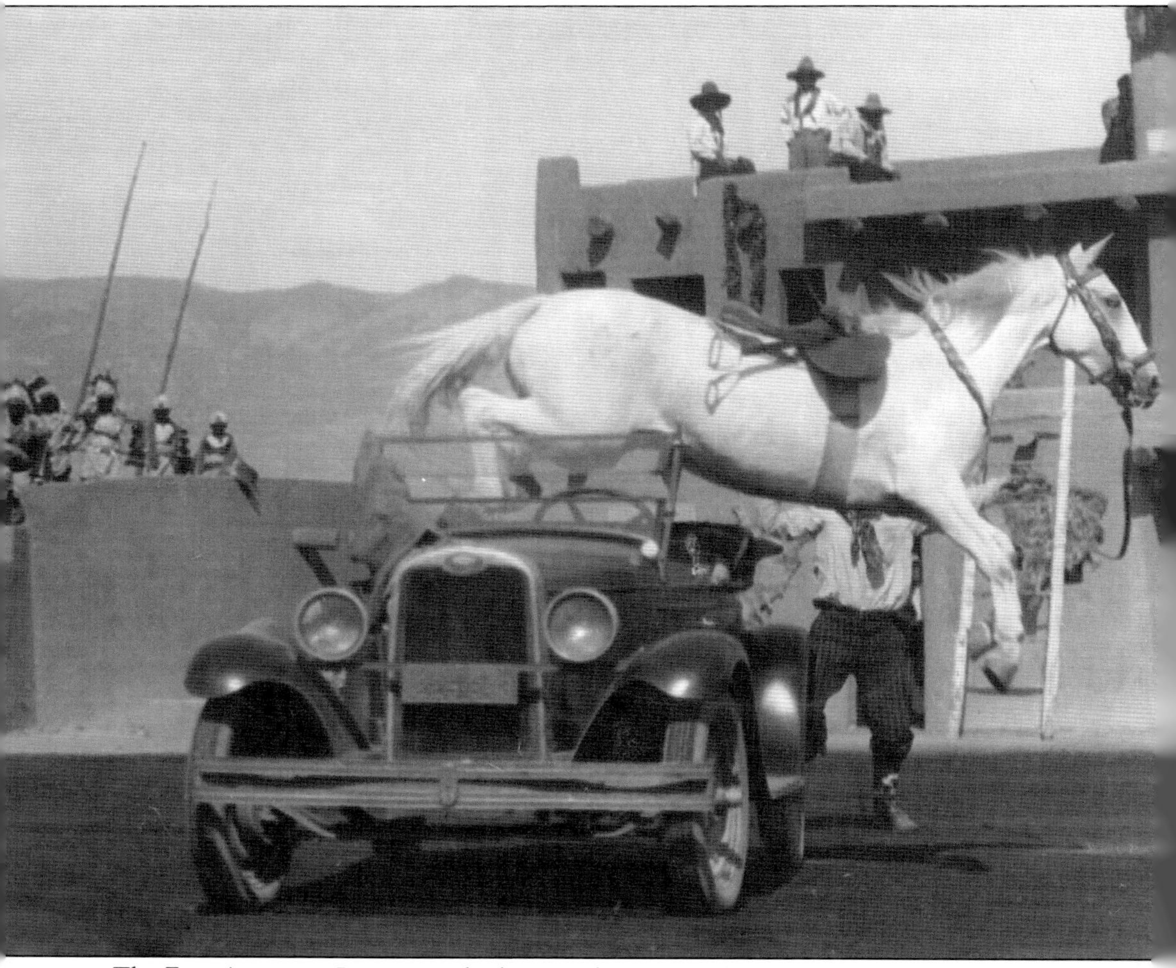

The First American Pageant took place at what is now the corner of Wyoming Boulevard and Central Avenue, which at the time was on the then desolate expanses of the far East Mesa. This 1928 photograph shows a horse jumping over the hood of a Ford truck to the amazement of onlookers. (CSWR.)

Three

The Clyde Tingley Era

In 1910, an engaged couple's train trip from Bowling Green, Ohio, to Arizona was cut short by a medical emergency, and Albuquerque's history was changed forever. Carrie Wooster, daughter of a wealthy Ohio family, suffered from tuberculosis and was in the company of her mother and fiancé when an acute attack forced the trio to stop in Albuquerque. They found the health care to be excellent and decided to go no farther. Carrie and Clyde Tingley were married on April 21, 1911. While Carrie Tingley recovered her health, Clyde became active in politics and was elected as city alderman in 1916—the first of many political positions he would hold in the next 40 years. He became a city commissioner in 1922 and served until elected governor of New Mexico in 1934 and 1936, but his attempts to change the state constitution to allow for a third term failed. Even so, his time as governor brought prominence to the state and much federal funding for post-Depression projects. Tingley returned to the city commission in 1939 and to his role as the chairman and ex-officio "mayor" until he resigned from political life in 1955. He died on Christmas Eve 1960.

Clyde Tingley's role in developing the city's park system was inestimable. He spearheaded the construction of Tingley Beach in 1931 and his close relationship with Pres. Franklin Roosevelt brought Works Progress Administration (WPA) projects such as Terrace Park, the Heights Community Center, and the Tingley Field baseball stadium. He quickly renamed Terrace Park as Roosevelt Park out of admiration for the president. Tingley's political influence was perhaps only matched by his flamboyance. While wearing his trademark linen suits and fedora, he utilized photo opportunities at every turn and posed with celebrities, beauty contestants, and even Santa Claus. Despite being a target for criticism and operating with a blend of country-style casualness and old-fashioned political strong-arming, Clyde Tingley always said, "Look at my record." That record was one with many lasting contributions, not the least of which was the children's hospital for which Carrie Tingley worked tirelessly and which today bears her name.

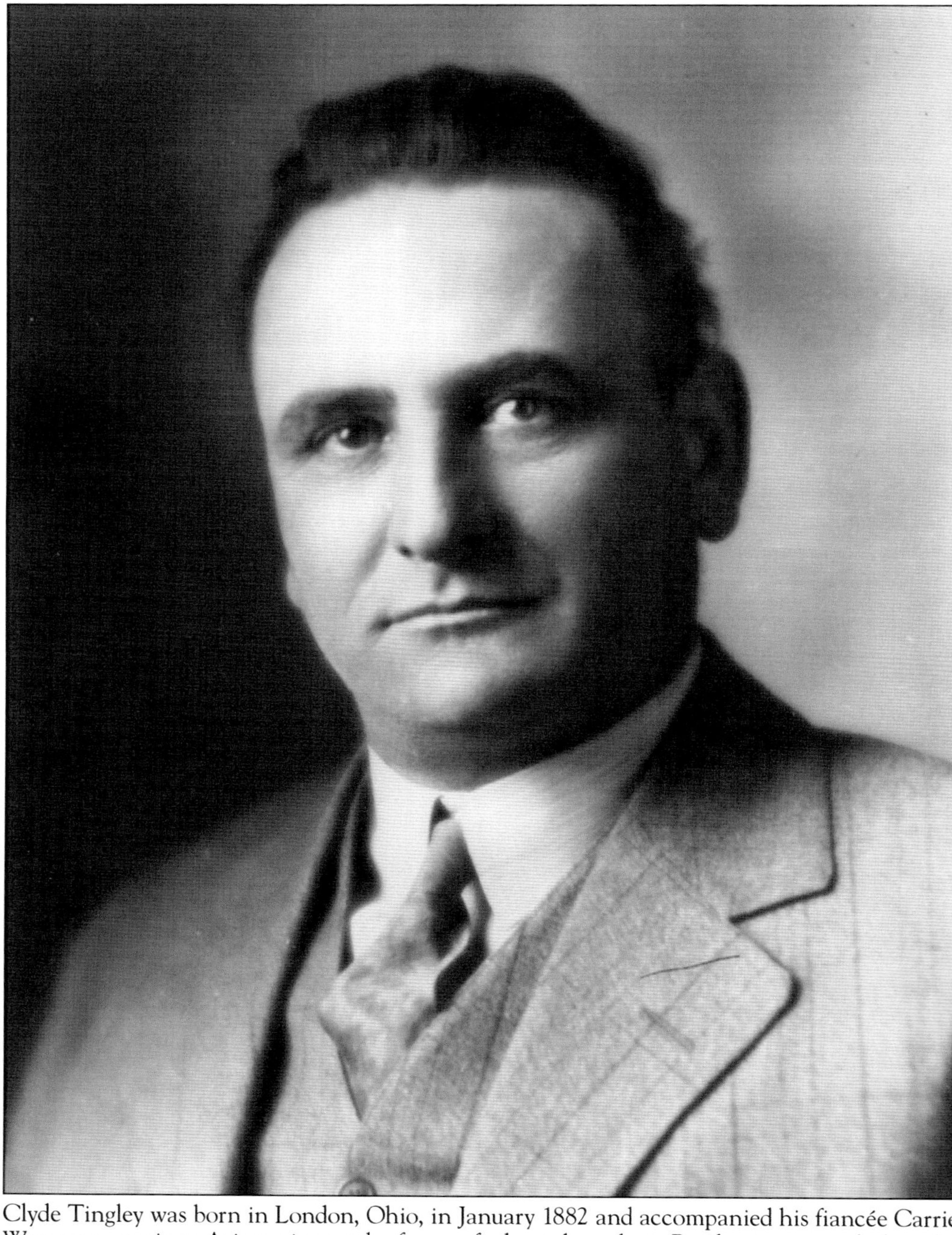

Clyde Tingley was born in London, Ohio, in January 1882 and accompanied his fiancée Carrie Wooster on a trip to Arizona in search of a cure for her tuberculosis. But fate intervened when she had an asthma attack in Albuquerque and the couple found excellent care. They decided to stay and were married in 1911. With Carrie's involvement in health care and Clyde in politics, they both had a profound effect on their new hometown. Clyde Tingley would serve in elected offices for 40 years. Tingley is shown in this c. 1925 formal portrait taken by photographer Alabama Milner. By this time, he had already served as alderman and had been elected "mayor" by virtue of being elected to lead the city commission. (AMPA.)

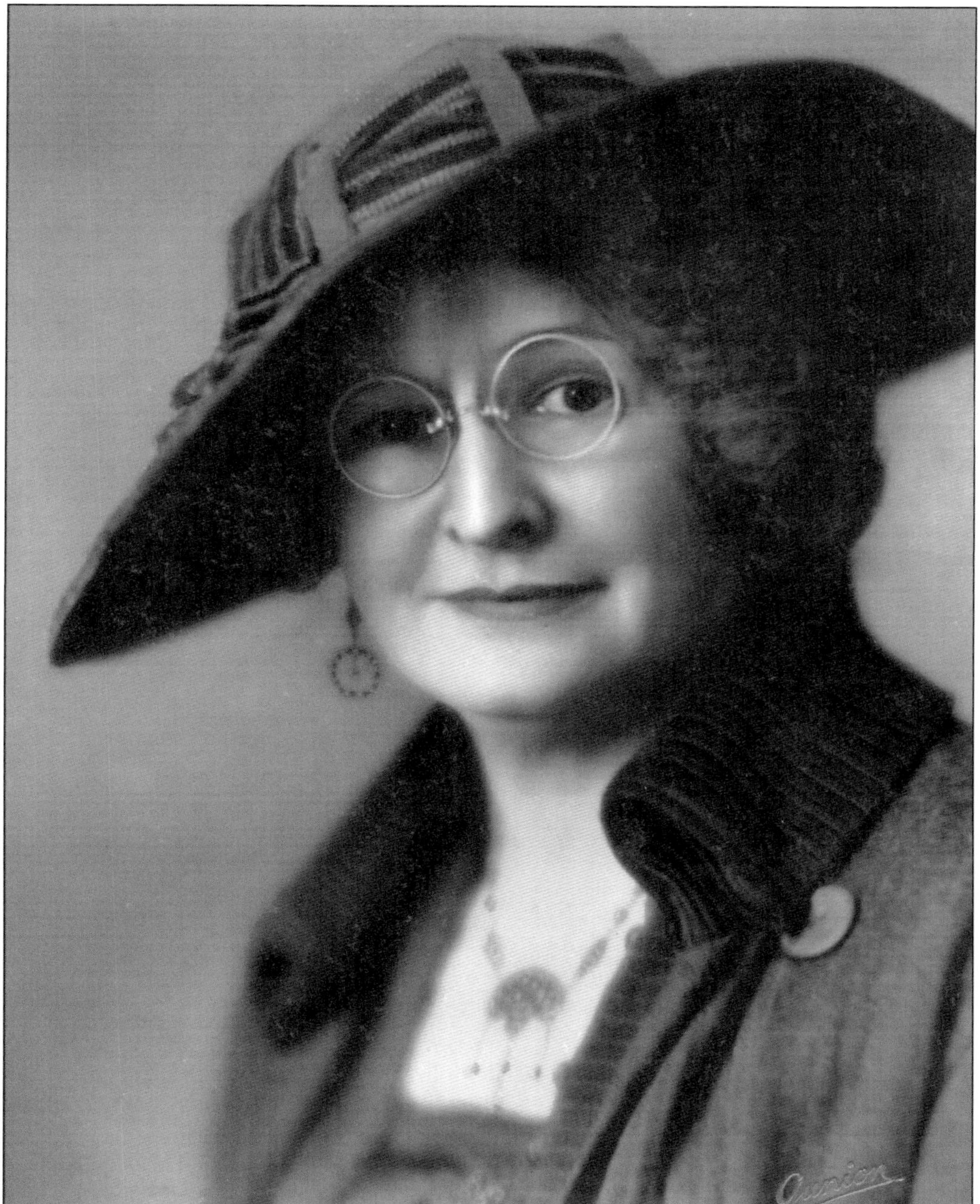

Carrie Wooster Tingley's own early-life battles with illness made her a passionate advocate for childhood health. After Clyde Tingley was elected governor of New Mexico, he helped establish hospitals all over the state. Carrie Tingley Children's Hospital was opened in 1937 in Hot Springs (later renamed Truth or Consequences) to care for young polio victims. The hospital moved to Albuquerque in 1981. This 1940s portrait by Gunion studios shows that Carrie Tingley was no shrinking violet alongside her powerful husband. (CSWR.)

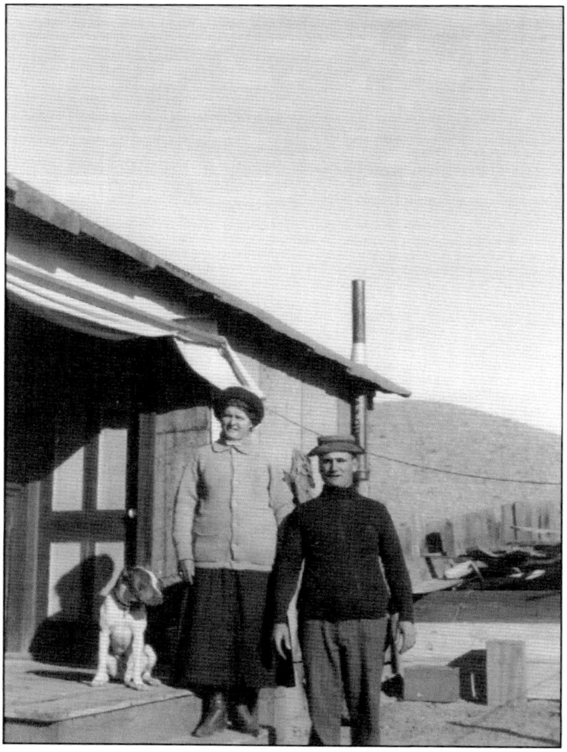

Soon after their arrival in Albuquerque, the newly wedded Clyde and Carrie Tingley pose for this portrait about 1912 with their dog in front of their cabin. At this time, Clyde had yet to venture into the world of politics. (AMPA.)

Carrie Tingley's own love of the outdoors is seen in this c. 1915 shot of her in a horse-drawn carriage, touring around at the base of the Sandia foothills. (AMPA.)

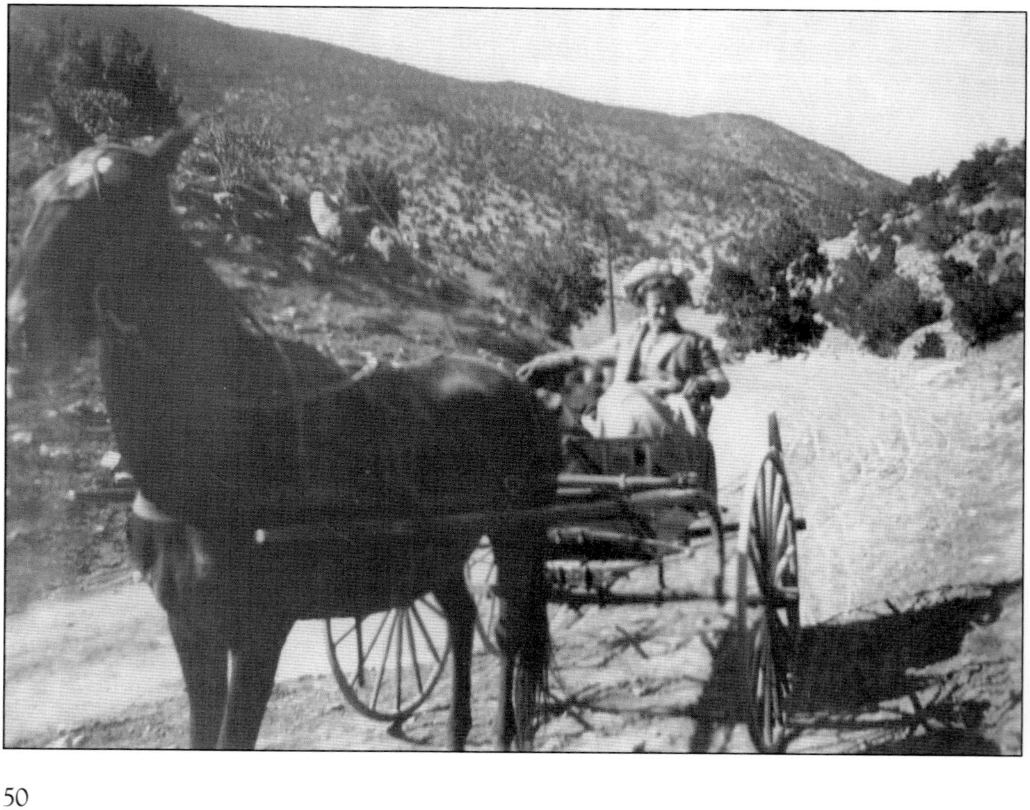

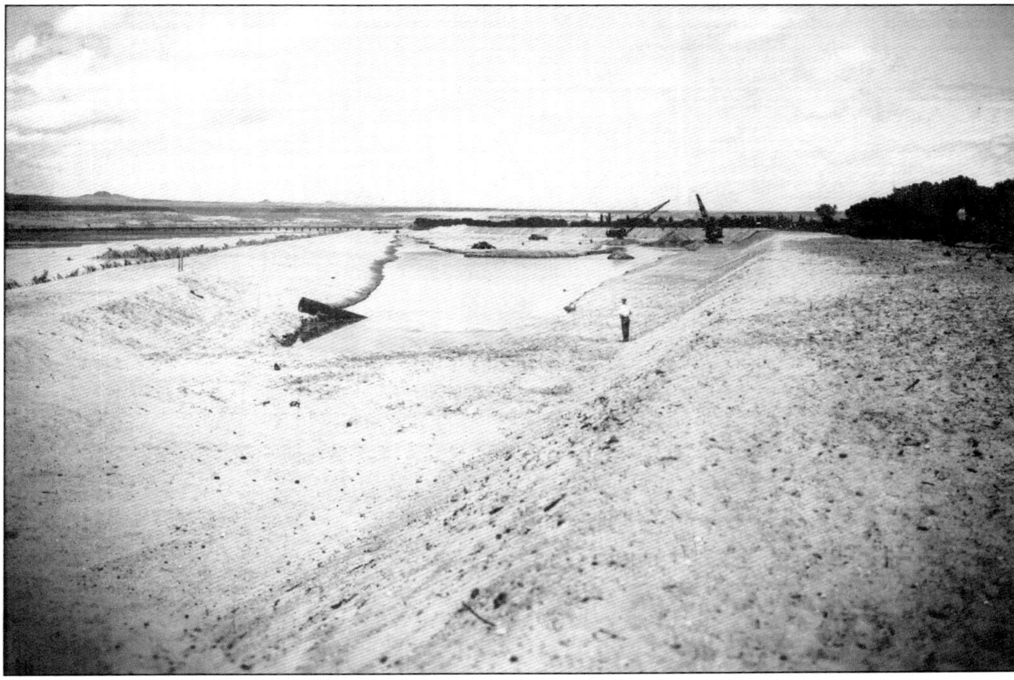

In 1931, Mayor Clyde Tingley urged the newly formed Middle Rio Grande Conservancy District to dredge a former city dump located between the country club and the Rio Grande to create a shallow linear lake. Working with Fred Burkholder, chief engineer of the Conservancy District, they ensured the job was finished in less than six months. This view looking northwest faintly shows the West Mesa volcanoes in the background. (AMPA.)

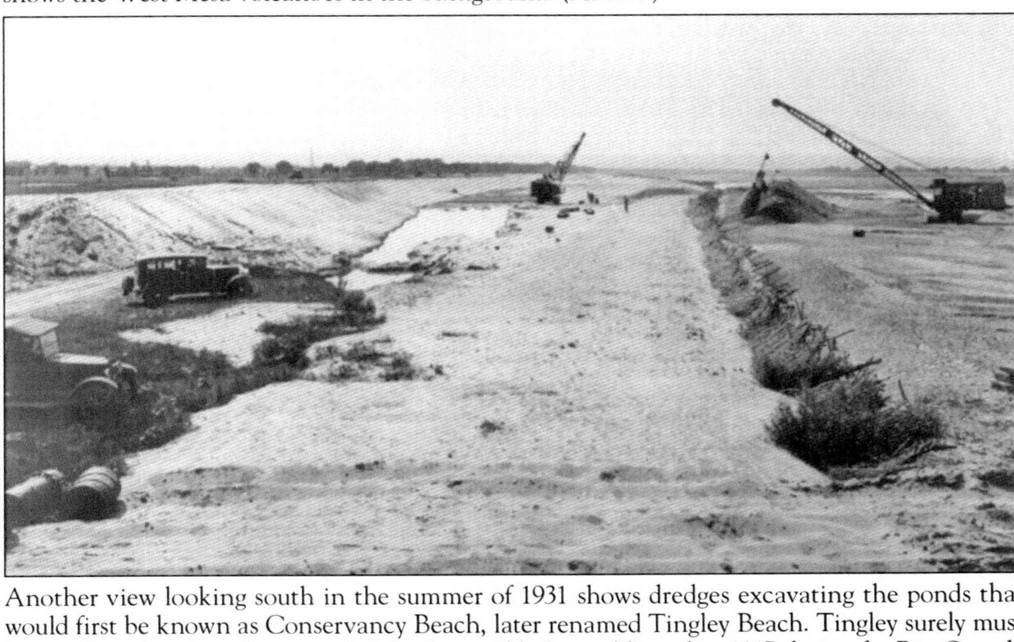

Another view looking south in the summer of 1931 shows dredges excavating the ponds that would first be known as Conservancy Beach, later renamed Tingley Beach. Tingley surely must have taken the idea of a riverside lake from Aldo Leopold's earlier 1917 design for Rio Grande Park. (AMPA.)

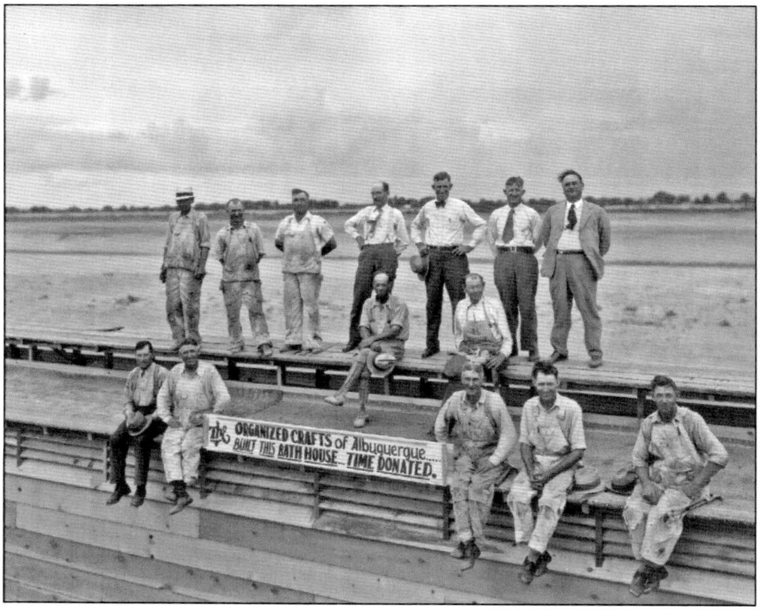

Clyde Tingley (standing, far right) was forced to pull together every resource he could find in order to construct the facilities needed for the new Conservancy Beach. During the Great Depression, cash was hard to come by, but he was able to obtain free labor from unions and donated materials from companies with which to build structures such as dressing rooms and bathhouses. (AMPA.)

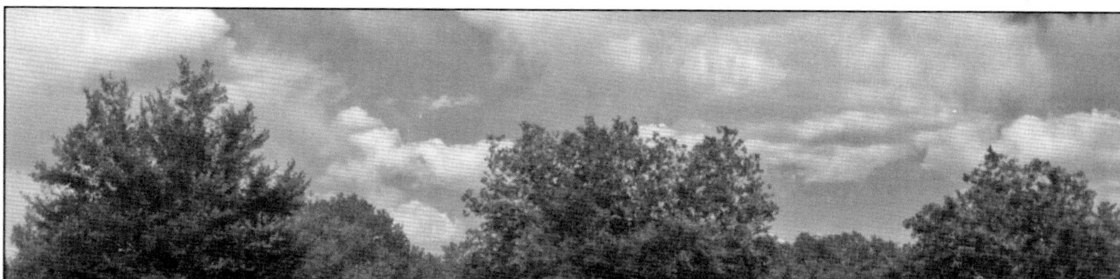

The success of Conservancy Beach was immediate. With waterslides, bathhouses, and lots of shoreline, it soon became the place to be seen in the summer months. Tingley Beach was a popular outdoor swimming pool for two decades until polio scares and health concerns closed it down in the early 1950s. (AMPA.)

Tingley Beach also featured a popular diving platform. During peak use, the city hired eight lifeguards to watch over swimmers. A later internal city commission memo complained, however, that the lifeguards were taking two-hour-long lunches that resulted in the diving tower often being closed. The lifeguards also "used abusive language when it rained" and there was "too much talking to girls and public necking." (AMPA.)

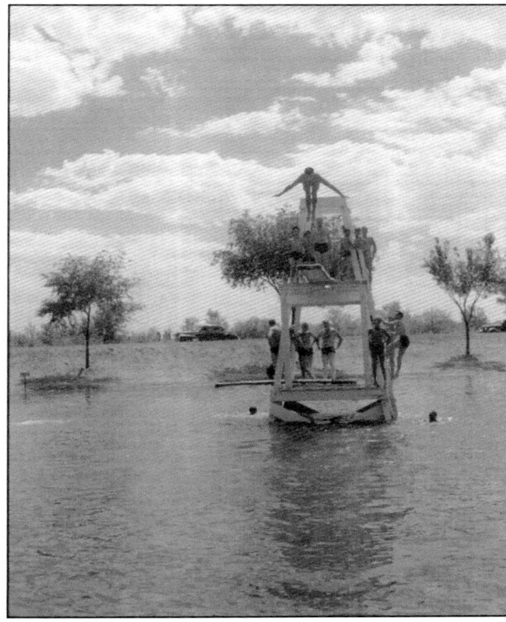

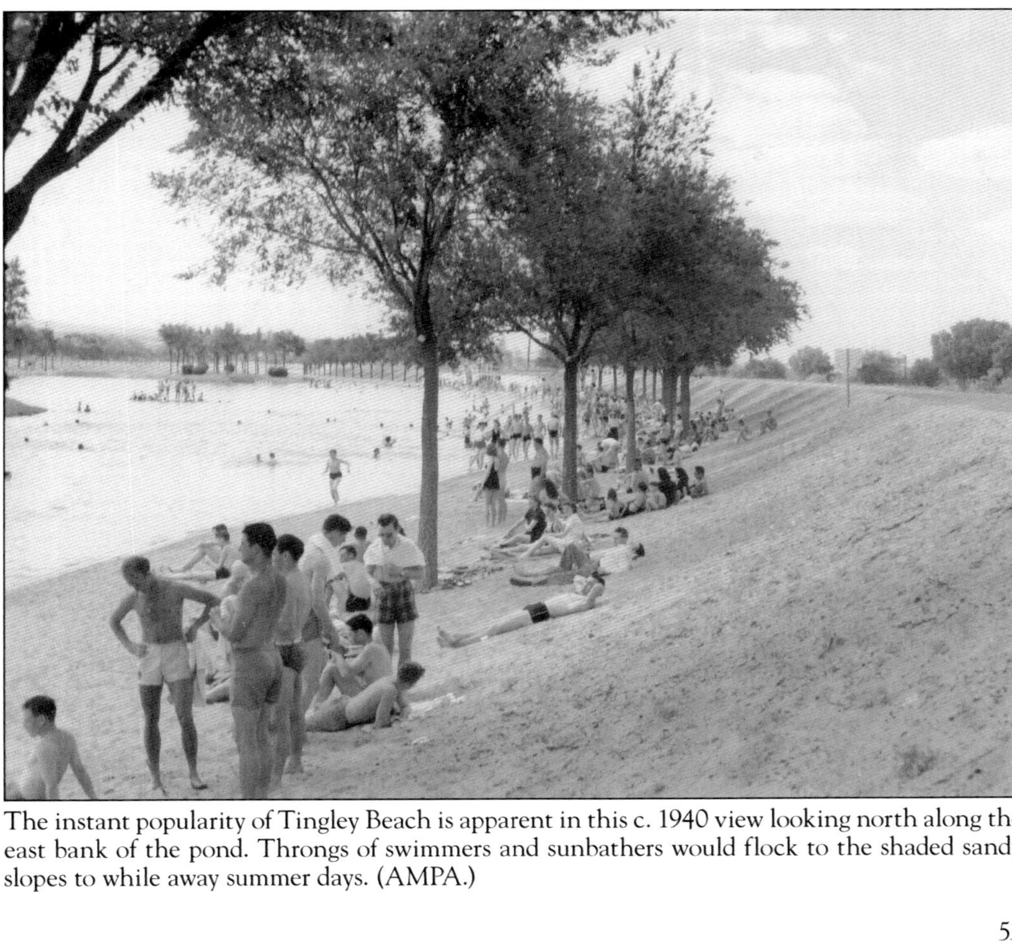

The instant popularity of Tingley Beach is apparent in this c. 1940 view looking north along the east bank of the pond. Throngs of swimmers and sunbathers would flock to the shaded sandy slopes to while away summer days. (AMPA.)

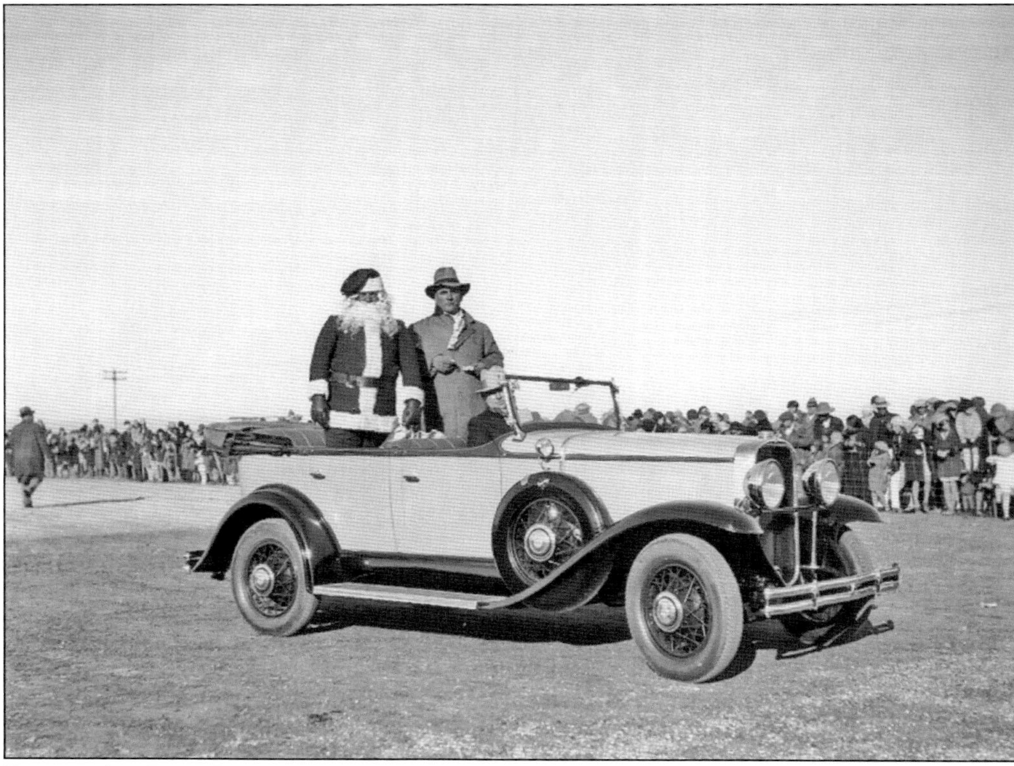

Despite the Great Depression, 1931 was a year that saw many gifts brought to the people of Albuquerque. At Christmas, Clyde Tingley invited a special guest to inaugurate the newly opened attraction at Conservancy Beach. Tingley is the man standing on the right. (AMPA.)

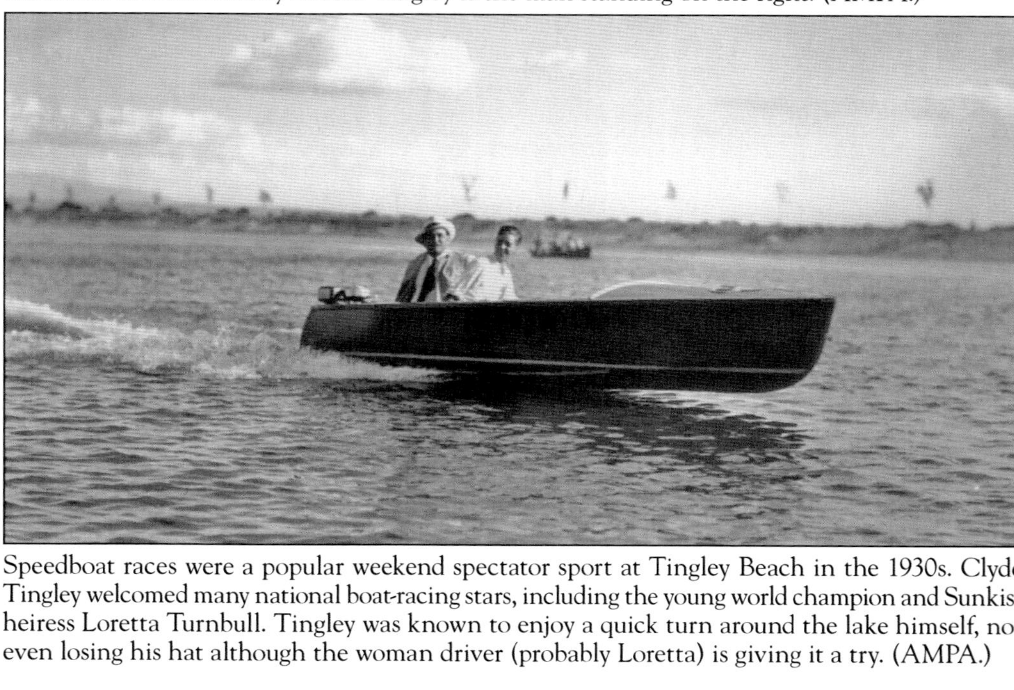

Speedboat races were a popular weekend spectator sport at Tingley Beach in the 1930s. Clyde Tingley welcomed many national boat-racing stars, including the young world champion and Sunkist heiress Loretta Turnbull. Tingley was known to enjoy a quick turn around the lake himself, not even losing his hat although the woman driver (probably Loretta) is giving it a try. (AMPA.)

In this 1930s photograph, Clyde Tingley seems to be taking his role as a beauty contest judge very seriously. (AMPA.)

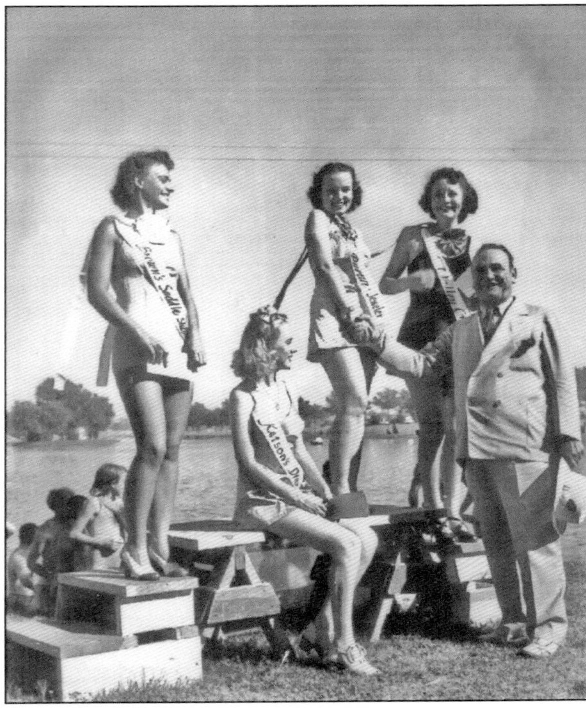

Clyde Tingley was never shy of the camera. He posed with movie stars, celebrities, politicians, and everyday people alike. On the set of *The Texas Rangers* in 1936, Tingley (far right) posed with, from left to right, stars Jack Oakie, Fred MacMurray, and Jean Parker. (CSWR.)

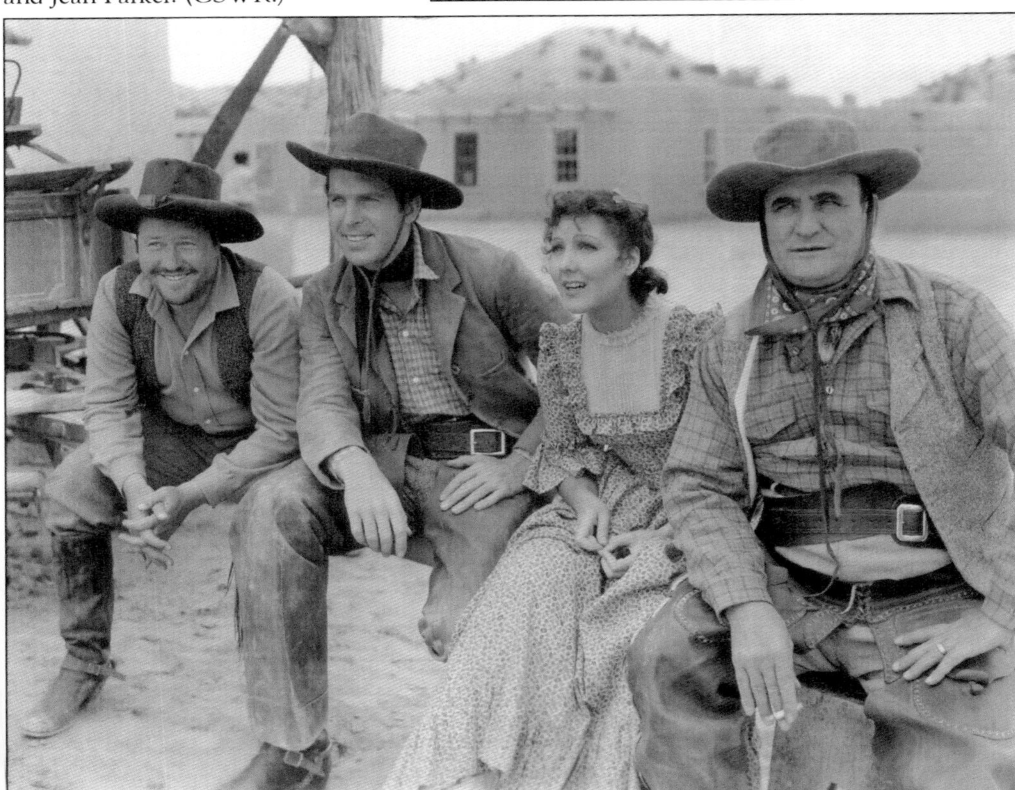

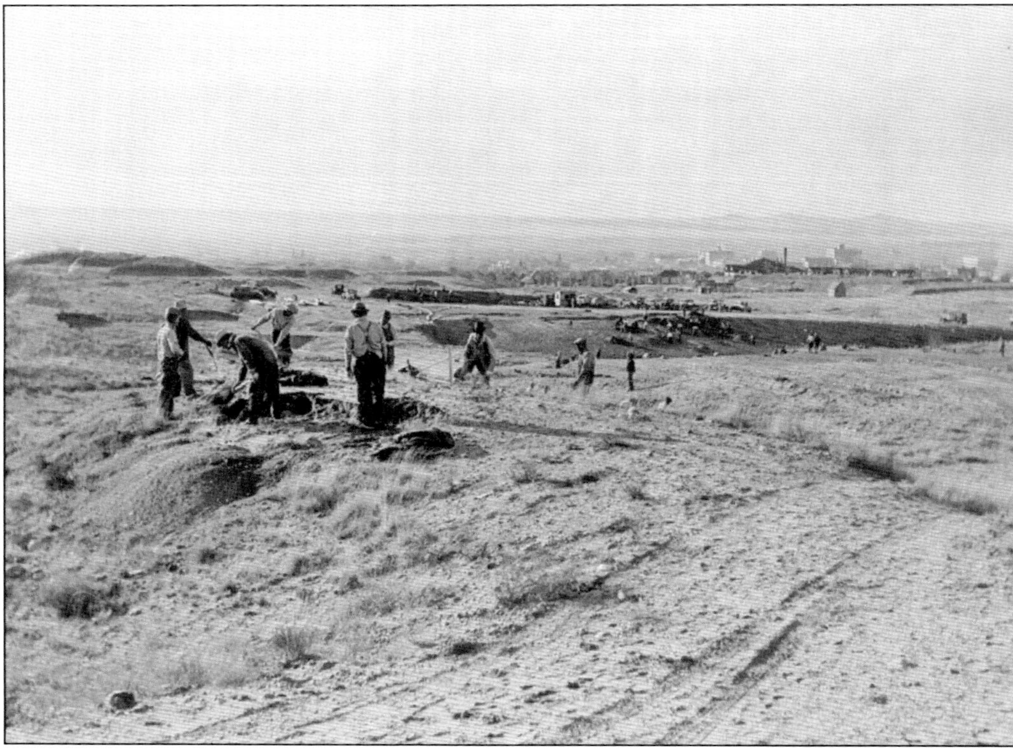

Following Franklin Roosevelt's election in 1932, ex-mayor and then governor Clyde Tingley initiated a campaign to bring public works projects and badly needed federal dollars to Albuquerque during the Depression. This scene shows work just beginning at Terrace Park in early 1934. Within months, Tingley wired President Roosevelt to ask him if the park could be named in honor of the "great service" the president had done for the country. (AMPA.)

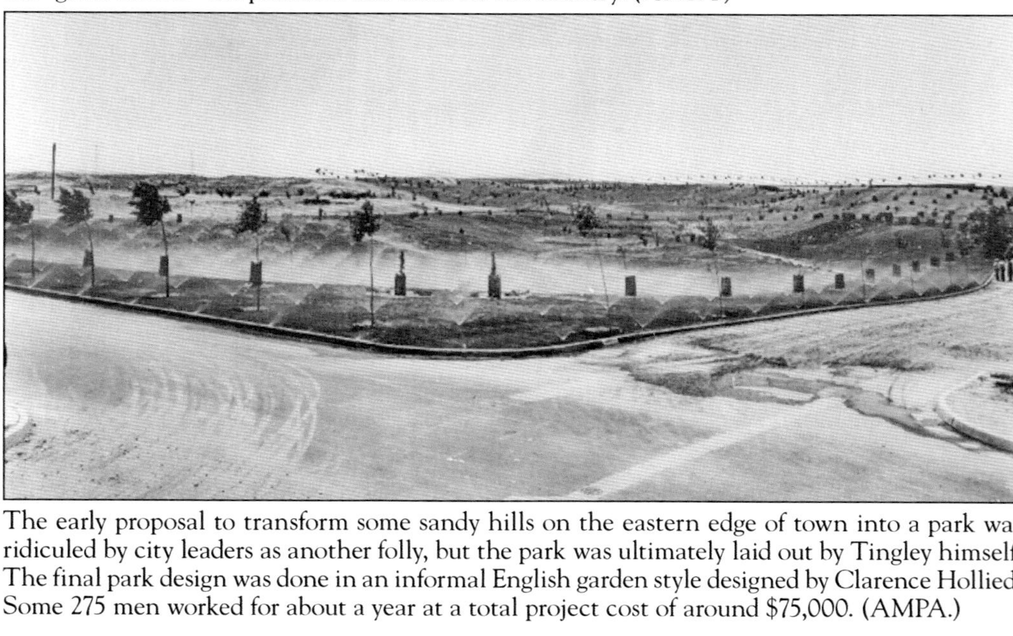

The early proposal to transform some sandy hills on the eastern edge of town into a park was ridiculed by city leaders as another folly, but the park was ultimately laid out by Tingley himself. The final park design was done in an informal English garden style designed by Clarence Hollied. Some 275 men worked for about a year at a total project cost of around $75,000. (AMPA.)

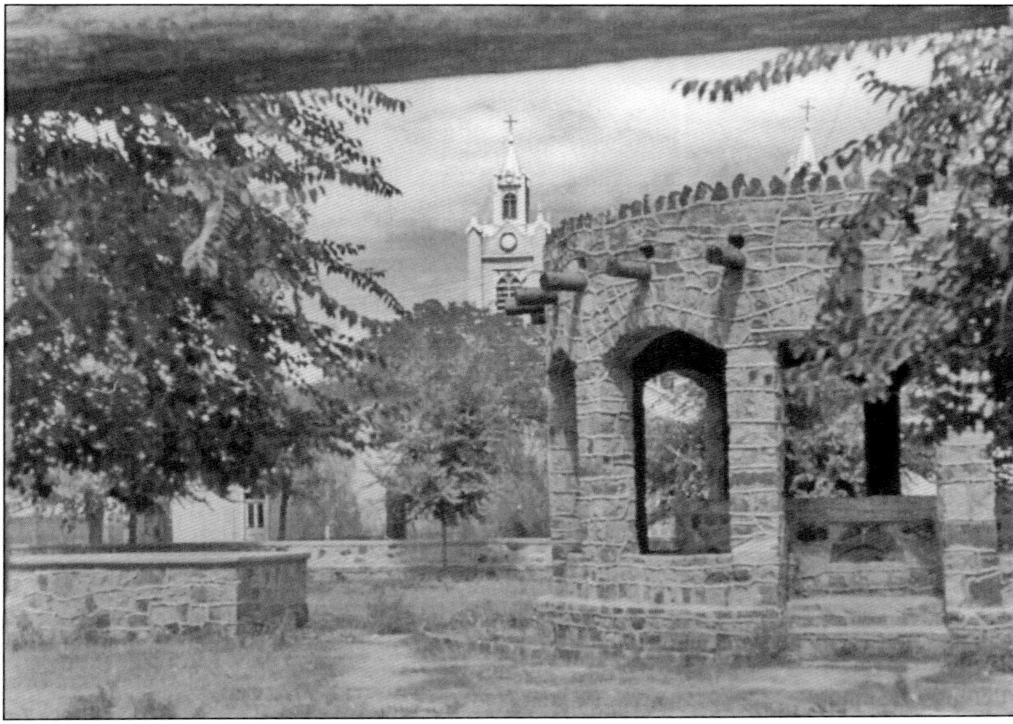

In the 1930s, the Civilian Conservation Corps (CCC) built this stone gazebo at the center of Old Town Plaza. As part of the WPA, the CCC was famous for fine stonework. But neighbors and residents hated the basalt walls enclosing the plaza and demanded it all be demolished. The gazebo only lasted a few years and was replaced by today's wooden structure. (AMPA.)

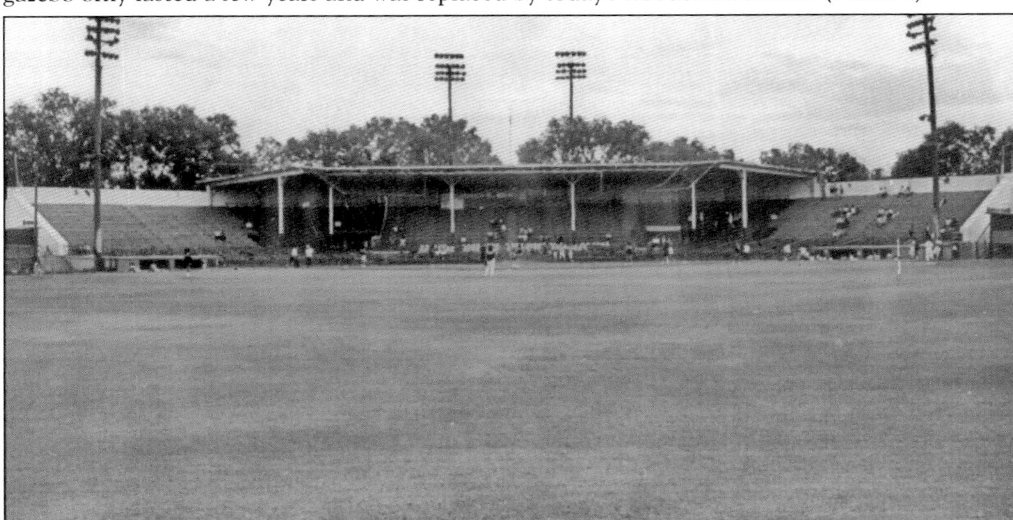

Another of Tingley's New Deal projects was a baseball stadium at Tenth Street and Atlantic Avenue (east of the present-day Rio Grande Zoo). The 3,000-seat stadium opened in 1937 at a cost of about $80,000. Fittingly, the outfield fence was an adobe wall. When a new stadium was built near the university, the concrete baseball that once adorned Tingley Field's entrance was moved to Isotopes Park. (AMPA.)

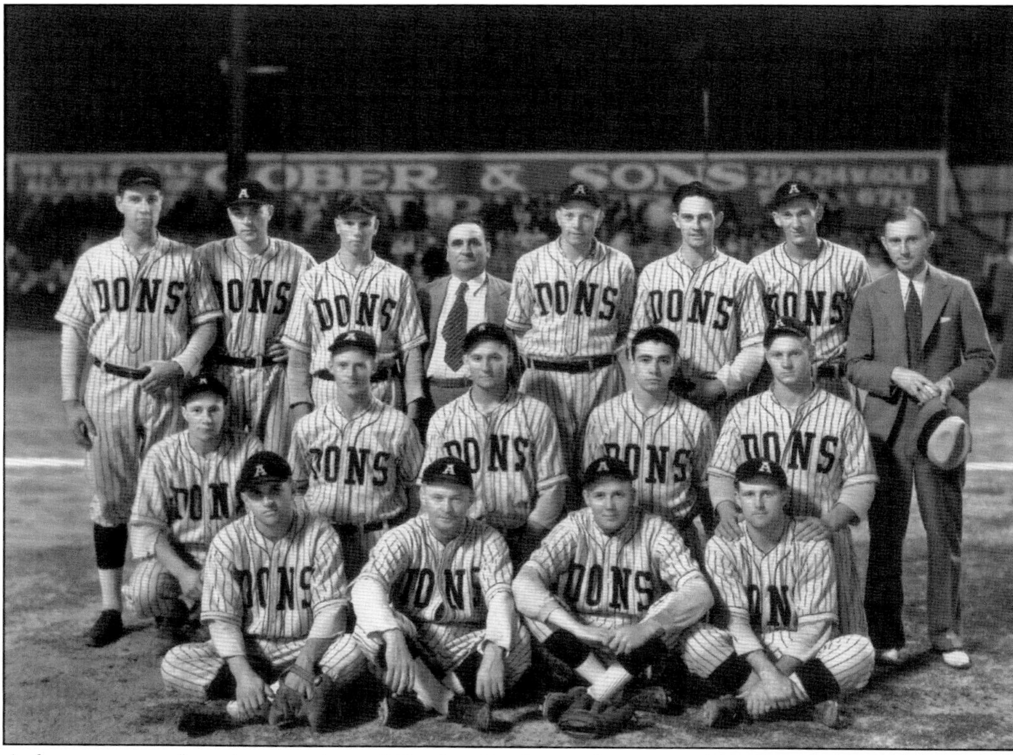

A few seasons after the opening of Tingley Stadium, the mayor (third row, center) poses with the Albuquerque Dons baseball team. The Dons would be replaced in 1947 by the Albuquerque Dukes, who played at Tingley Field until 1968. (AMPA.)

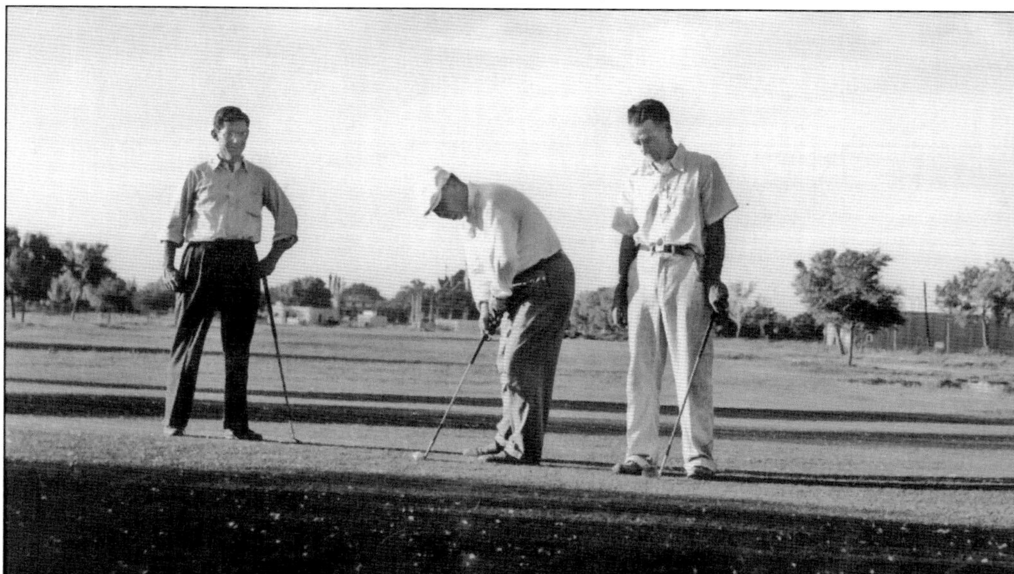

A golfing threesome of unidentified men is shown in this c. 1940 image shot at Albuquerque Country Club, one of the few local courses at which to play during that time. (AMPA.)

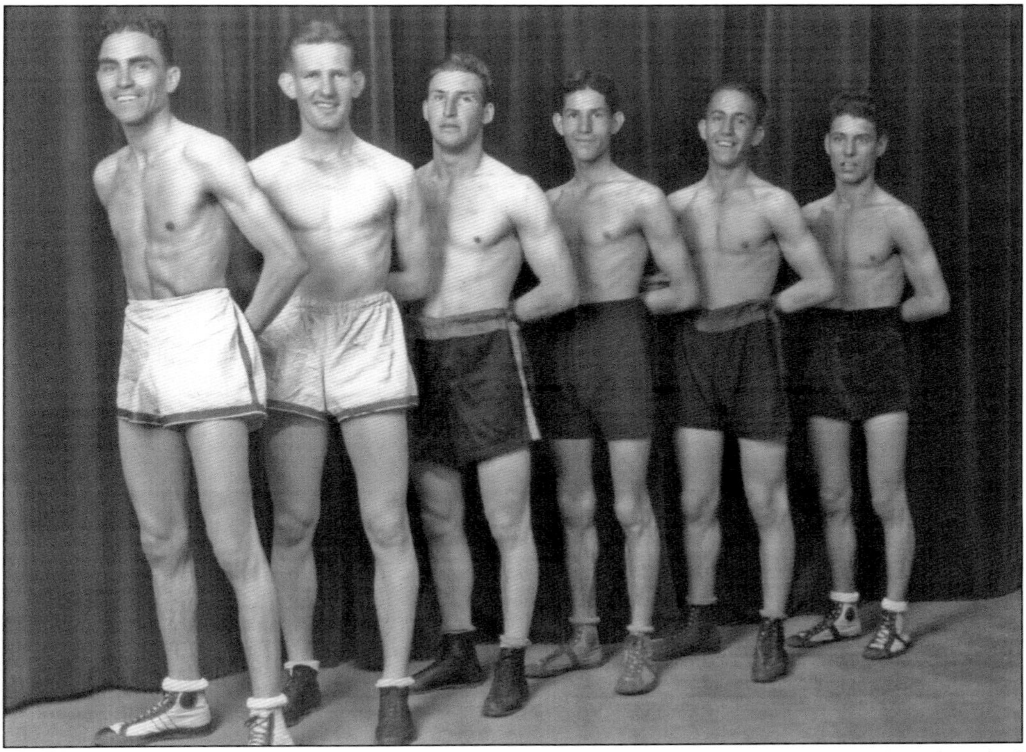

Albuquerque has long been known as a major boxing town. This portrait of a group of unidentified boxers was taken at the Brooks Studio about 1930. (AMPA.)

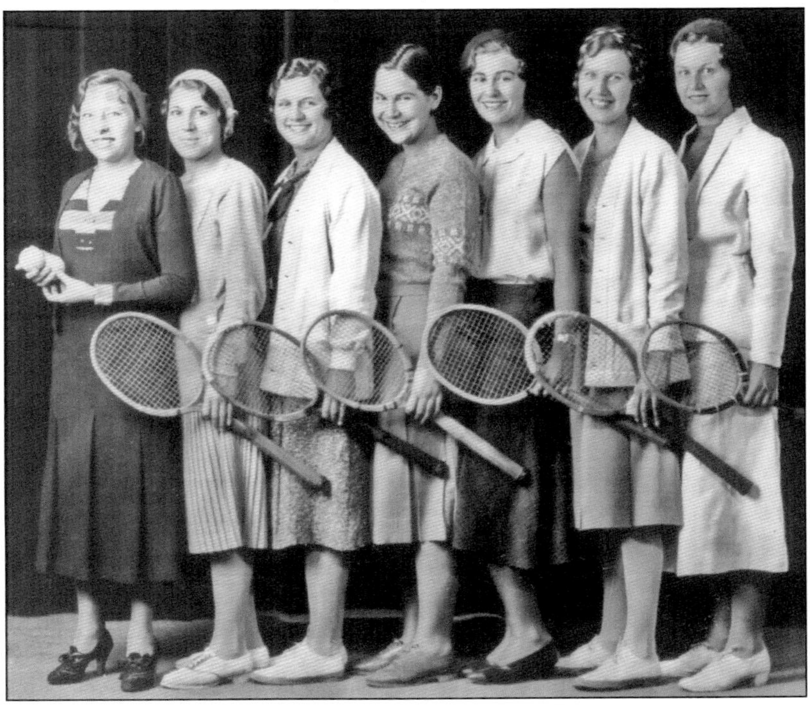

Women's tennis was evidently a somewhat more formal affair, featuring waistcoats and low heels, as seen in this Brooks Studio portrait taken about 1930. (AMPA.)

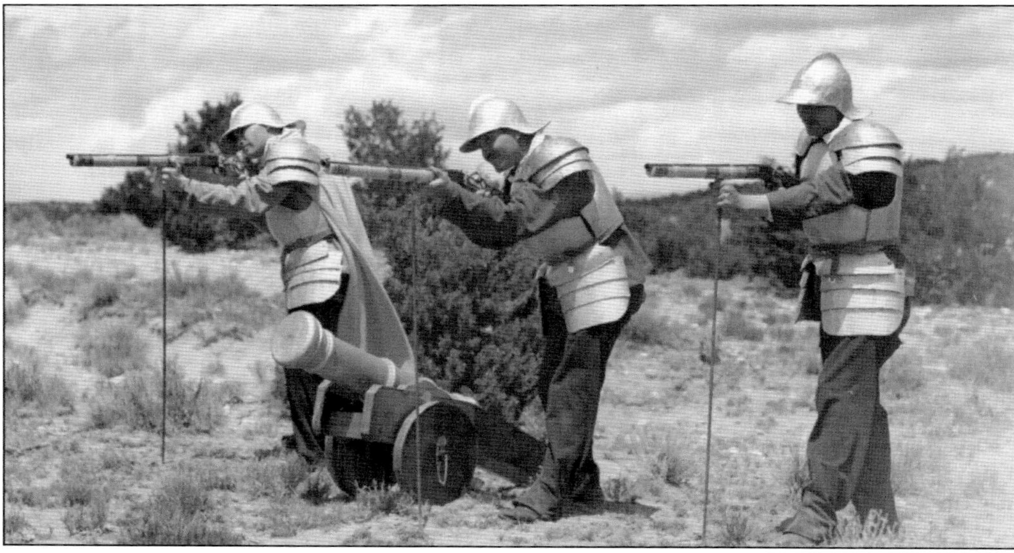

The first Europeans and nonnatives to enter the Rio Grande valley were members of the Francisco Vázquez de Coronado expedition of 1540–1542. Coronado's expedition was the largest land-based enterprise launched by imperial Spain west of the Mississippi. As the 400th anniversary of the exploration neared, the University of New Mexico embarked on a search for Coronado sites in the Albuquerque area in the late 1930s. Convinced that such evidence was to be found near Bernalillo, scholars succeeded in having Coronado State Monument created. As part of the quadricentennial celebrations, reenactments were popular. Above, a group of men demonstrate the firing of a primitive musket known as an arquebus. Below, a soldier aims a crossbow, still a medieval weapon of choice in Coronado's day. Recently, substantial evidence of the expedition has been found on park land near the Rio Grande in northern Albuquerque. (Both, AMPA.)

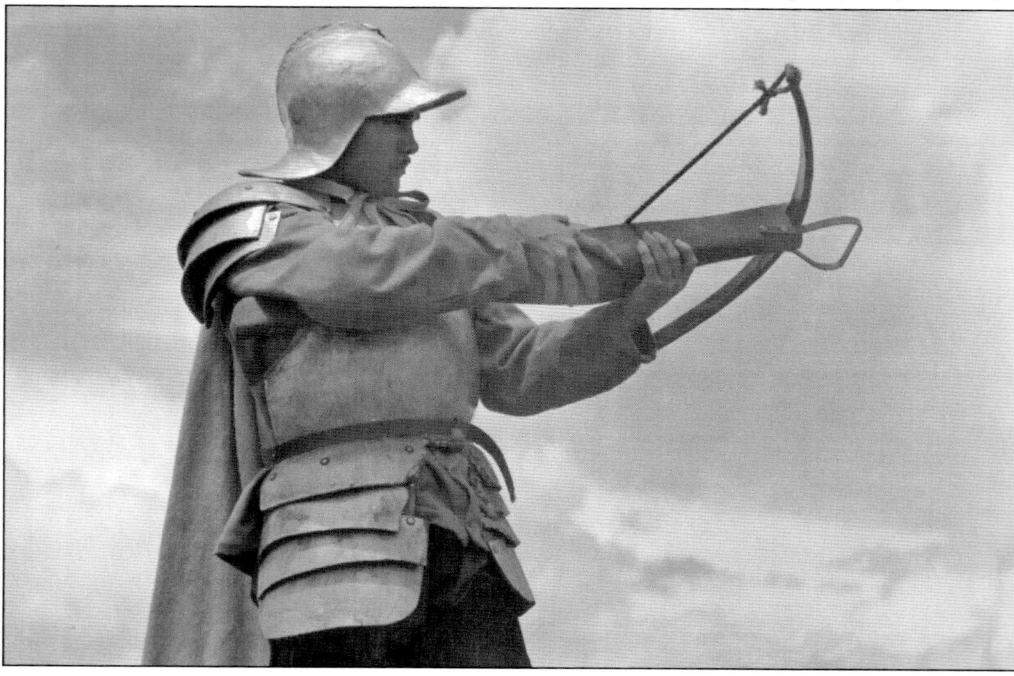

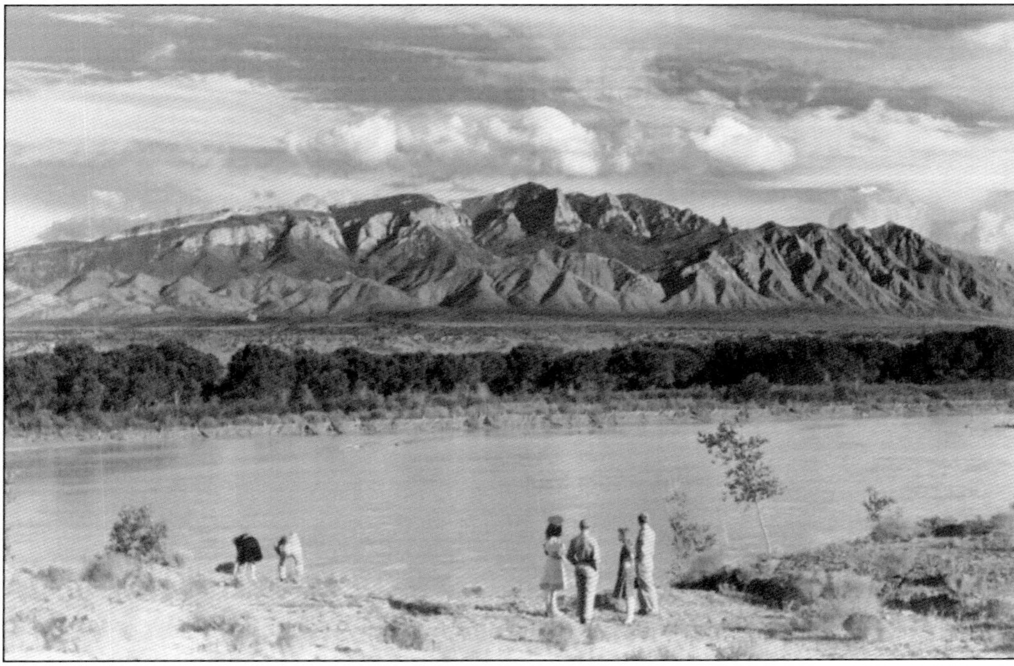

This view of the Rio Grande and the Sandia Mountains was shot by photographer Jeffrey McDaniel in the 1940s from the newly established Coronado State Monument. While this view was similar to what Coronado might have seen 400 years earlier, little physical evidence points to the location as having the expeditionary significance once thought. (AMPA.)

By 1940, Albuquerque's population had grown to over 35,000. This aerial view to the south shows the country club and Barelas residential areas with the railroad to the far left-hand side. The Rio Grande has a wide floodway with several islands and is spanned by the Barelas Bridge. (AMPA.)

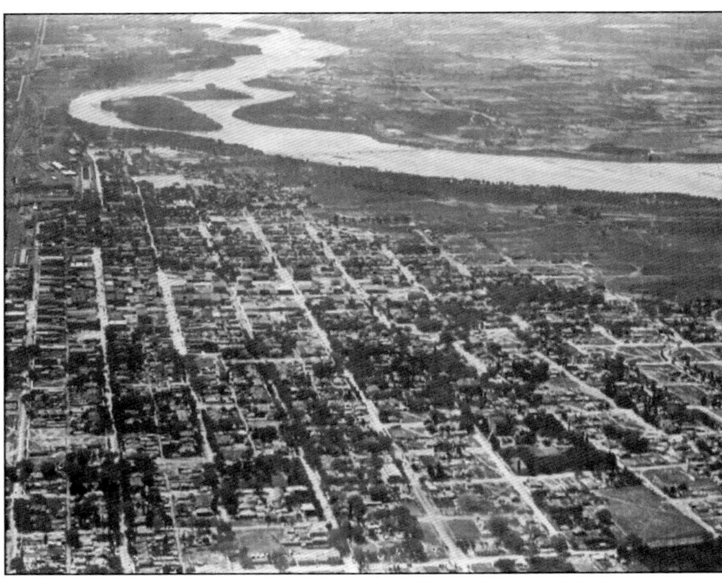

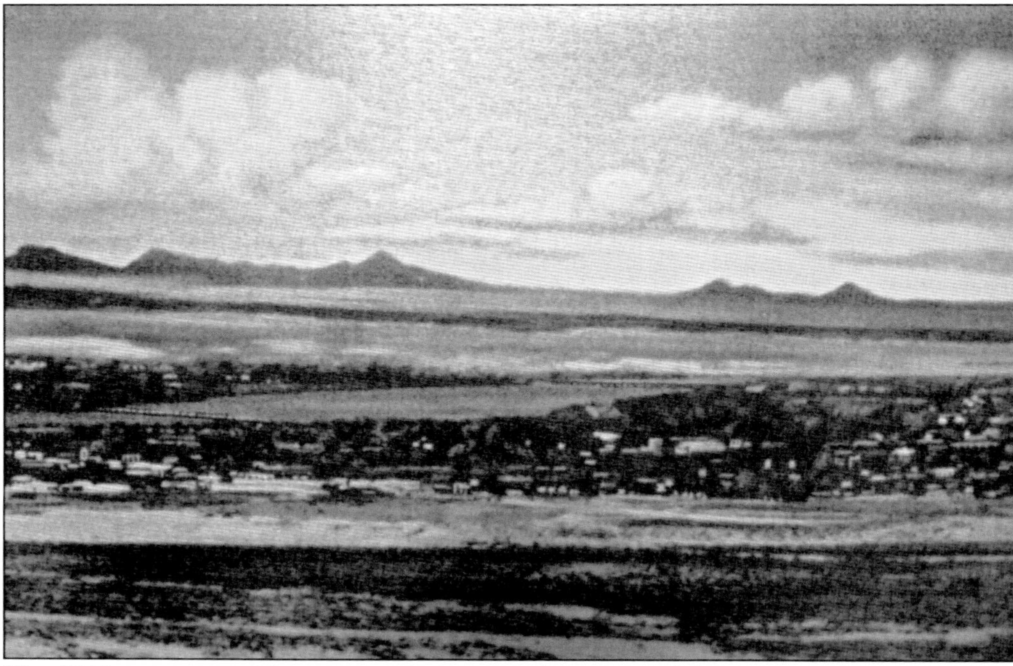

This 1940s-era postcard shows a view looking northwest toward the Rio Grande, the West Mesa volcanic escarpment, the mesa top, and the volcanoes from southeastern Albuquerque. While none of these landforms was formally protected at the time, this view somewhat predicts what areas would be necessary for future Open Space preservation plans yet to come. (Albuquerque Library Special Collections.)

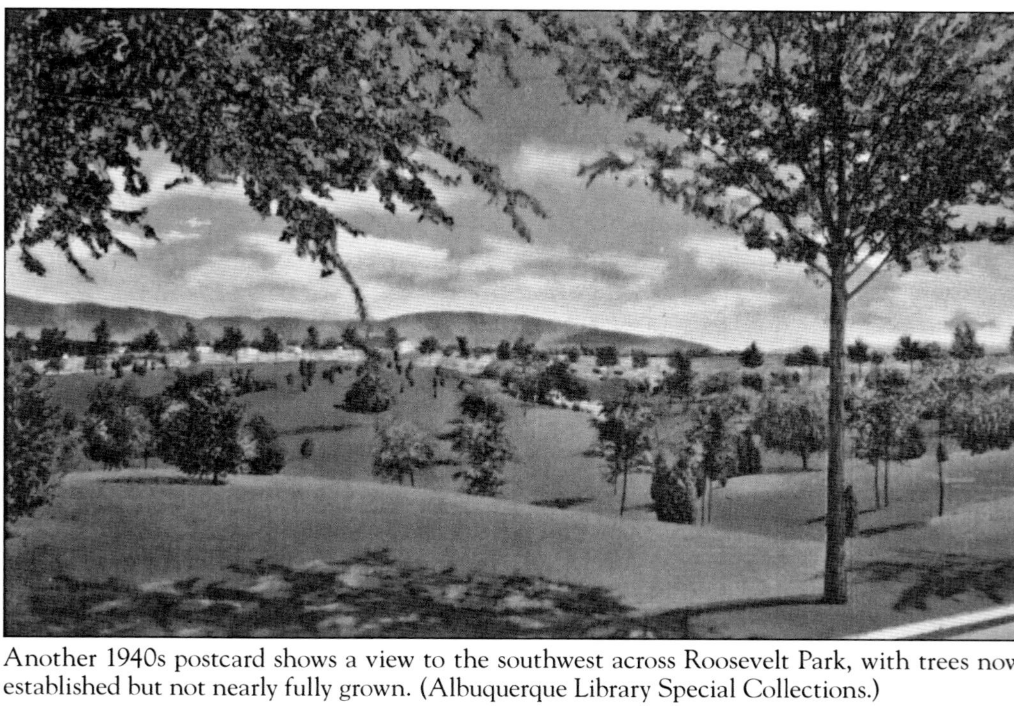

Another 1940s postcard shows a view to the southwest across Roosevelt Park, with trees now established but not nearly fully grown. (Albuquerque Library Special Collections.)

Four

A Department is Born

Following World War II, with many veterans returning and with a nationwide building effort under way, Albuquerque found itself with a growing need for recreation and an expanding list of assets to meet that need. Prewar civic projects built under the Works Progress Administration included Terrace/Roosevelt Park (1933–1934), Tingley Field/Stadium (1936–1939), improvements to Rio Grande Park/Zoo (1936), Heights Community Center courtyard (1936), a wading pool at Tingley Beach (1937), landscaping Forest Park (1936) and other parks (1939), and the construction of University Golf Course (1940), to name but a few.

From 1930 to 1940, the WPA expended nearly $27 million on Albuquerque-area projects. The Rio Grande Zoo, for example, had expanded from its modest beginnings in 1925, when, according to the May 1949 edition of the *Albuquerque Progress*, it started with "two bears, two lions, a snake, and a bobcat," to become the only public zoo within 475 miles.

After the war, the city built Bataan Memorial Park in 1947, Hyder Park in 1948, and Coronado Park in 1949 in rapid succession. Community centers, playgrounds, and tennis courts added to the amenities that the city had to offer. In 1948, all of these programs were organized into a new agency called the Parks and Recreation Department, and Irene Teakell was named its first director.

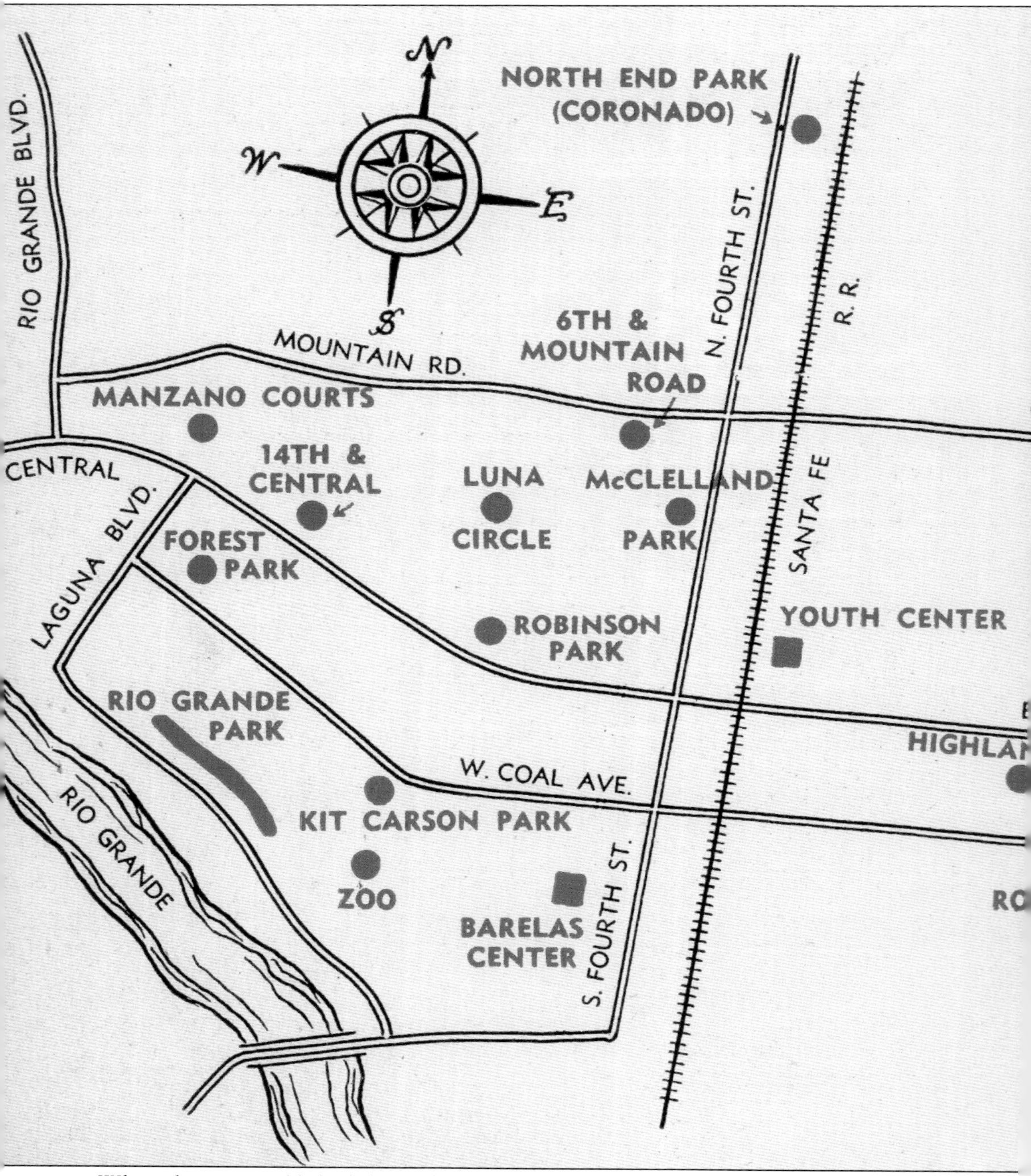

When the city established the Parks and Recreation Department in 1948, it proudly boasted, "Albuquerque has 21 municipal parks and recreation areas." The important integration of community centers (such as Barelas, Heights, and the Youth Center) with more traditional turfed park areas is clear as an original goal of the new department. The important early parks—Robinson, Highland, McClellan, and Roosevelt—are highlighted along with the new additions of Bataan,

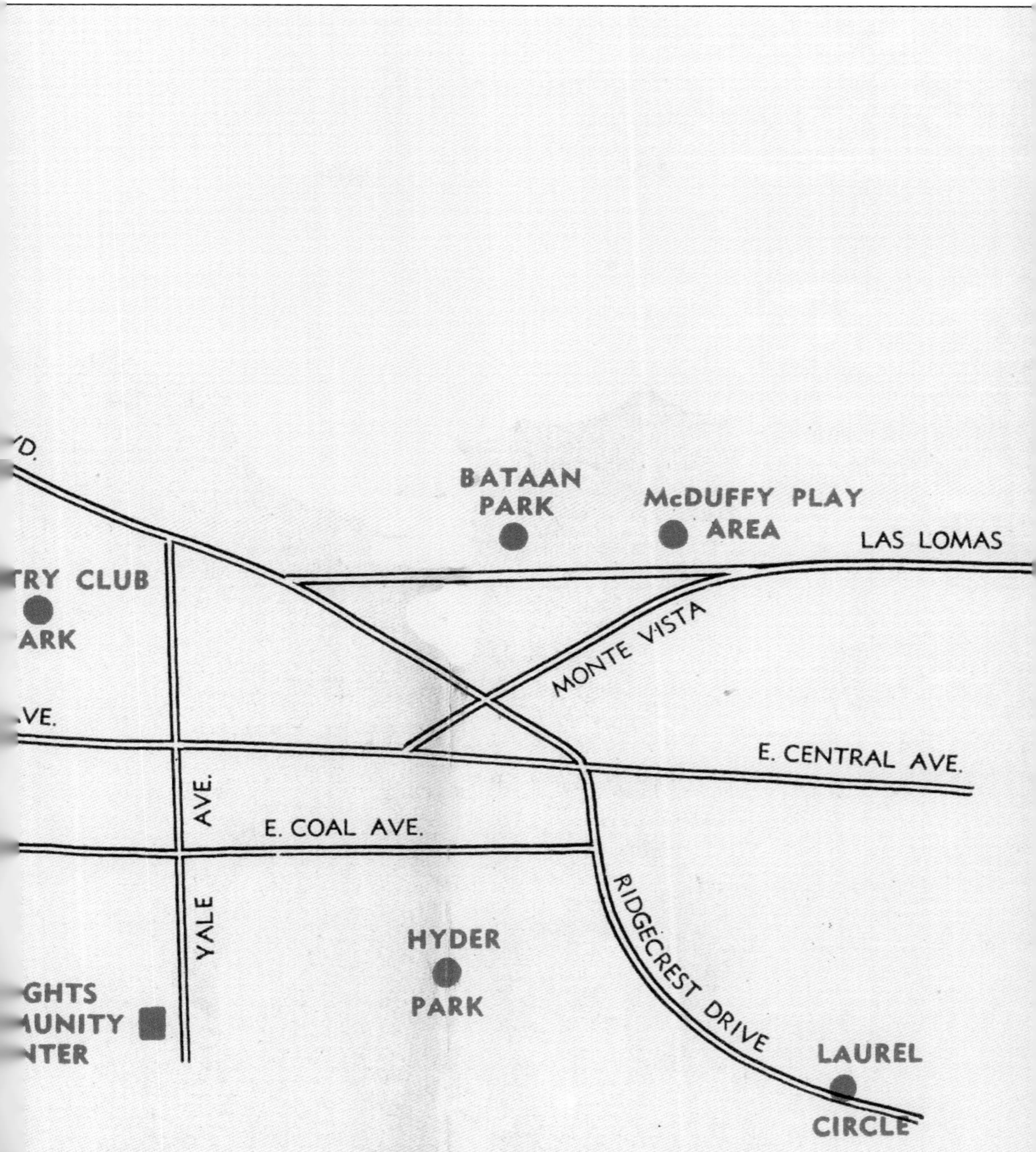

Hyder, and Coronado. Smaller parks such as Forest, Luna Circle, Laurel Circle, and McDuffie play area are included. This map was created for the July 1949 "Municipal Recreation" volume of *Albuquerque Progress*, a monthly 16-page booster magazine published by Albuquerque National Bank. *Albuquerque Progress* was produced from 1933 until 1957. (AMPA.)

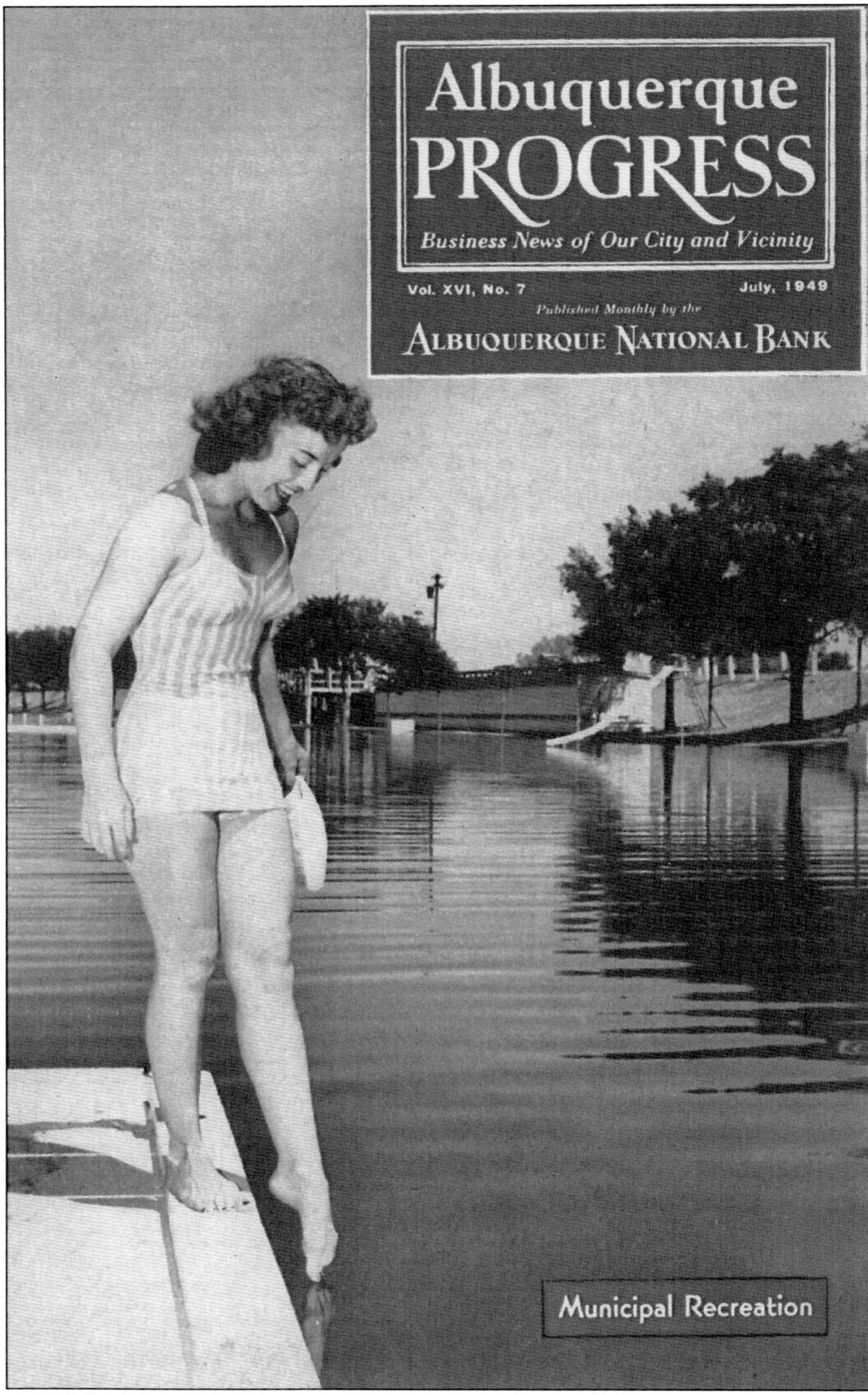

The cover of the May 1949 "Municipal Recreation" edition of *Albuquerque Progress* shows Jean Pitchford testing the waters at Ernie Pyle Beach (formerly called Tingley Beach). *Albuquerque Progress* would devote its entire editions to different topics, and the newly created department rated its very own issue. (Albuquerque Library.)

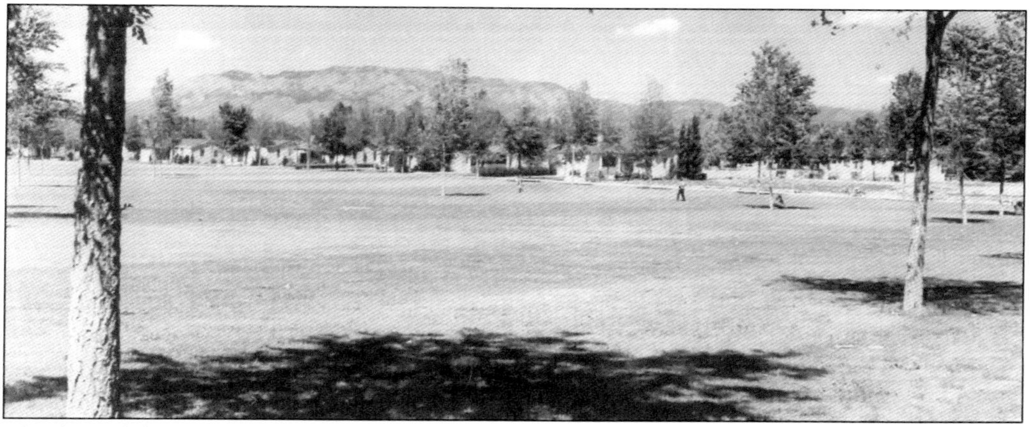

The first of the post–World War II parks to be built with a more expansive layout was Bataan Memorial Park. It was named Bataan Park in 1943 by the Albuquerque City Commission "for the super-human sacrifices endured . . . that freedom and liberty of mankind shall be preserved." This 1949 view shows the park soon after construction in honor of the many New Mexican soldiers subjected to the horrific Bataan Death March. (AMPA.)

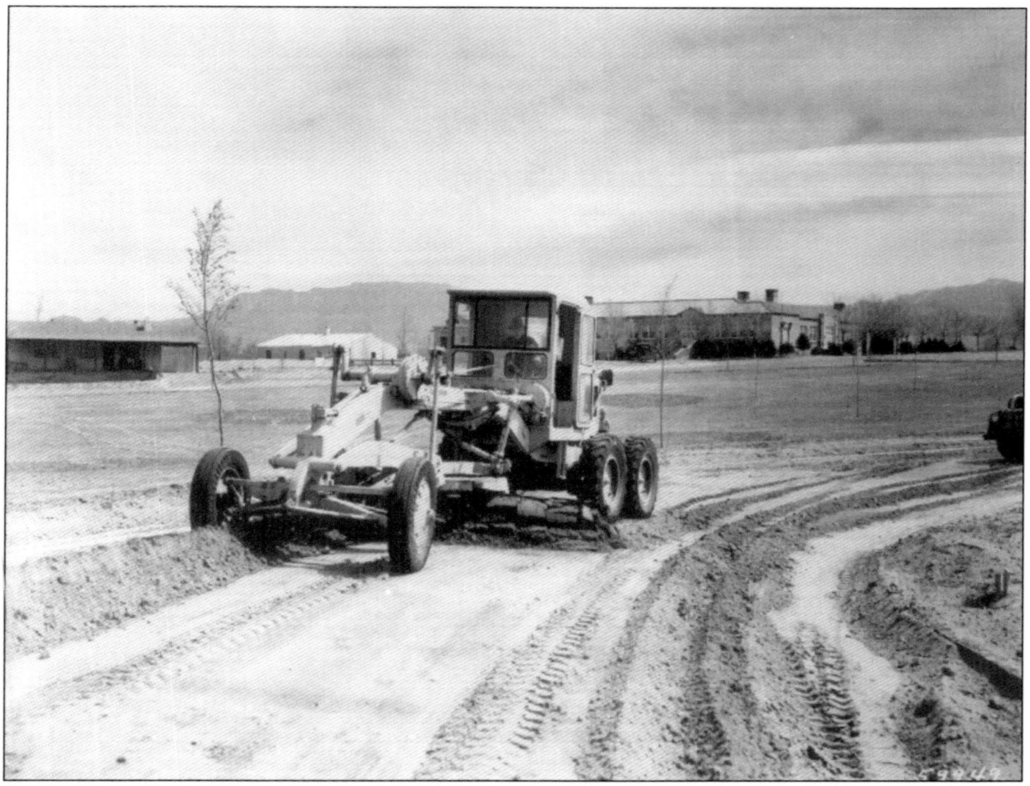

A post–World War II building boom resulted in a handful of new, larger, and more open parks being built. Here, a grader takes another pass at leveling the ground for Hyder Park in 1948. Bandelier Elementary School, built a few years earlier, is in the background. (AMPA.)

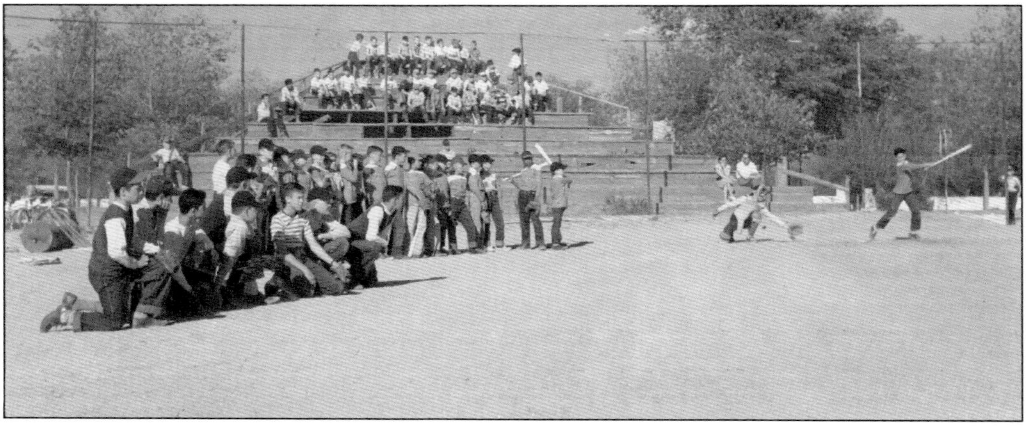

Despite the postwar addition of new parks in Albuquerque, there was still a lack of places for formalized youth sports in the growing city. As a result, schools and community centers offered the most popular venues for league games and summer activities. Here, a peewee baseball game is played at Heights Community Center in 1949. (AMPA.)

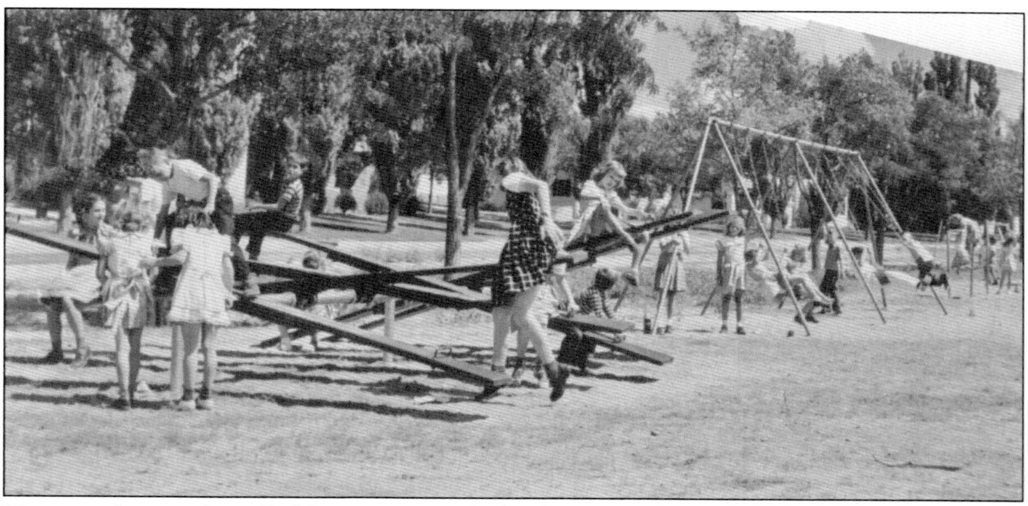

Playgrounds were also called "nursery grounds" but by any name served the vital need for children to get exercise outside on swings, teeter-totters, or monkey bars, as caught in this action at Heights Community Center. (AMPA.)

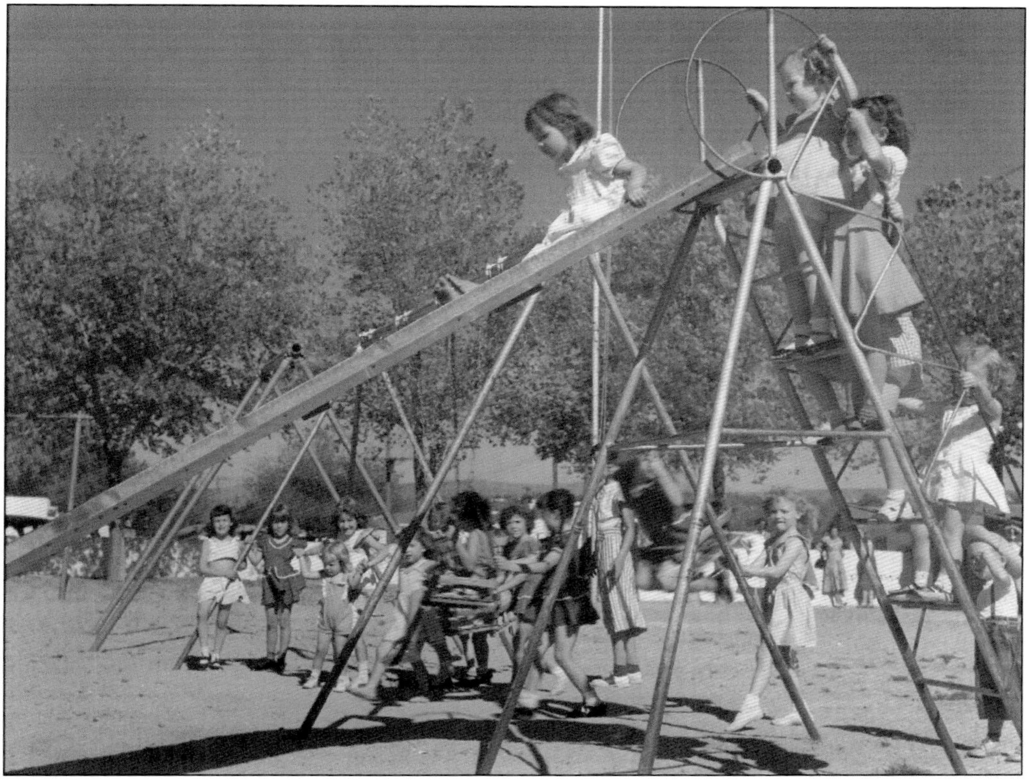

Developed playgrounds were important to meet the needs of the very first of the baby-boom generation of children. In the 1949 photograph above, throngs of girls line up for a turn on the slides and swings at Heights Community Center while moms look on in the background. Below is a view of the wading pool and sandbox at Heights Community Center. (Both, AMPA.)

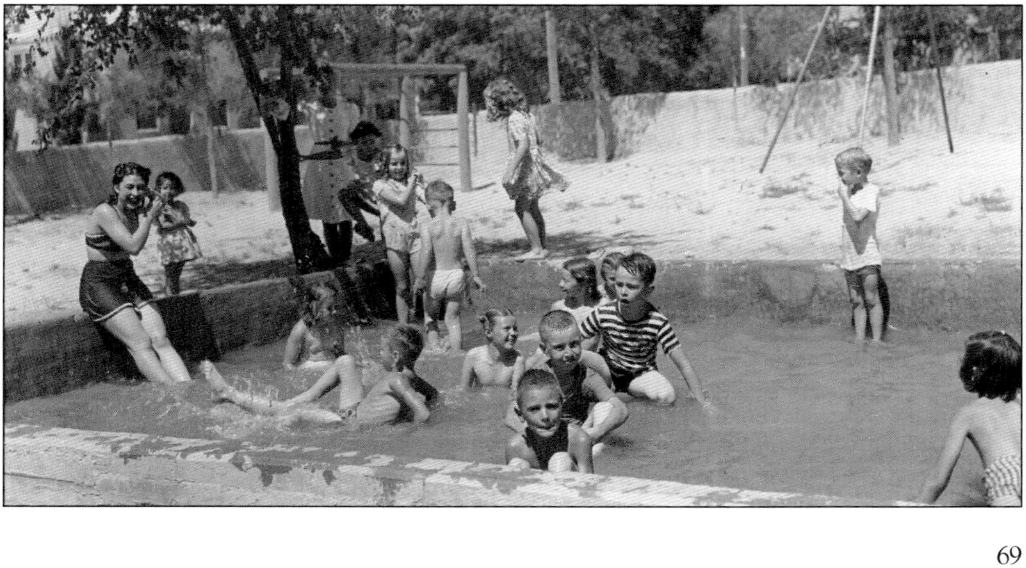

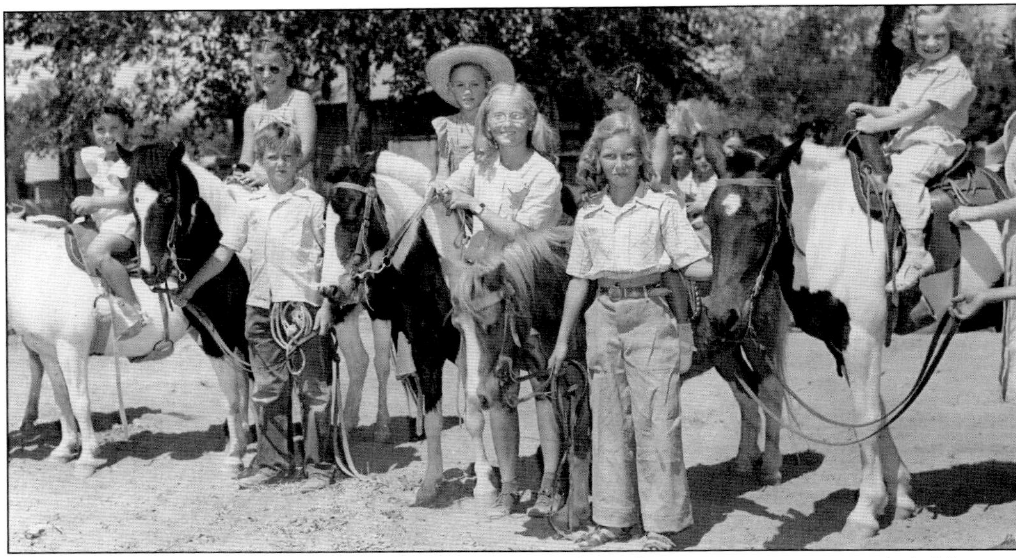

Advertised summertime activities offered at various parks and community centers included "tennis, softball, marbles, shuffleboard, and picnicking at the cook-out areas." Here, girls and boys line up with their ponies on a group excursion. (AMPA.)

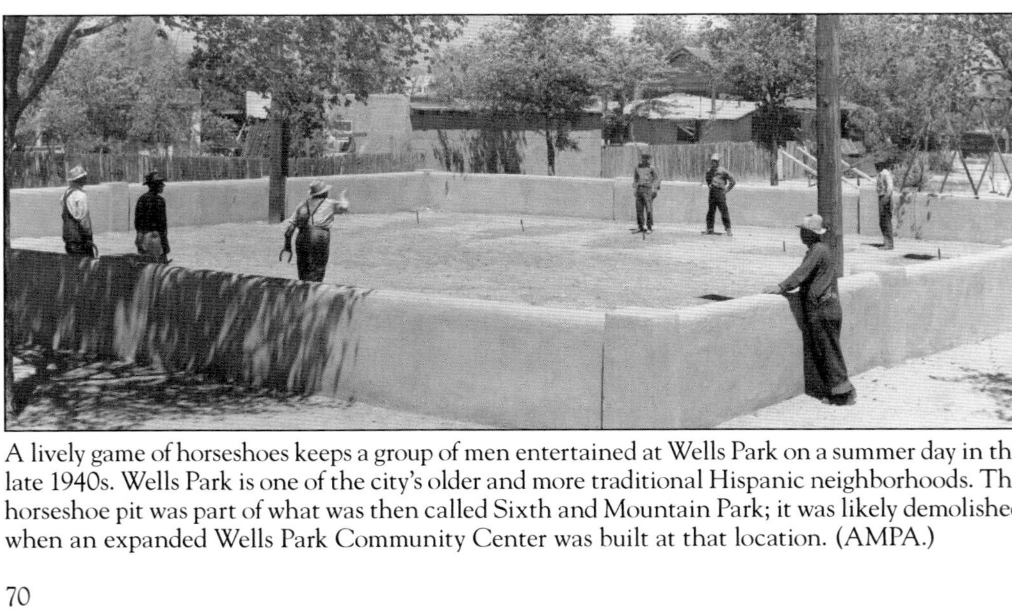

A lively game of horseshoes keeps a group of men entertained at Wells Park on a summer day in the late 1940s. Wells Park is one of the city's older and more traditional Hispanic neighborhoods. The horseshoe pit was part of what was then called Sixth and Mountain Park; it was likely demolished when an expanded Wells Park Community Center was built at that location. (AMPA.)

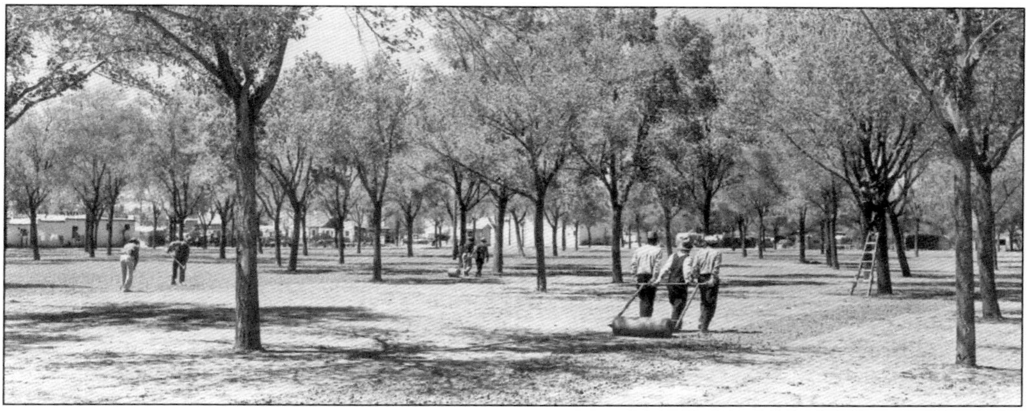

Workers from the newly formed Parks Department are shown putting finishing touches on the city's latest addition to the park system in 1949. Coronado Park, also known as North End Park, was built at Second Street and McKnight Avenue, then on the northern edge of the city. (AMPA.)

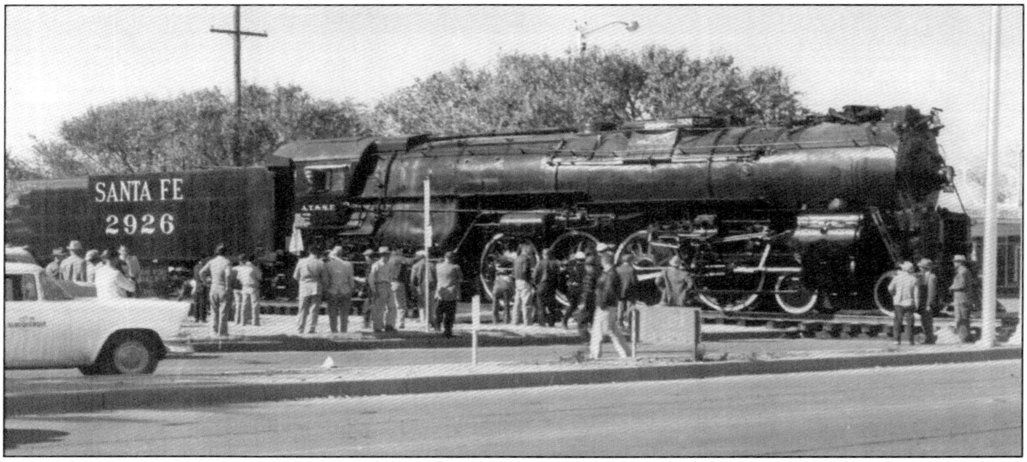

In 1956, the Atchison, Topeka, and Santa Fe Railway donated steam locomotive engine no. 2926 to the City of Albuquerque. The 250-ton engine had logged over one million miles in less than 10 years of service, including passenger runs to the Grand Canyon. The city landmark was removed in 2000 for restoration and inclusion in a planned railroad museum. This 1956 image shows the official installation ceremonies at Coronado Park. (AMPA.)

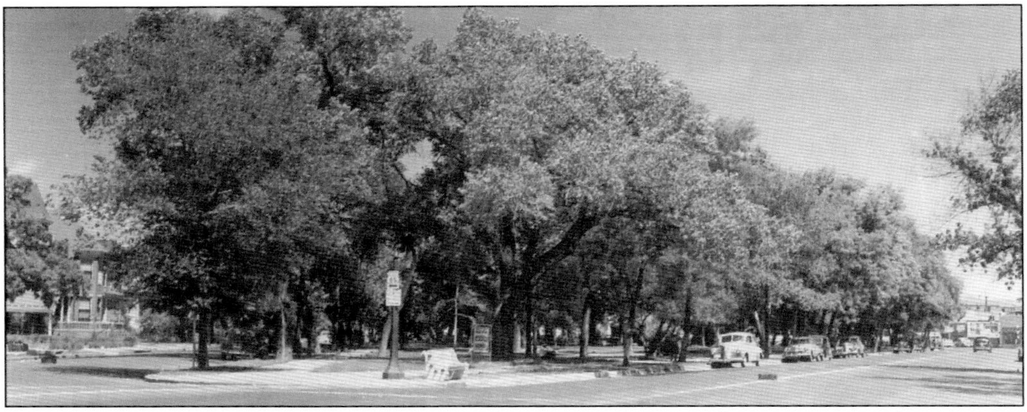

The 1949 "Municipal Recreation" issue of *Albuquerque Progress* shows a view looking east at Robinson Park, the city's oldest formal green space, then about 70 years old. (AMPA.)

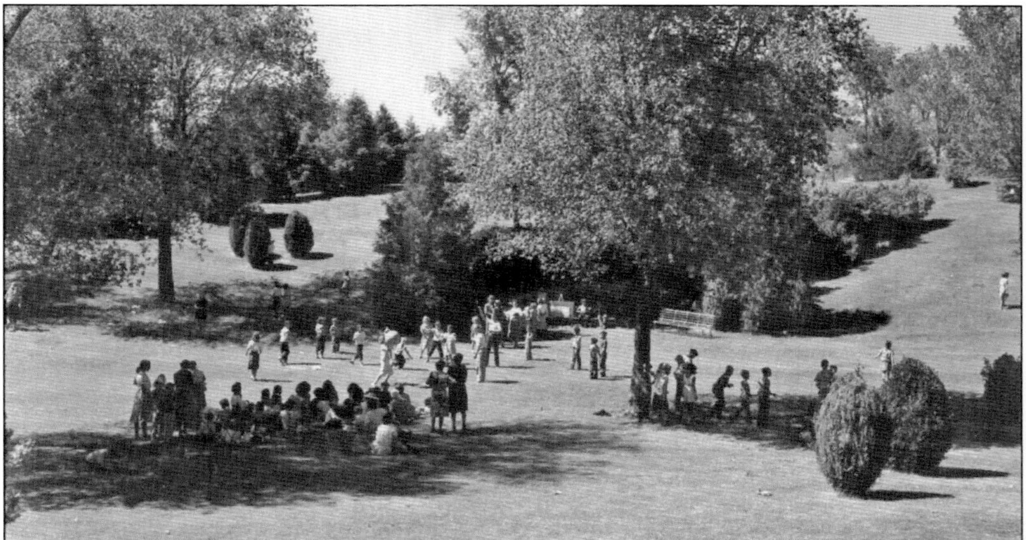

Similarly, an image of an outdoor group at Roosevelt Park around 1948 shows the maturing trees and landscape at one of the city's flagship recreation spots. (AMPA.)

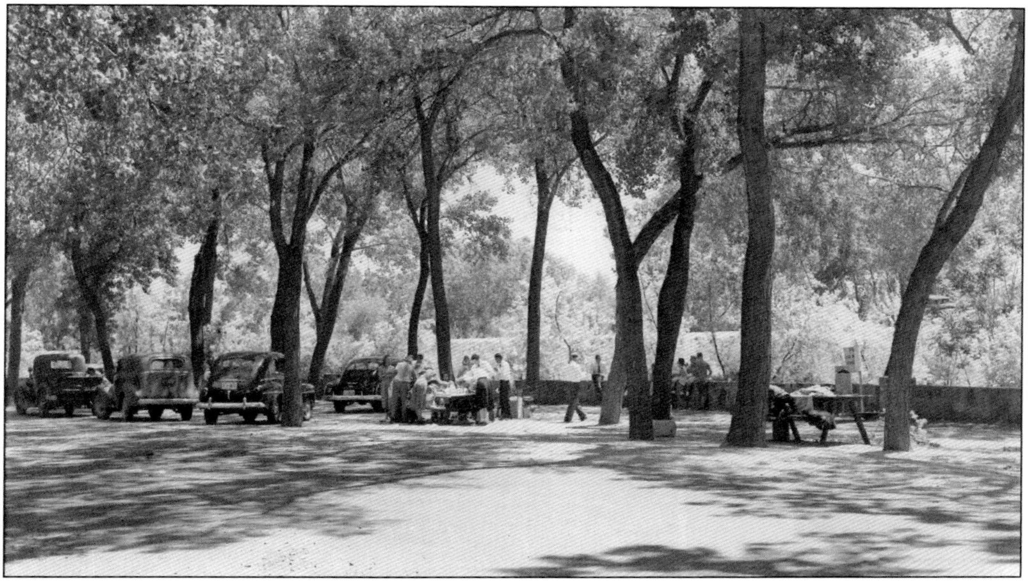

In the 1949 recreation issue of *Albuquerque Progress*, it is reported that in the "summer the parks are often so well-filled with picnickers that there is hardly room for spreading another picnic lunch." This view looking southwest across Kit Carson Park shows why the monthly publication boasted that "Albuquerque is noted for its many beautiful parks and landscaped areas." (AMPA.)

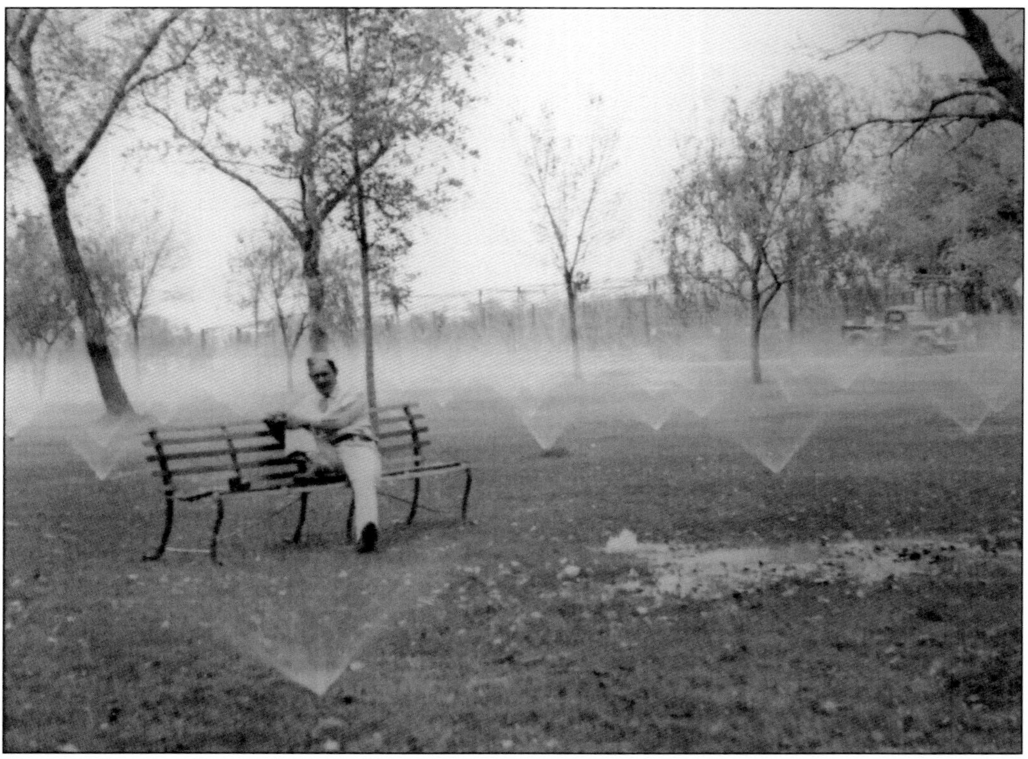

Not minding at all that the sprinklers are running, an unidentified man relaxes on a bench at what appears to be Kit Carson Park in this late-1940s photograph. (AMPA.)

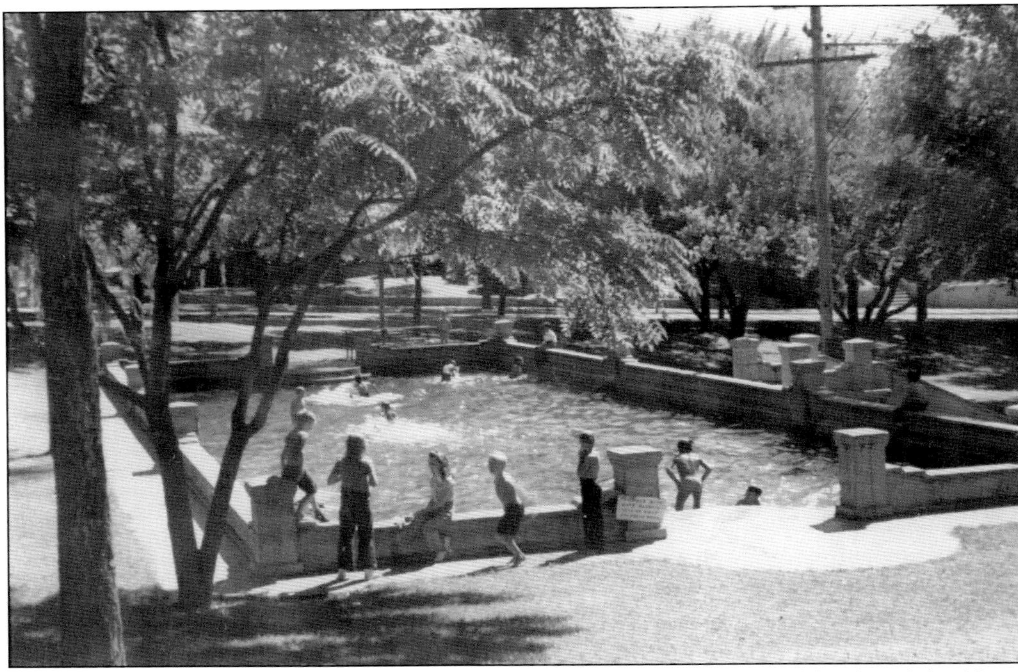

By the 1940s, the crumbling, smaller kidney-shaped wading pool at Highland Park had been replaced by a larger rectangular wading pool. This c. 1945 photograph shows the newer pool in full use, but it, too, would soon experience problems and was used as an informal tennis court after being filled in during winter months. (AMPA.)

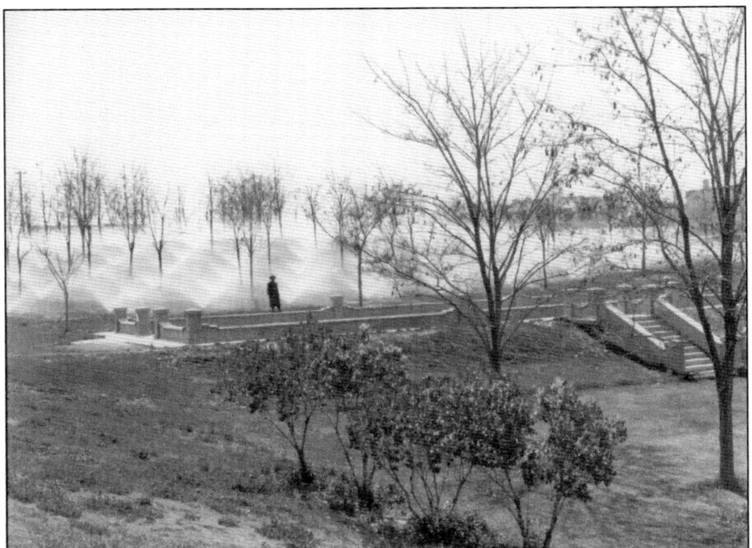

A 1940s southeast view across Highland Park shows terracing of the landscape. In its heyday, Highland was known as the shadiest spot in the city and was also the host park for the city's official Christmas tree. The man standing in a raincoat amidst the sprinklers may be a parks worker. This eastern half of the park was demolished in 1959 to make way for Interstate 25. (AMPA.)

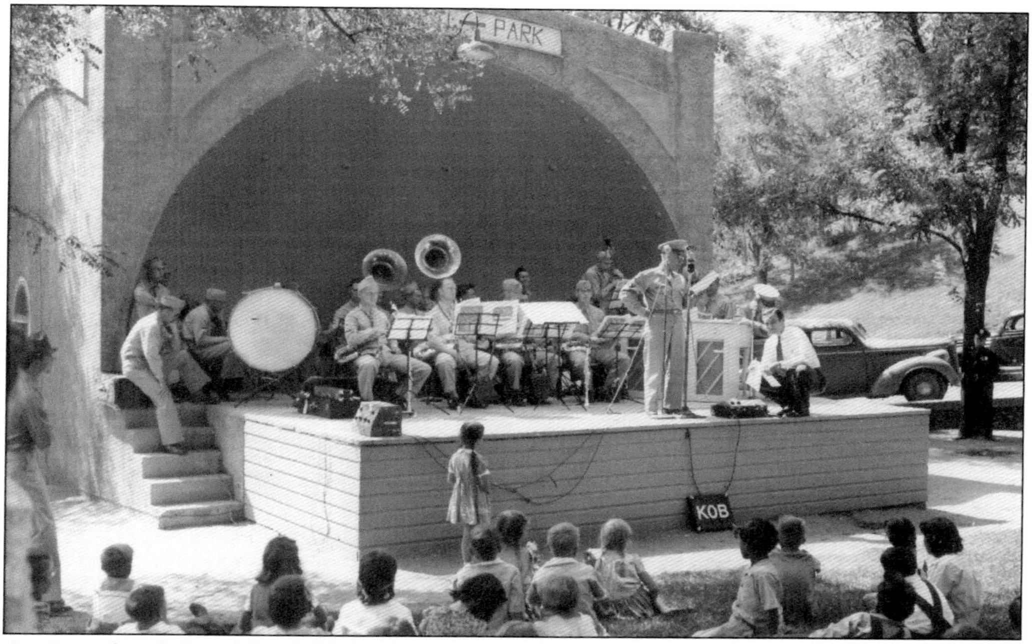

An Army band played for children and parents alike at the Highland Park band shell during the summer of 1944. The performances must have aired live over KOB radio, which started broadcasting in 1932. The band shell was designed to reflect sounds and was built at the northeast corner of Silver Avenue and Elm Street. It was torn down before Interstate 25 was built in 1959. (AMPA.)

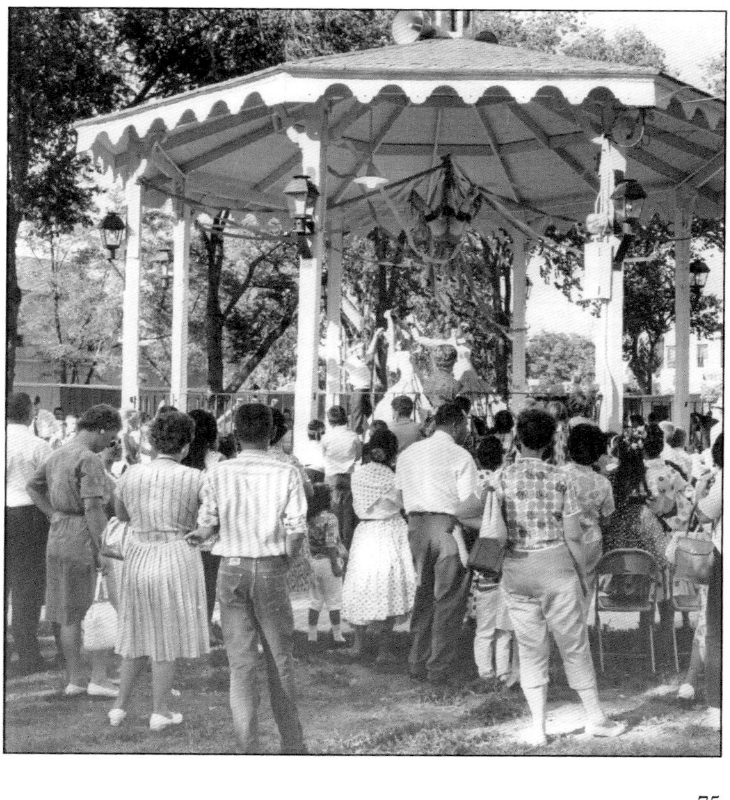

After a stone gazebo was built in Old Town Plaza in the 1930s by the Civilian Conservation Corps, it was soon torn down due to the outcry of residents. The gazebo was replaced by a more graceful and formal-looking wooden octagon with iron railings. In this 1956 scene, tourists and locals take in a traditional dance demonstration. (AMPA.)

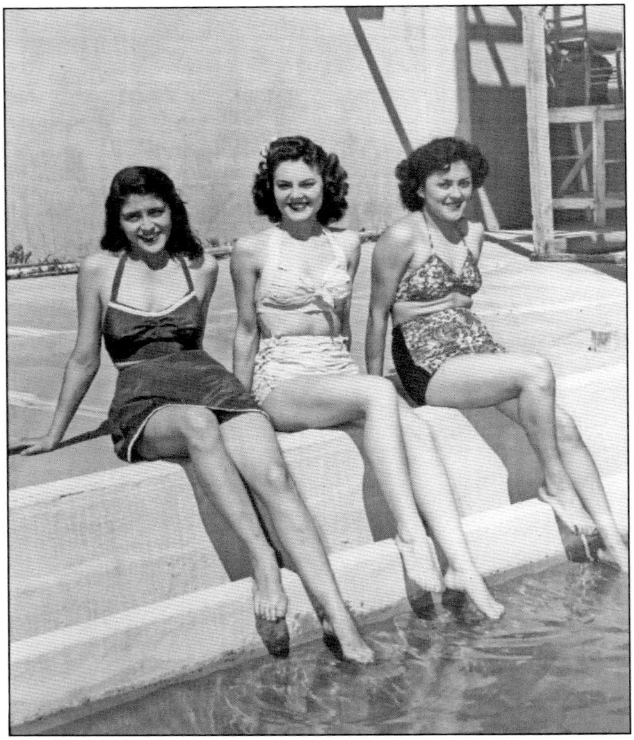

Following the polio scares of the early 1950s, Ernie Pyle Beach (renamed from Tingley Beach) suffered several closures. It ultimately never recovered as a place where hundreds of people could enjoy swimming and sunbathing. Instead, the city began to develop a number of smaller pools whose water quality could be closely regulated. In the photograph at left, a trio of unidentified women sunbathe at an unknown location (possibly Sunport Pool). Taken in May 1950, the photograph below shows members of the "Acapulco Swimming Club" congregating at the Sunport Pool on Columbia Drive and Gibson Boulevard. (Both, AMPA.)

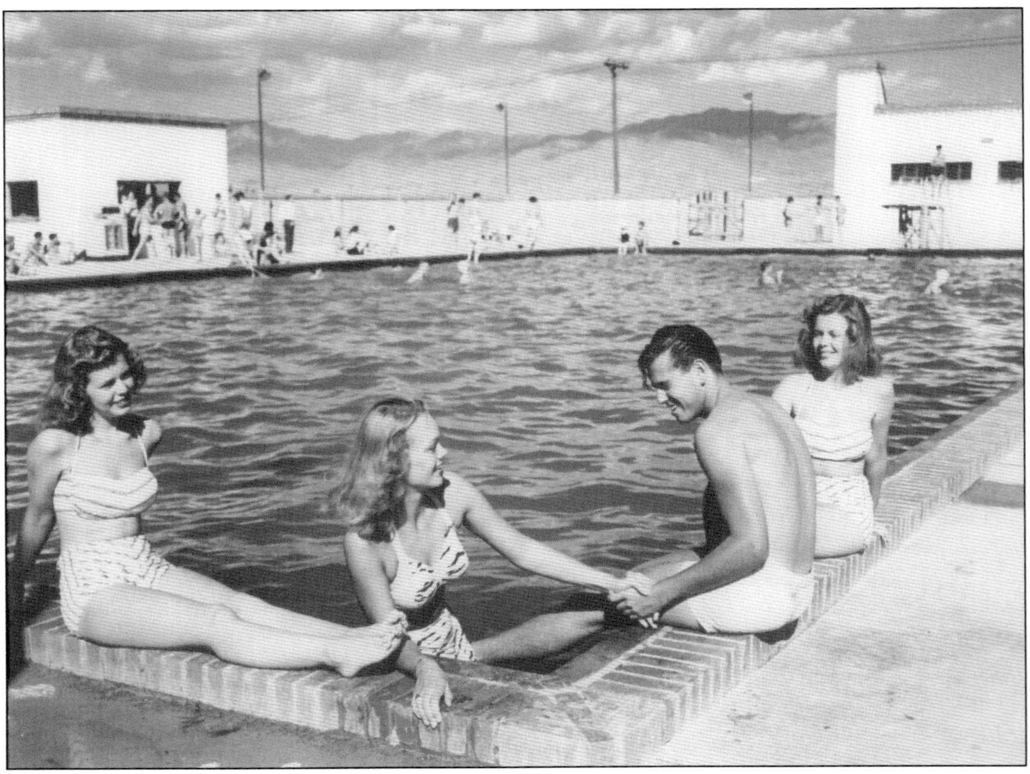

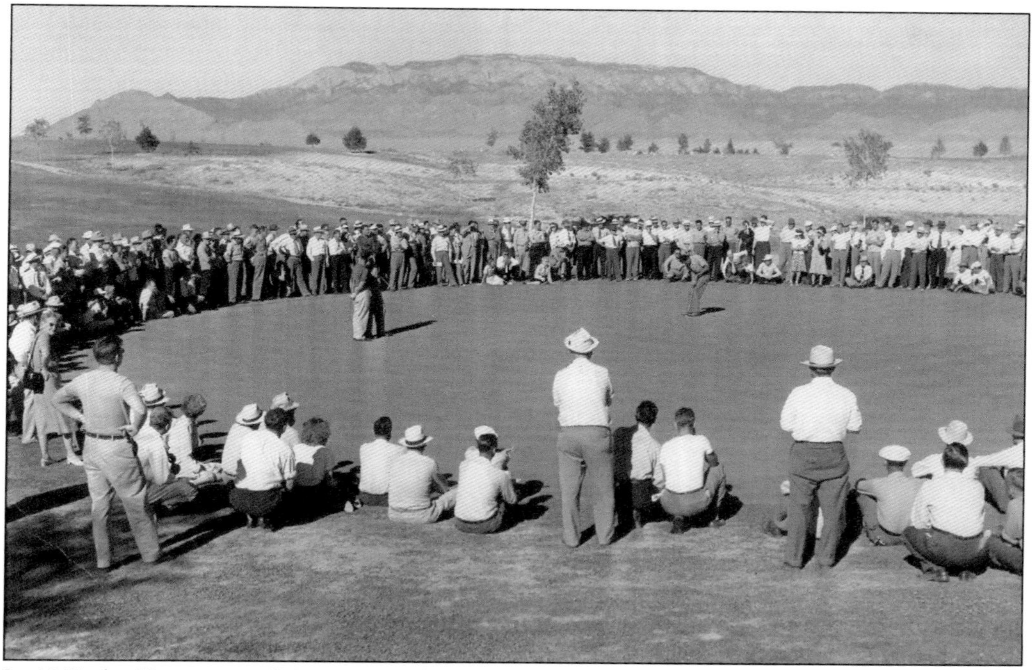

In 1947, the University of New Mexico hosted the Albuquerque Open at its new "north course," completed in 1942 under the design of William H. Tucker. This view looking west at the 16th green shows a group, including one of golf's stars of the day, nightclub singer Jimmy Demaret. The flamboyant Demaret won the following year's 1948 Albuquerque Open, one of 31 tour victories that included three Masters' titles. (AMPA.)

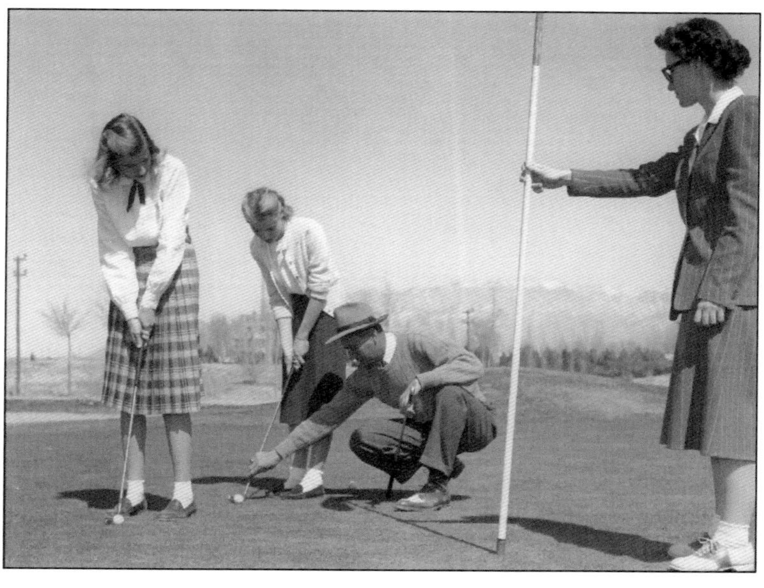

The university also offered women's golf instruction at the north course, as shown in this 1948 photograph. (AMPA.)

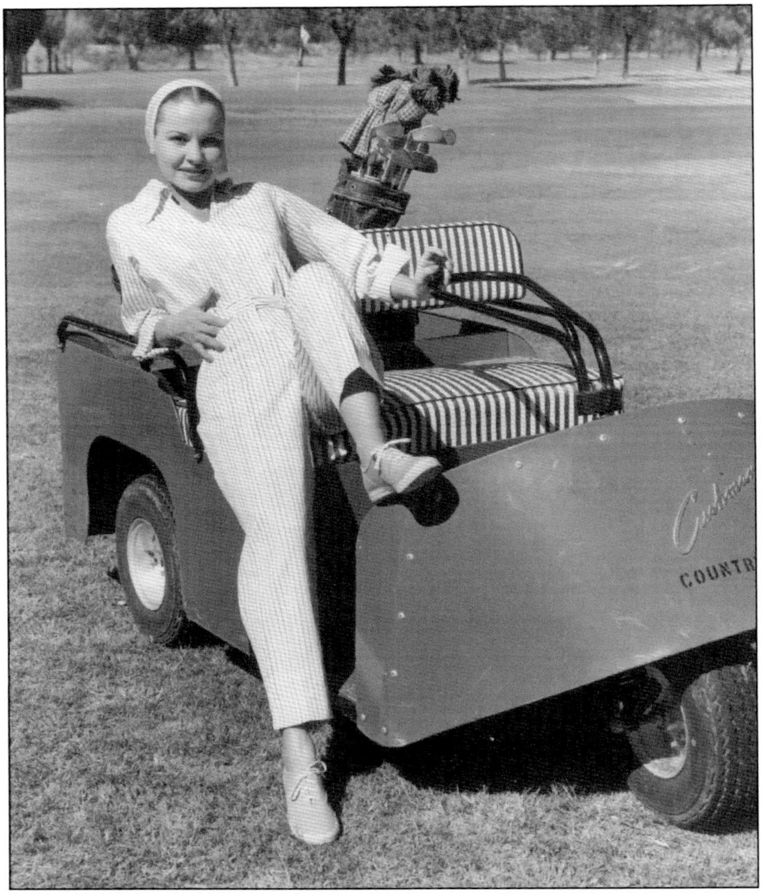

The fashionable side of golf apparel is displayed by this unidentified model posing on a contemporary Cushman golf cart at the Albuquerque Country Club in a photograph taken about 1955. (AMPA.)

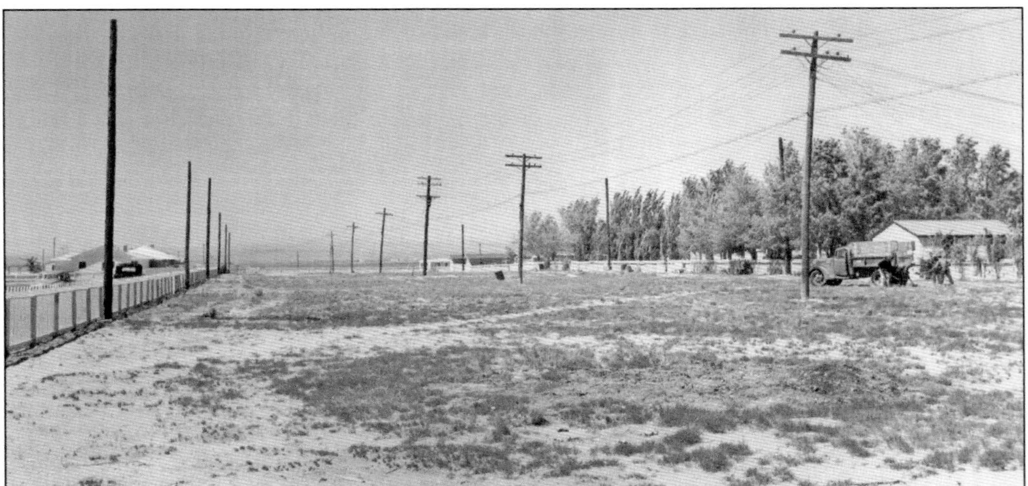

This c. 1940 image is a view looking northwest at the completely barren setting of what would one day become McDuffie Park, or Hidden Park. Post-Depression developer Charles McDuffie and his wife, Martha, sold the land for $1 to the city in hopes that the area would be landscaped and turned into a park. The photograph appears to show park workers starting that project. (AMPA.)

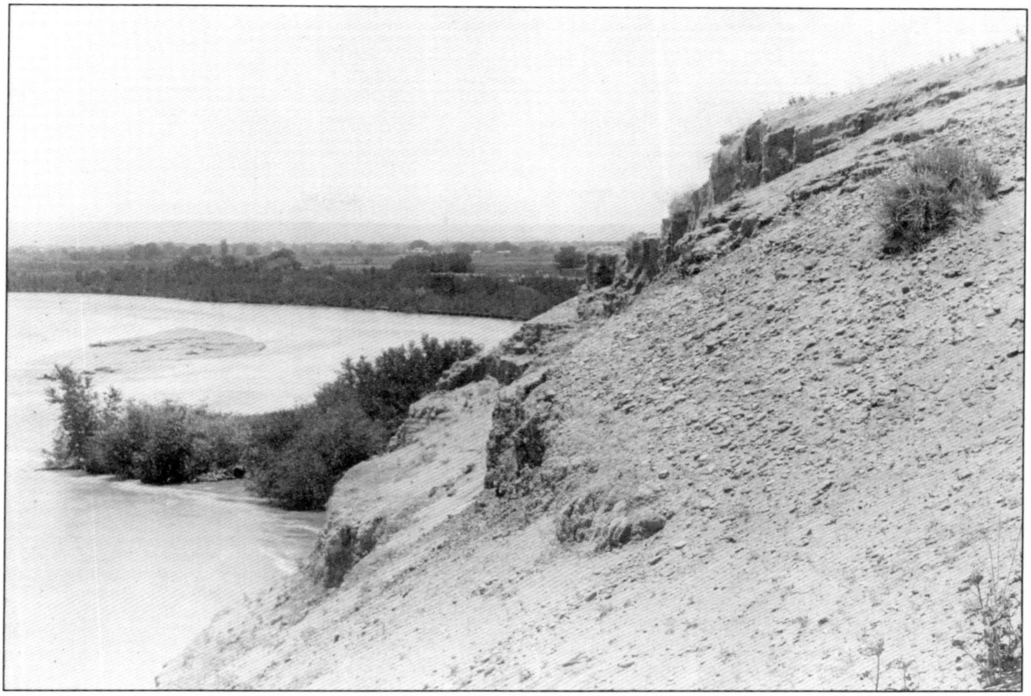

This view looking south along the bluffs of the Rio Grande's west bank was taken about 1940. Interstate 40 would be constructed just south of this location in the early 1960s. (CSWR.)

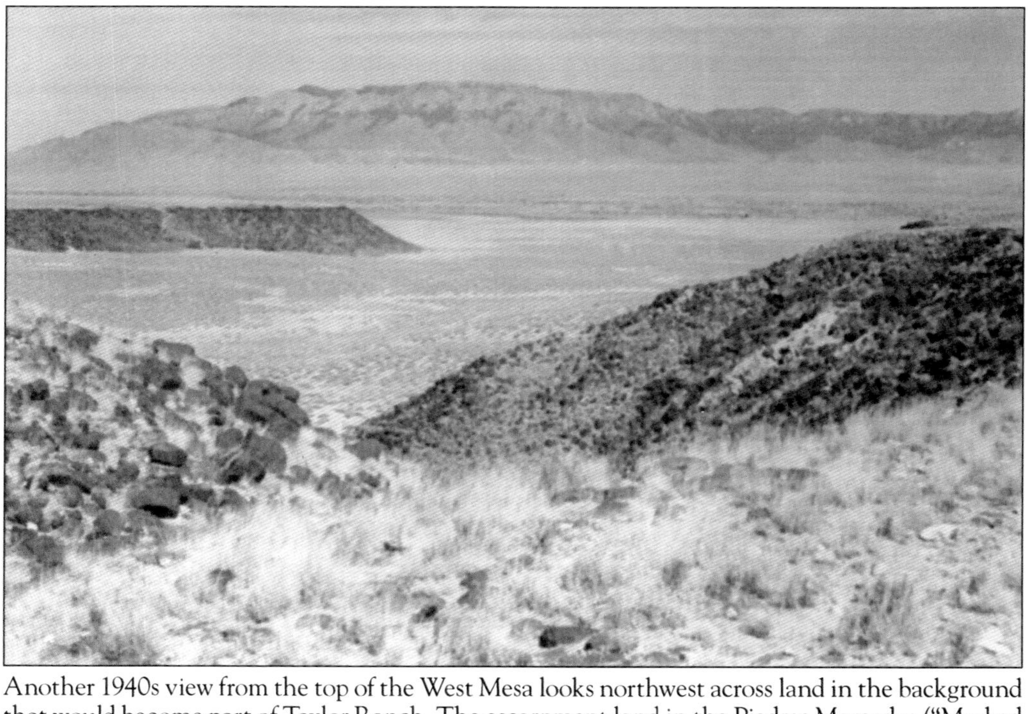

Another 1940s view from the top of the West Mesa looks northwest across land in the background that would become part of Taylor Ranch. The escarpment land in the Piedras Marcadas ("Marked Rocks") Canyon would eventually be included in Petroglyph National Monument. (AMPA.)

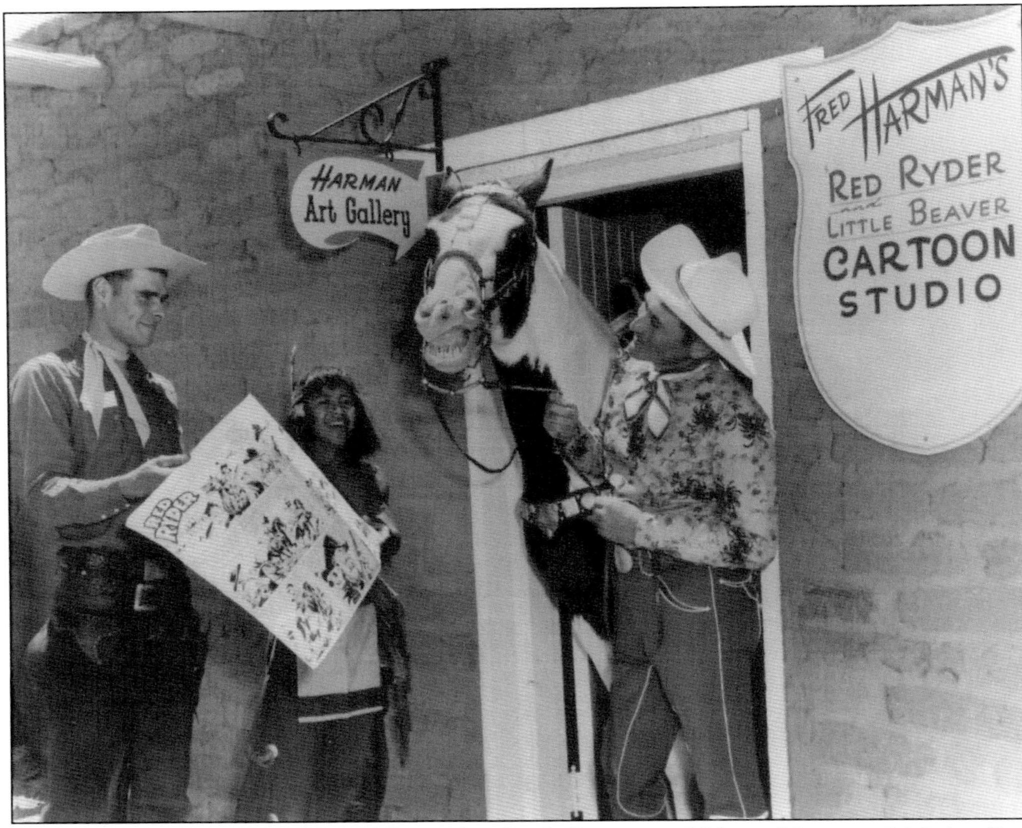

Dave Saunders (left), Arnold Vigil (center) as Little Beaver, and Monte Montana (right) as Red Ryder pose at Fred Harman's cartoon studio at Little Beavertown. Opening to a crowd of 15,000 in June 1961, the $3-million venture had short-lived success because future construction of Interstate 40 did not include good access to the park. Harman paid off his debts to salvage the Little Beaver name, and the amusement park was dismantled soon thereafter. (AMPA.)

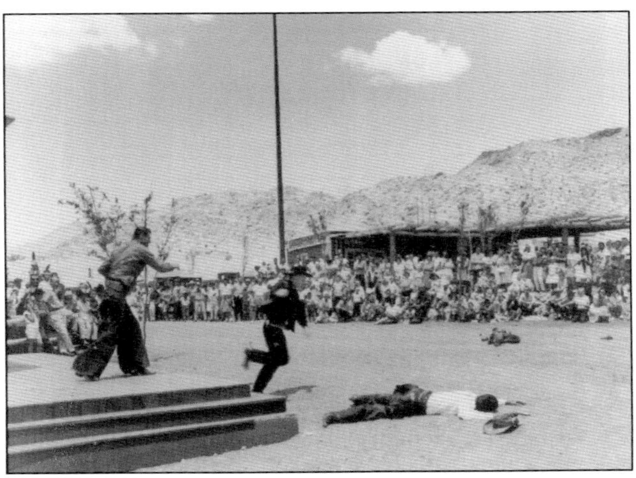

Little Beavertown was an amusement park that creators Howard Hull and *Red Ryder* cartoonist Fred Harman envisioned would have a draw nearly equal to that of Disneyland. Located on Route 66 at the mouth of Tijeras Canyon before tourists arrived in Albuquerque, the 44-acre tract featured Western towns, Indian artisans, and a miniature railroad. In this early-1960s photograph, Dave Saunders (left) knocks out Waco Williams in a mock gunfight. (AMPA.)

Five

"The Most Beautiful Backdrop a City Could Have"

The story of Albuquerque's open space is, in a sense, millions of years in the making. The Sandia Mountains contain granites over a billion years old; and the Rio Grande valley, one of five rift valleys in the world, is filled with sediments two miles deep. The lava flows, volcanoes, and basalt escarpments of the West Mesa are much younger at about 200,000 years old but contain as much recent exposed structural geology as any volcanic landscape on the continent. All of these incredible landscape features are as much a part of Albuquerque as the skyline is to New York City. Into this setting came the first peoples in the New World, leaving behind a cultural sequence over 12,000 years long and filled with momentous developments such as the creation of thousands of sacred petroglyph symbols, the arrival of the first European-led expeditions in the Southwest, colonization, revolt, and resettlement through land grants.

The desire to preserve land in its natural state has stirred Albuquerque's people for decades. Large areas of native land, then called regional parks, were acquired by the city throughout the 1960s. This set the stage for a future system of wild lands that would be called "Open Space." But it was communitywide opposition to land development proposals that produced the Open Space system that exists today. Activist groups worked to save the West Mesa and the volcanoes and to preserve the Rio Grande's cottonwood forest and Sandia foothills. Those disparate ideas were brought together as the Open Space Task Force at the urging of Phillip Tollefsrud, an engineer whose life ended before he could see the results of what he had set in motion. Hundreds more activists would step in to further the cause of preservation. Elected officials, too, from mayors to city councilors, stepped in a critical moments and found funds to buy endangered land as Open Space. The citizens of Albuquerque have shown consistent support by approving special taxes and every Open Space land purchase bond issue in the past 35 years. Together, the famous and the countless, the inspired and the tireless, have created one of the finest Open Space programs in the nation.

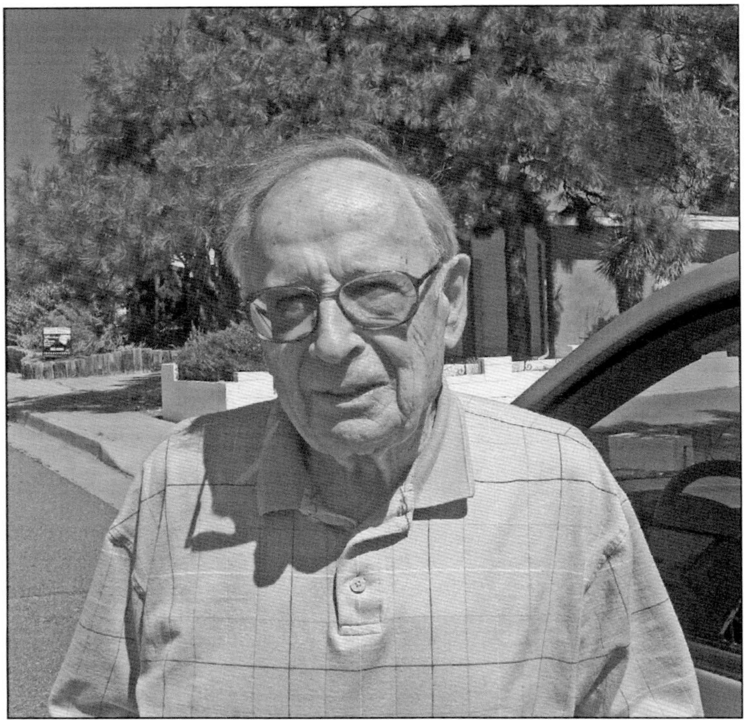

Serving from 1954 through 1979, Bob Burgan was the second director of the Parks Department. Starting at age 36, he instituted professional standards while being a quiet visionary. He especially valued starting the Open Space Program, helping acquire 8,000 acres of federal land in little over a decade. Burgan was 89 when this photograph was taken September 2007; the next day, he left Albuquerque after living there for 60 years.

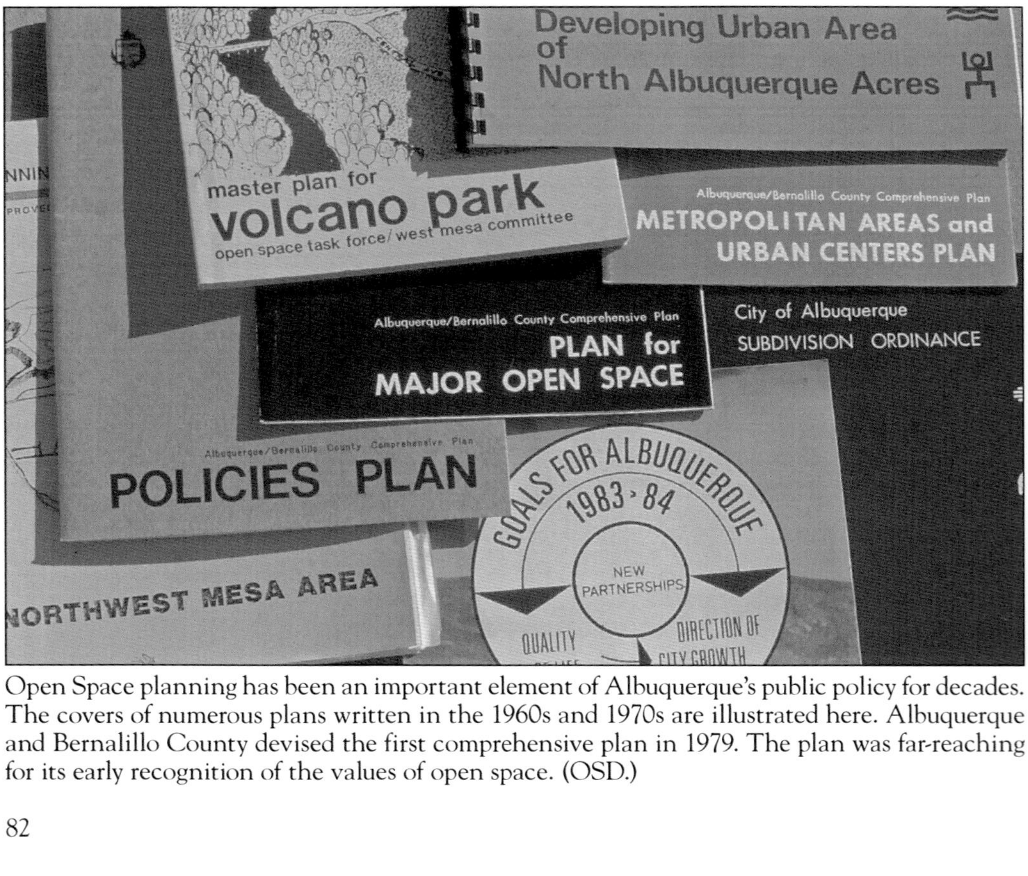

Open Space planning has been an important element of Albuquerque's public policy for decades. The covers of numerous plans written in the 1960s and 1970s are illustrated here. Albuquerque and Bernalillo County devised the first comprehensive plan in 1979. The plan was far-reaching for its early recognition of the values of open space. (OSD.)

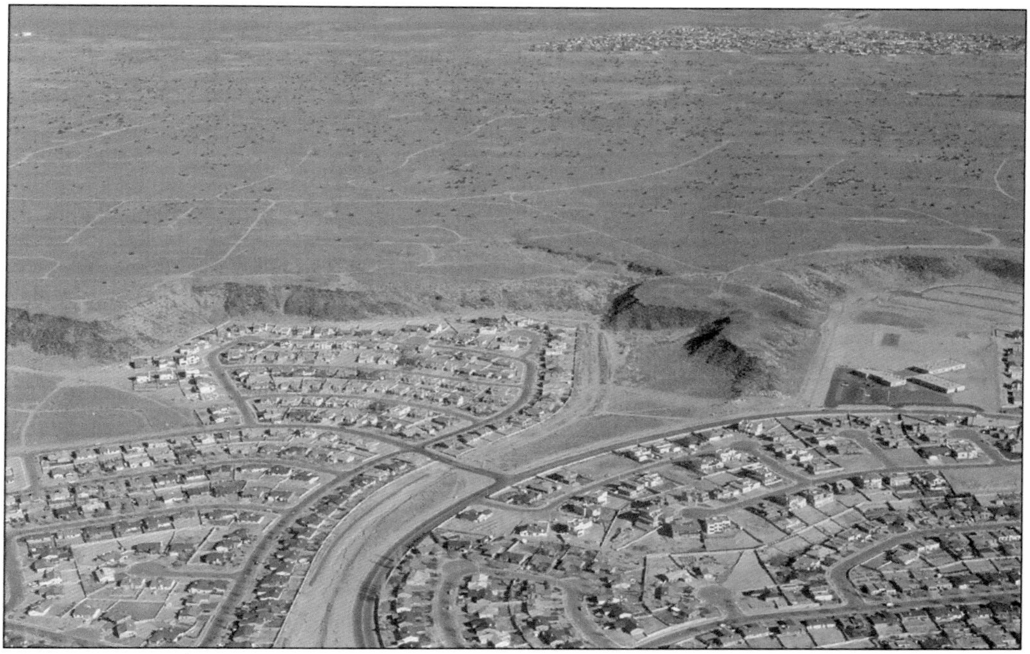

The next comprehensive plan revision in 1988 devoted an entire section to Open Space policies. One vital policy was to "shape the urban form," that is, to define the edges of the city and create natural areas where the landforms warranted it. This March 1985 aerial shows the urban growth of Taylor Ranch stopping at the base of the West Mesa's volcanic escarpment. (OSD, Joel Wooldridge.)

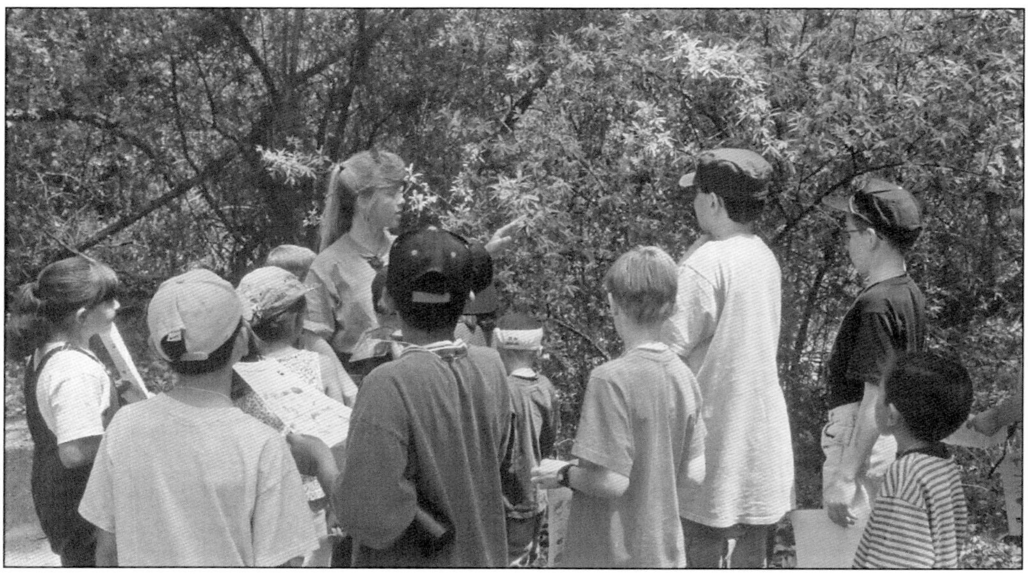

Environmental education has always been an important part of the Open Space Program. Future generations will inherit the land, make decisions about resources, vote, and pay taxes. Children of Albuquerque are taught about the environment at an early age in the hope that they will continue a preservation ethic. In this May 1999 photograph, Bonnie Schmader instructs a class on a field trip to the Sandia foothills. (OSD.)

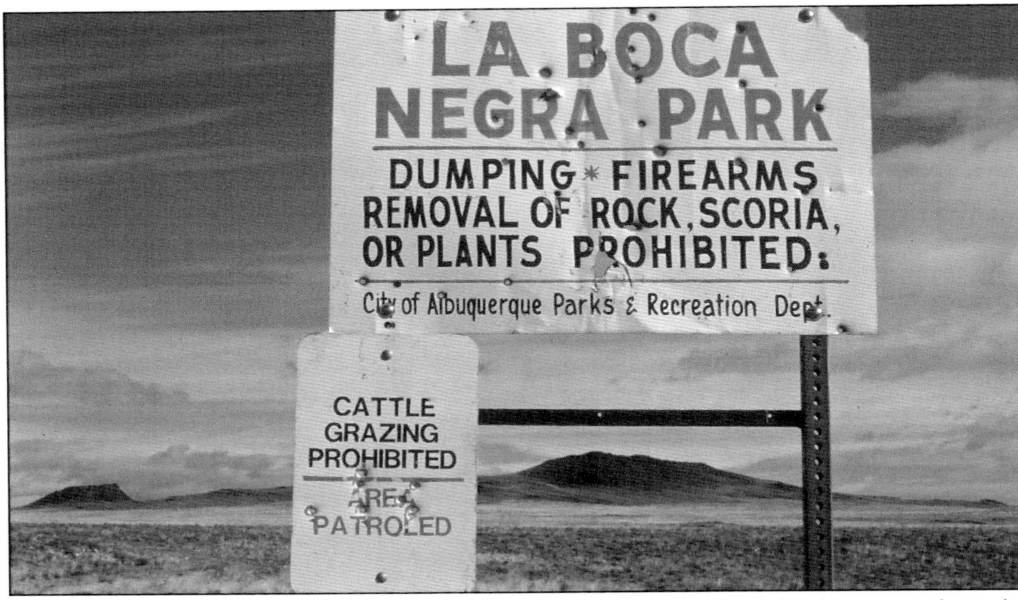

The City of Albuquerque was highly successful in acquiring surplus federal property from the Bureau of Land Management (BLM), creating the basis for today's Open Space system. One such tract comprised 1,527 acres east of the volcanoes called La Boca Negra Park, obtained from 1961 to 1965 under Bob Burgan. Much of the land is now within the boundaries of Petroglyph National Monument. Regulation signs have always been a popular target for shooters. (OSD, Rex Funk.)

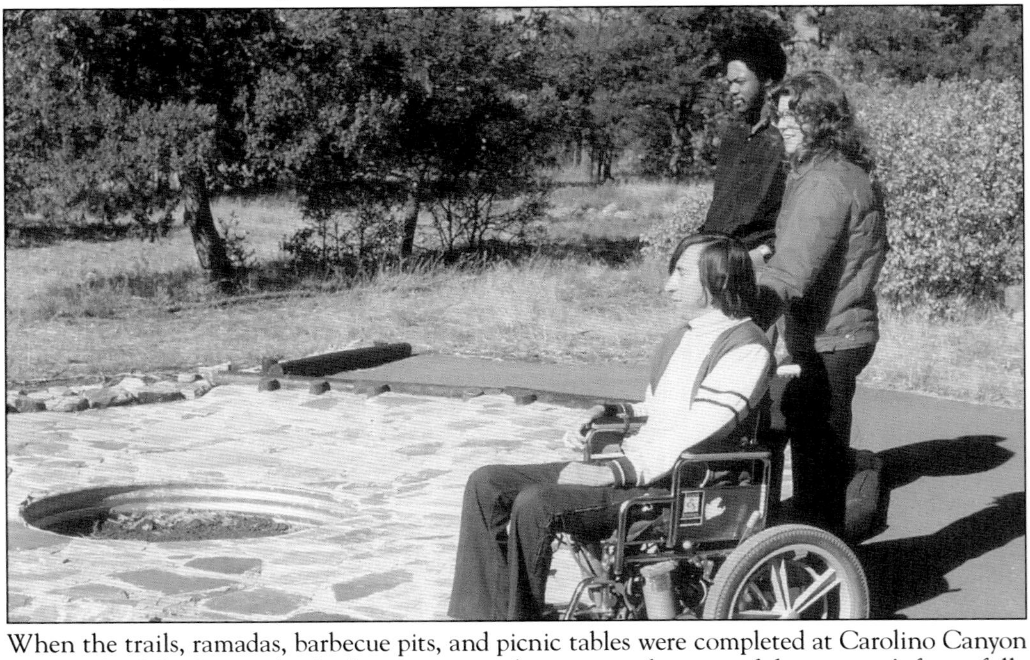

When the trails, ramadas, barbecue pits, and picnic tables were completed at Carolino Canyon Park in the fall of 1979, the facility was instantly recognized as one of the country's finest fully accessible outdoor recreation sites. Carolino Canyon had been obtained from the Bureau of Land Management in the mid-1960s and developed into a group reservation area. The park is nine miles south of the village of Tijeras. (OSD.)

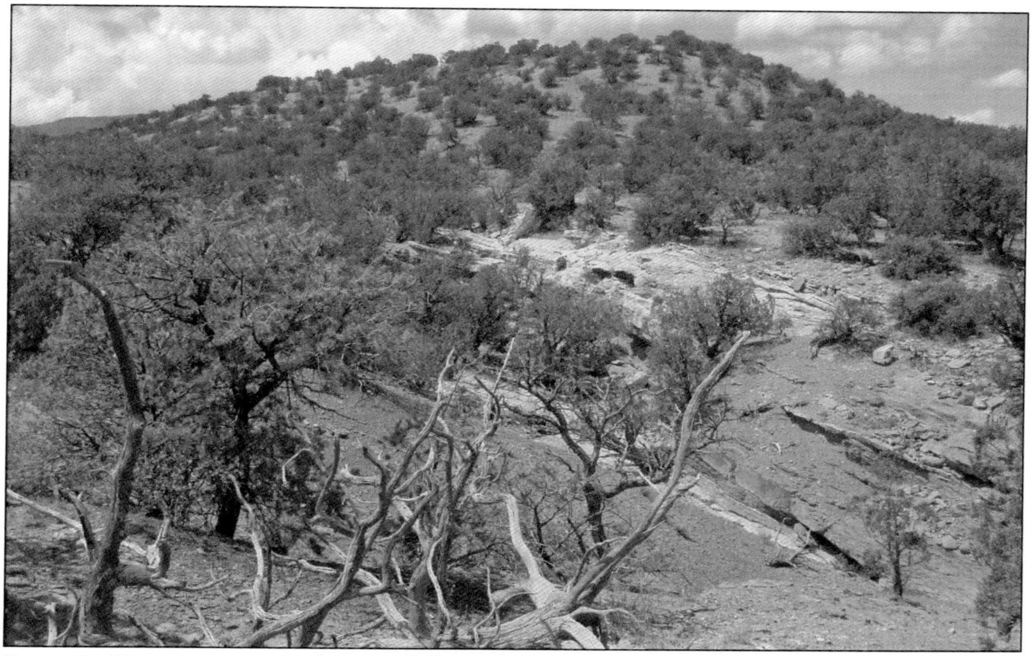

Burgan's efforts to secure surplus parcels from the Bureau of Land Management during the 1960s stretched into neighboring Sandoval County. When asked why the City of Albuquerque would have interests so far away, he replied, "No other municipality is capable of doing the job." Today, Open Space holdings in Sandoval County include 560 acres in Placitas and 1,180 acres near Golden, obtained from 1964 to 1967 (pictured above). (OSD.)

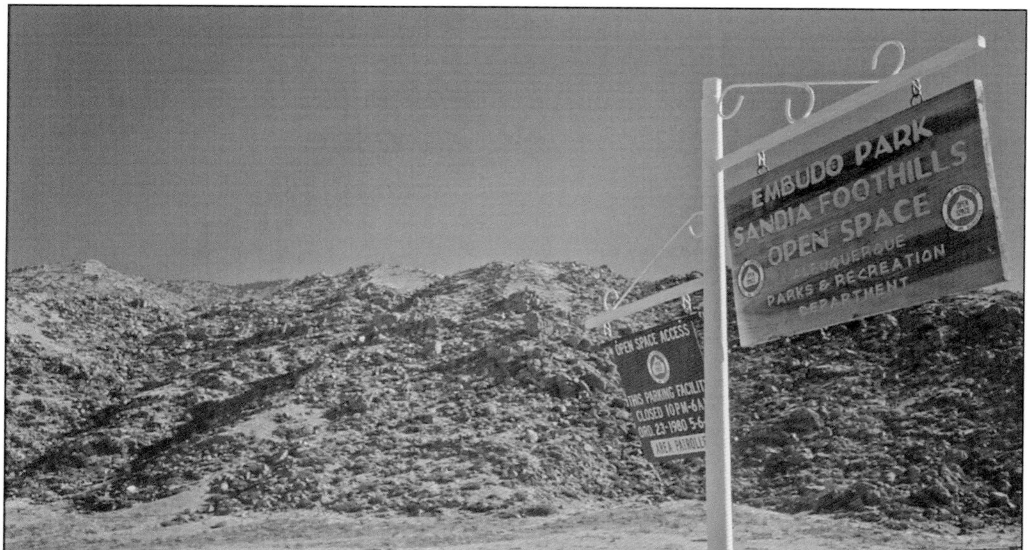

By the late 1970s, acquisition of land at the foothills of the Sandia Mountains included tracts near Glenwood Hills, Rebonito, and Sandia Heights. Open Space parking and access to several key areas in the foothills had been completed by early 1985, as shown in this view of the Embudo Canyon trailhead. (OSD.)

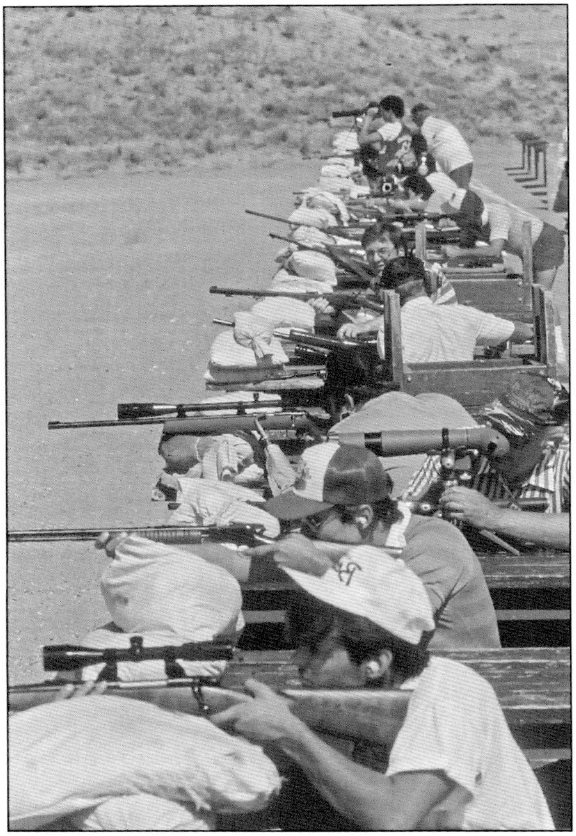

Shooting Range State Park was one of the finest of its kind to be built in the Southwest when it was completed in 1979. Located on 4,596 acres of BLM surplus lands, it remains one of the premier public ranges and has been popular for various events, national competitions, and rifle association–sponsored shoots. In this photograph taken in July 1989, every bay on the 100-meter rifle range is full. (OSD.)

This aerial view looking north towards Vulcan, the largest of the Albuquerque volcanoes, was taken in May 1984. The Albuquerque volcanoes were formed about 210,000 years ago when cracks opened up in the earth's surface and lava poured out in extensive flows covering about 25 square miles. The volcanoes were the last features to form, when the lava thickened and piled up into cones. (OSD.)

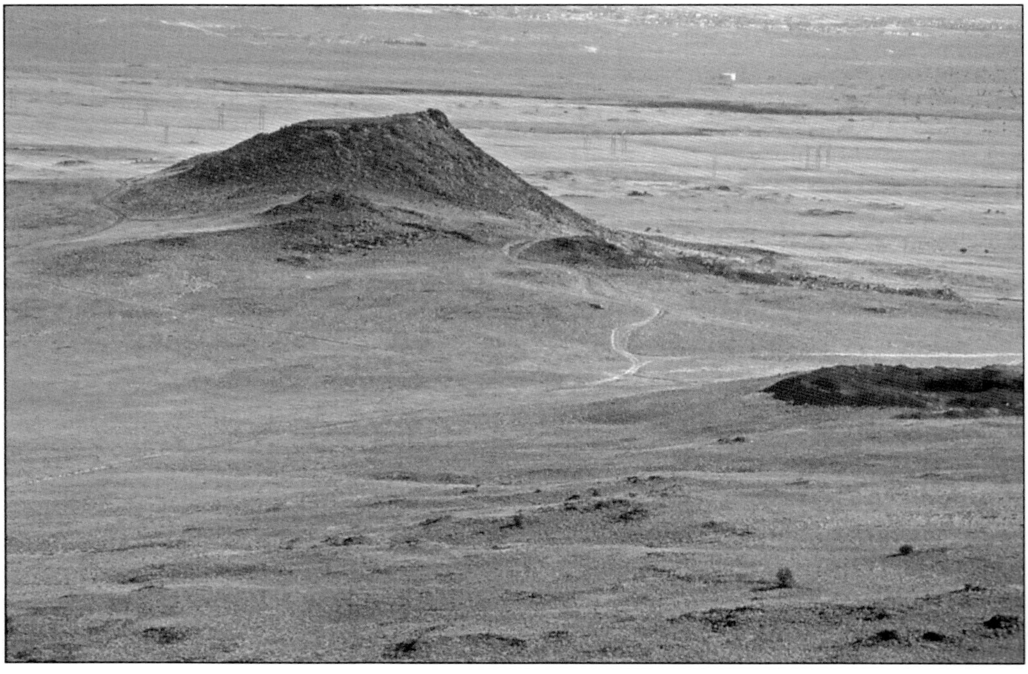

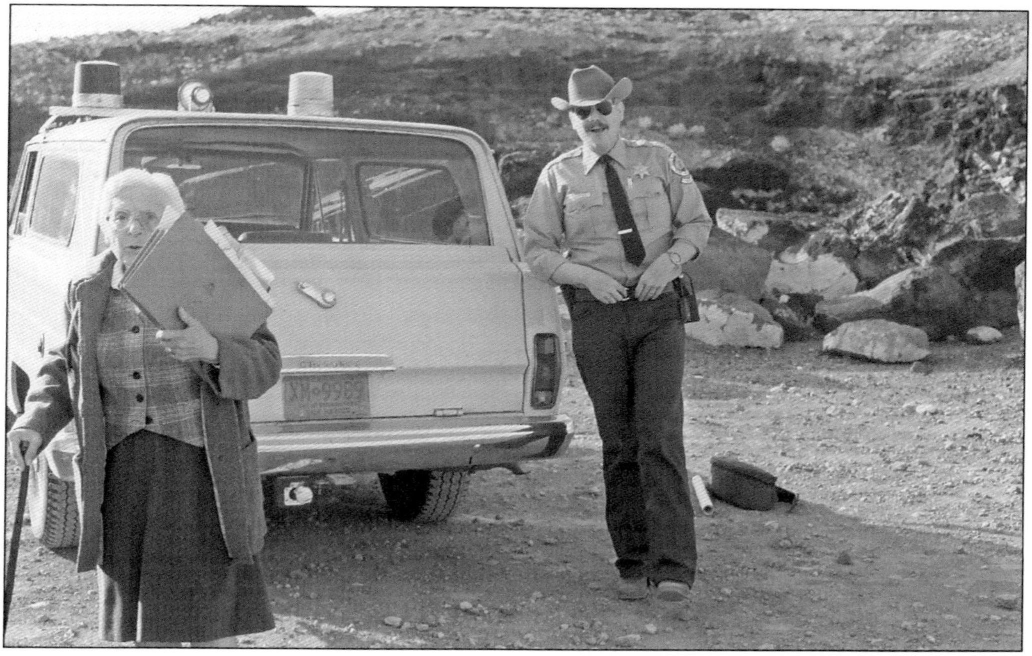

Occasionally, the crusade of one person becomes synonymous with her cause. Ruth Eisenberg was known simply as the "Volcano Lady." She demanded that Mayor Kinney and city councilors save the volcanoes from planned development and ensured thousands of acres were put into permanent open space. This April 1984 photograph shows Eisenberg, then 85, touring one of the newly acquired volcanoes as an Open Space ranger looks on. (OSD, Rex Funk.)

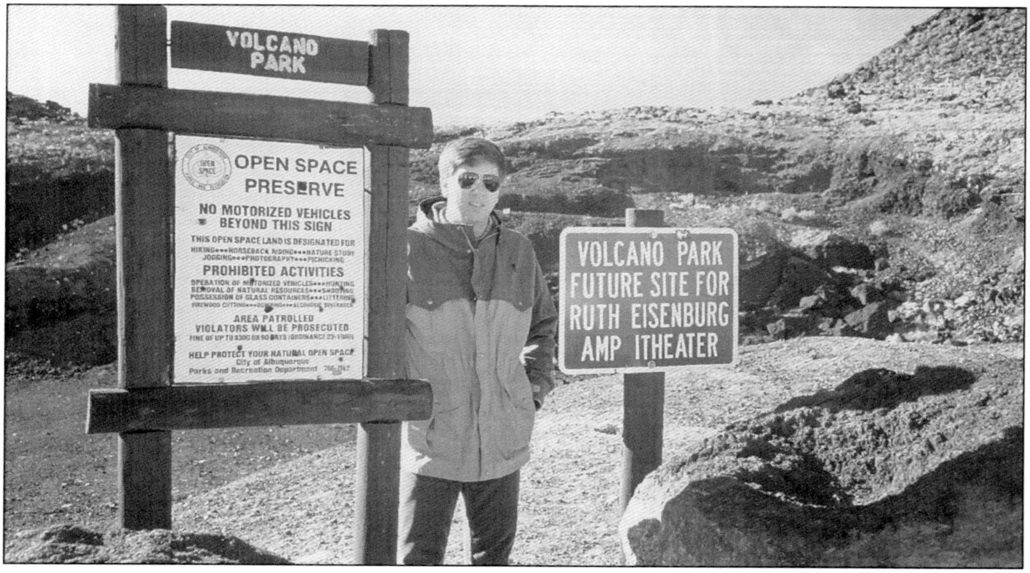

Jay Hart became the second Open Space superintendent, succeeding Rex Funk in 1995. Overseeing construction of facilities at places such as the Elena Gallegos Picnic Area and Carolino Canyon, Hart had been with the Open Space Program since its inception. He is shown here in a late-1980s photograph beside a sign declaring the site of a planned Ruth Eisenberg Memorial Amphitheater. (OSD, Rex Funk.)

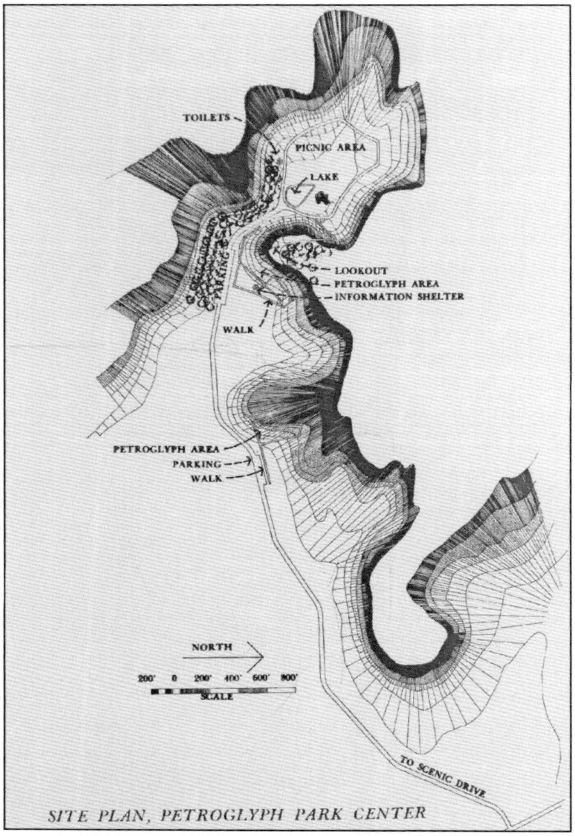

By the late 1960s, plans identified possible locations for a future petroglyph state park and park sites along the Rio Grande. The plan was ambitious, as Rio Grande Park would not be created for another 15 years. While the preferred location for a petroglyph park (pictured) was near Paradise Hills, landowner Horizon Corporation balked, and an alternative location at Taylor Ranch became Indian Petroglyph State Park in 1973. (OSD.)

Original Indian Petroglyph State Park was built in 1973 on land donated to the City of Albuquerque by developer D.W. Falls. Falls dedicated 73 acres for a city park, but the setting, along with its hundreds of petroglyphs, was more suited for a cultural preservation purpose. When the state park opened, it was well ahead of its time nationally for its interpretation of sacred images and for providing accessibility. (OSD.)

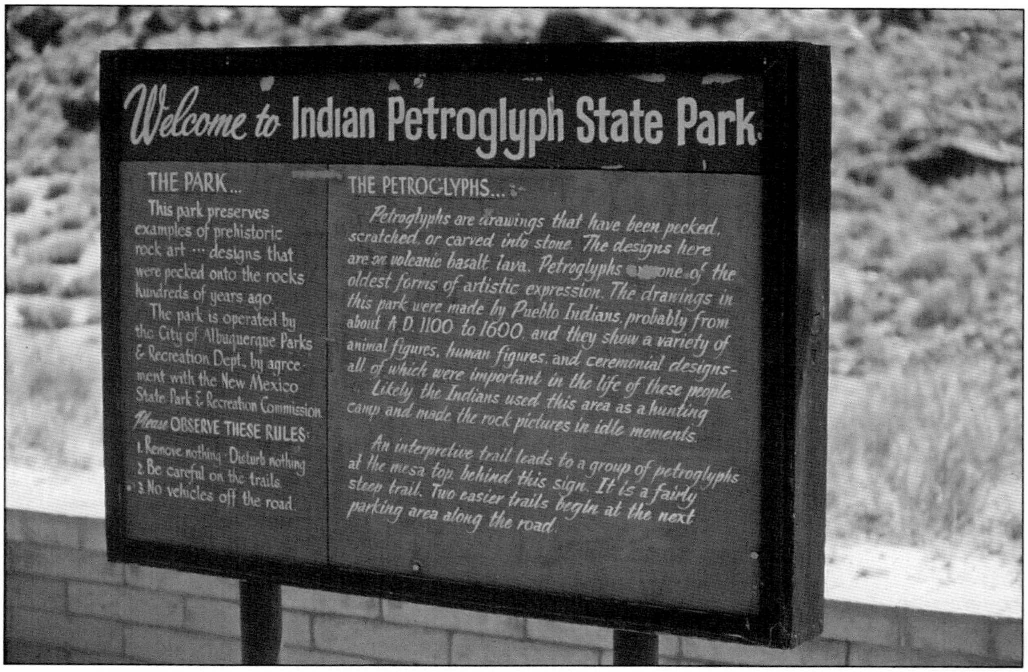

Petroglyphs are images carved into rock by traditional community members to convey messages of prayer, healing, or power. The setting, orientation, and context of each petroglyph also carries meaning. The 17-mile-long West Mesa escarpment of Albuquerque's volcanic cliffs contains an estimated 20,000 or more petroglyphs, the majority of which were left as offerings by Pueblo peoples living in the Rio Grande valley 500 to 700 years ago. (OSD.)

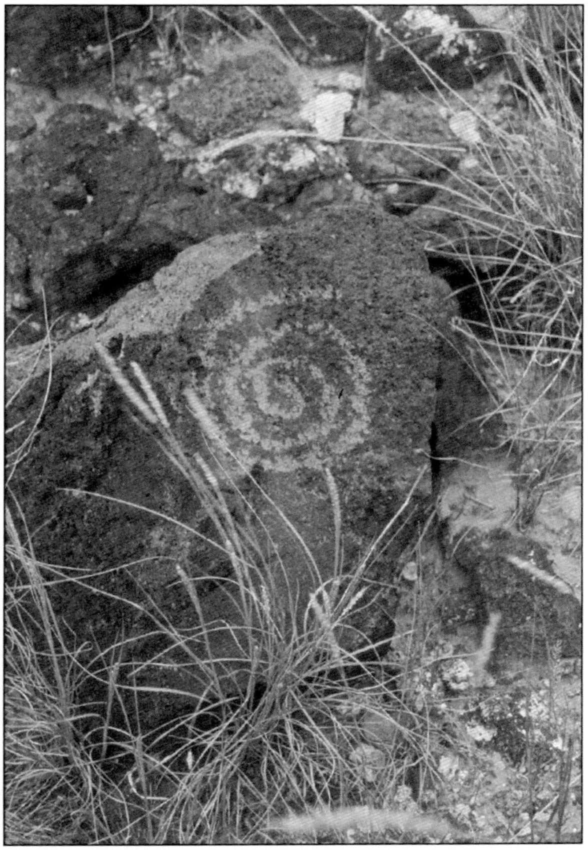

Shortly after completion of a 1,100-acre survey of the West Mesa escarpment in the summer of 1985, results were released estimating the presence of more than 15,000 petroglyphs and 65 archaeological sites. In recognition of the area's vast cultural significance, it was placed in the National Register of Historic Places. Here, the author conducts an on-site television interview in September 1985. (OSD, Rex Funk.)

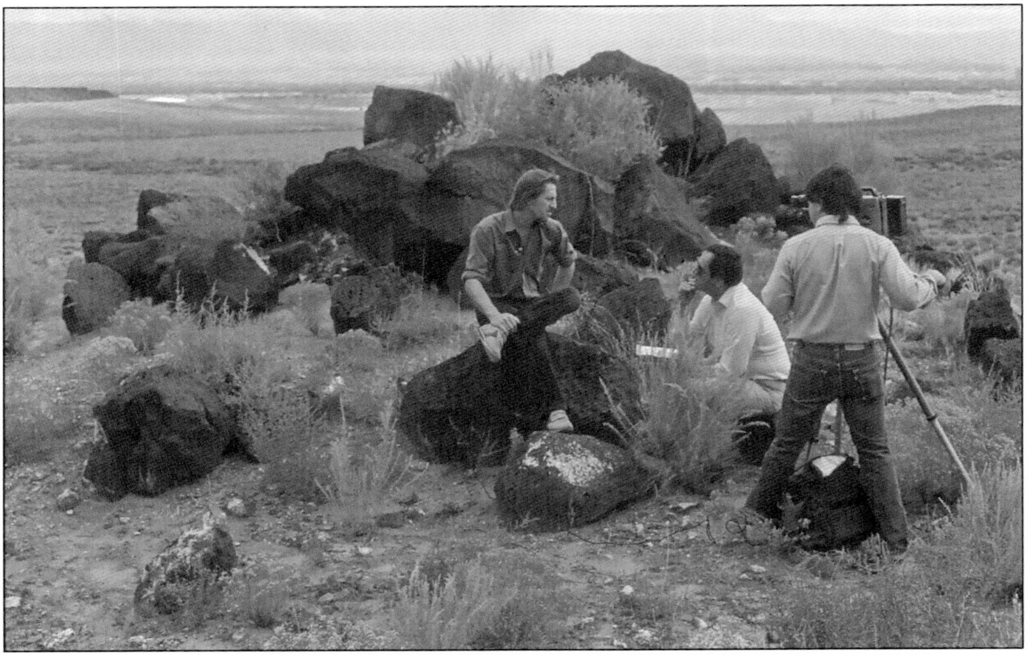

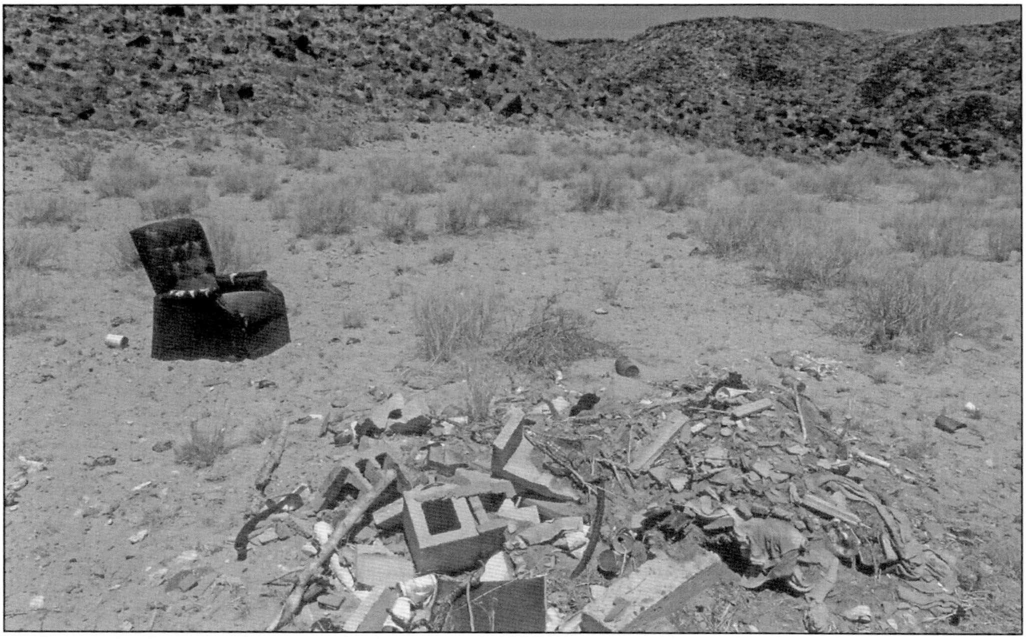

Major trash dumping was prevalent in many areas of the West Mesa escarpment, as shown in this July 1984 image. Contractors building near Paradise Hills created a virtual surface landfill, and irresponsible dumping remains a problem on private West Mesa lands even today. (OSD, Rex Funk.)

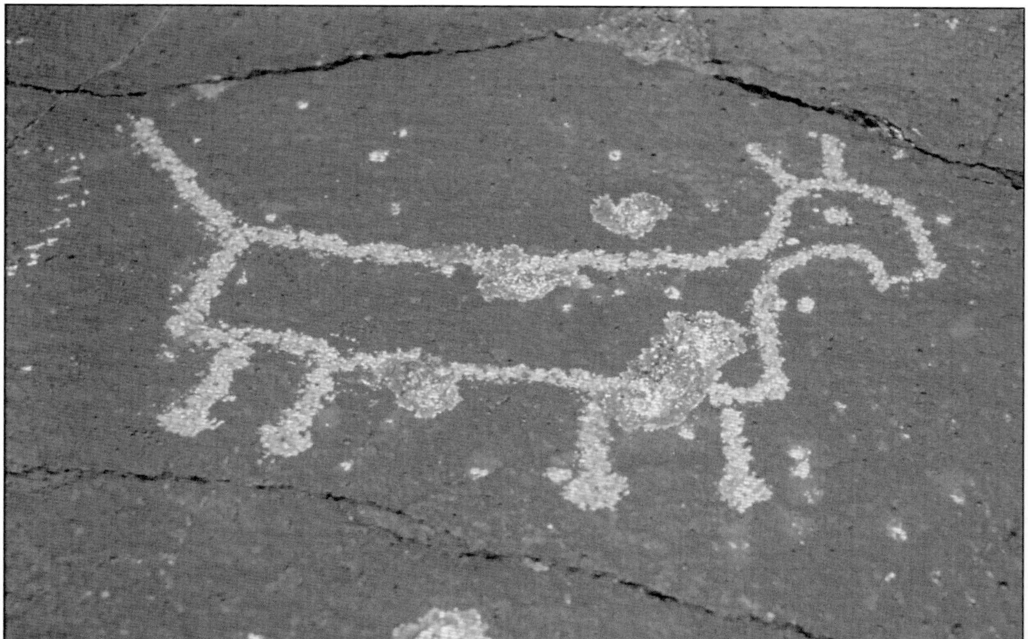

Other forms of damage were extreme and irreversible. This 1985 photograph of a mountain lion shows the effects of intentional gunshots. Landscapers also frequently removed the large basalt boulders from private land along the volcanic escarpment. (OSD, Matt Schmader.)

Follow-up studies and surveys in 1986 continued to document the importance of areas such as Piedras Marcadas Canyon and its associated arroyos. Evidence of archaic hunters, pre-Columbian agricultural features, thousands of petroglyphs, and 19th-century sheepherding sites were all recorded in areas south of Paradise Hills. A newspaper article from November 13, 1986, reports the findings and the city's attempts to acquire the nearby Piedras Marcadas pueblo. (*Albuquerque Journal.*)

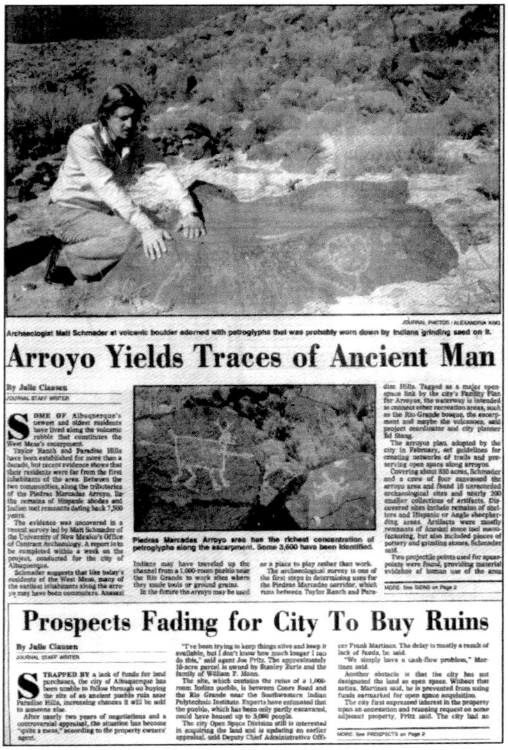

JOURNAL PHOTOS / ALEXANDRA KING

Archaeologist Matt Schmader at volcanic boulder adorned with petroglyphs that was probably worn down by Indians grinding seed on it.

Arroyo Yields Traces of Ancient Man

By Julie Clausen
JOURNAL STAFF WRITER

SOME OF Albuquerque's newest and oldest residents have lived along the volcanic rubble that constitutes the West Mesa's escarpment.

Taylor Ranch and Paradise Hills have been established for more than a decade, but recent evidence shows that their residents were far from the first inhabitants of the area. Between the two communities, along the tributaries of the Piedras Marcadas Arroyo, lie the remains of Hispanic abodes and Indian tool remnants dating back 7,500 years.

The evidence was uncovered in a recent survey led by Matt Schmader of the University of New Mexico's Office of Contract Archaeology. A report is to be completed within a week on the project, conducted for the city of Albuquerque.

Schmader suggests that like today's residents of the West Mesa, many of the earliest inhabitants along the arroyo may have been commuters. Anasazi Indians may have traveled up the channel from a 1,000-room pueblo near the Rio Grande to work sites where they made tools or ground grains.

In the future the arroyo may be used as a place to play rather than work.

The archaeological survey is one of the first steps in determining uses for the Piedras Marcadas corridor, which runs between Taylor Ranch and Paradise Hills. Tagged as a major open-space link by the city's Facility Plan for Arroyos, the waterway is intended to connect other recreation areas, such as the Rio Grande bosque, the escarpment and maybe the volcanoes, said project coordinator and city planner Ed Stang.

The arroyos plan, adopted by the city in February, set guidelines for creating networks of trails and preserving open space along arroyos.

Covering about 330 acres, Schmader and a crew of four canvassed the arroyo area and found 18 unrecorded archaeological sites and nearly 200 smaller collections of artifacts. Discovered sites include remains of shelters and Hispanic or Anglo sheepherding areas. Artifacts were mostly remnants of Anasazi stone tool manufacturing, but also included pieces of pottery and grinding stones, Schmader said.

Two projectile points used for spearpoints were found, providing material evidence of human use of the area

Piedras Marcadas Arroyo area has the richest concentration of petroglyphs along the escarpment. Some 3,600 have been identified.

MORE: See SIGNS on Page 2

Prospects Fading for City To Buy Ruins

By Julie Clausen
JOURNAL STAFF WRITER

STRAPPED BY a lack of funds for land purchases, the city of Albuquerque has been unable to follow through on buying the site of an ancient pueblo ruin near Paradise Hills, increasing chances it will be sold to someone else.

After nearly two years of negotiations and a controversial appraisal, the situation has become "quite a mess," according to the property owners' agent.

"I've been trying to keep things alive and keep it available, but I don't know how much longer I can do this," said agent Joe Fritz. The approximately 10-acre parcel is owned by Stanley Zuris and the family of William F. Mann.

The site, which contains the ruins of a 1,000-room Indian pueblo, is between Coors Road and the Rio Grande near the Southwestern Indian Polytechnic Institute. Experts have estimated that the pueblo, which has been only partly excavated, could have housed up to 3,000 people.

The city Open Space Division still is interested in acquiring the land and is updating an earlier appraisal, said Deputy Chief Administrative Officer Frank Martinez. The delay is mostly a result of lack of funds, he said.

"We simply have a cash-flow problem," Martinez said.

Another obstacle is that the city has not designated the land as open space. Without that action, Martinez said, he is prevented from using funds earmarked for open space acquisition.

The city first expressed interest in the property upon an annexation and rezoning request on some adjacent property, Fritz said. The city had no

MORE: See PROSPECTS on Page 2

Isaac "Ike" Eastvold moved to Albuquerque from Riverside, California, in 1985. A preservationist who helped save Mojave Desert intaglios (huge ancient symbols drawn into the desert pavement), Eastvold dove immediately into the issues surrounding the West Mesa escarpment. He formed the activist group Friends of the Albuquerque Petroglyphs and worked tirelessly for protection and national status of the area by researching, writing, educating, and testifying. (OSD, Matt Schmader.)

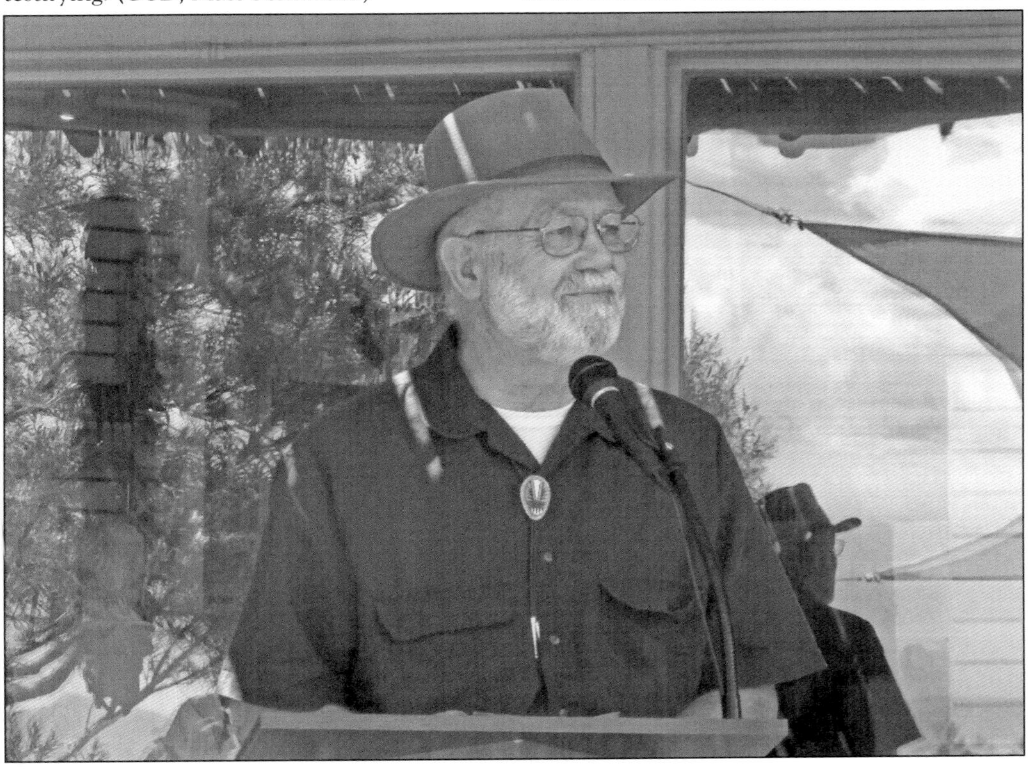

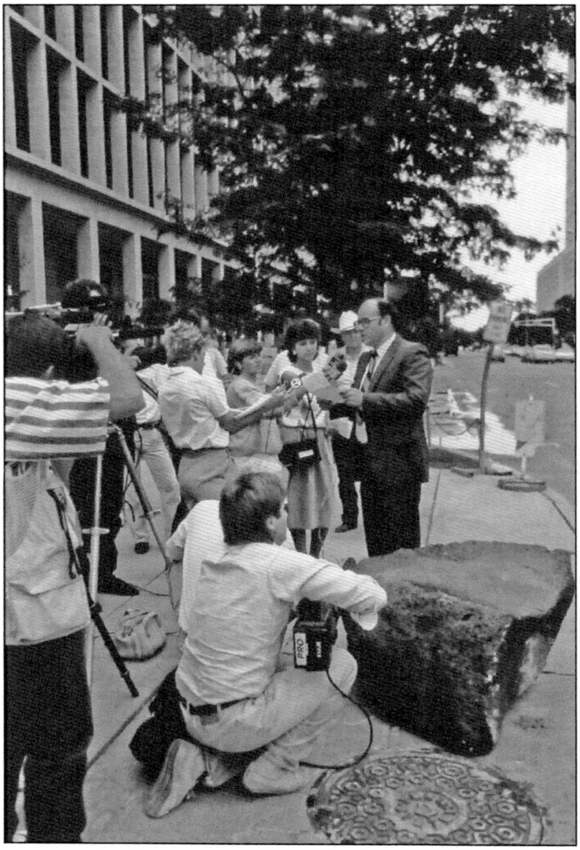

Landowners' rights were a major concern as the real possibility of a new national monument on Albuquerque's west side drew closer. Out of frustration over what might become of their development plans, landowners such as Max Kiehne (right, wearing tie) decided to take action. On September 4, 1987, Kiehne hired a crew to remove a basalt boulder with a mountain lion petroglyph from his property. (OSD.)

The petroglyph-bearing boulder was delivered to the steps of city hall amid much media publicity. In this image, Ike Eastvold, leader of the community group Friends of the Albuquerque Petroglyphs, takes photographs while the boulder is hoisted onto the sidewalk. Max Kiehne later gave a speech denouncing any proposals that would take private land to create a new national monument. (OSD.)

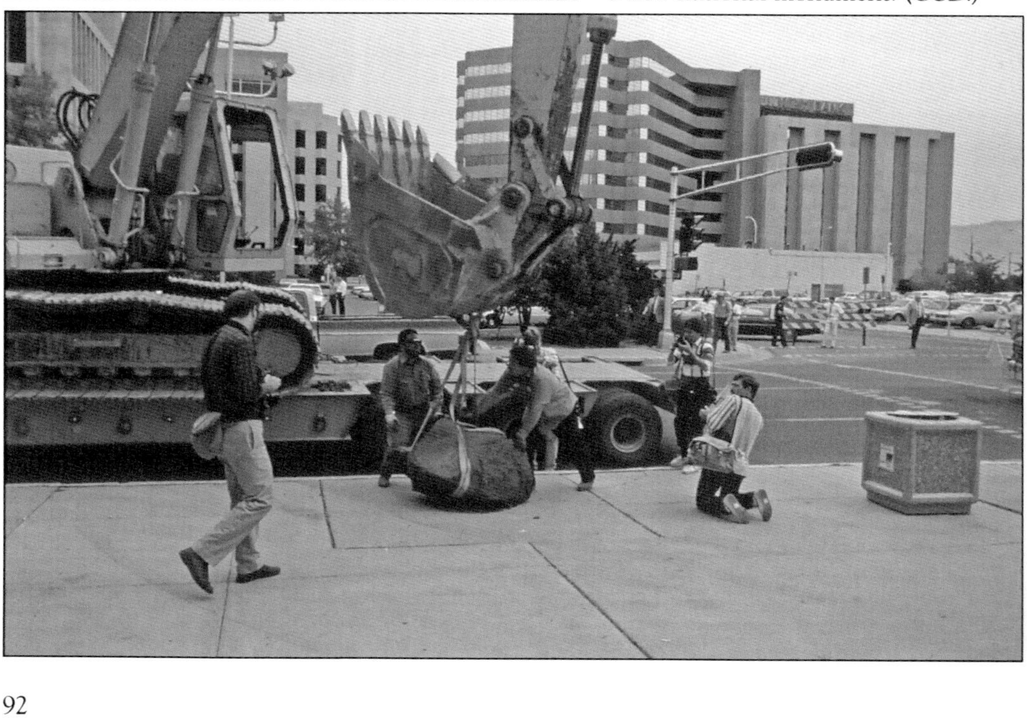

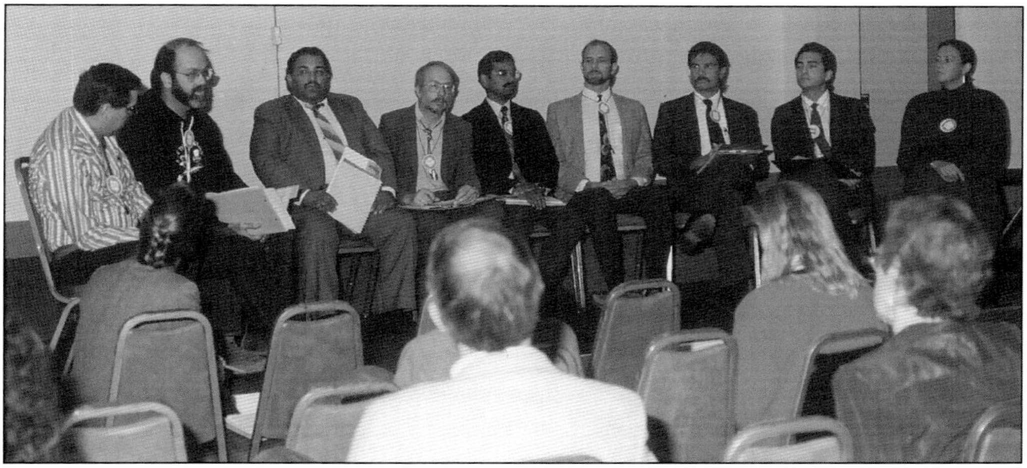

Albuquerque hosted a national Open Space conference in 1989. With congressional field hearings being conducted by the National Park Service (NPS) and the promise of a new national monument looming, protection and interpretation of petroglyphs was a timely topic. A panel discussion included, from left to right, Cliff Anderson, Ike Eastvold, Joe David Montano, Mark Money, Kapil Goyal, Jack Cloud, John Myers, Leroy Chavez, and the Open Space Division's Barbara Baca. (OSD.)

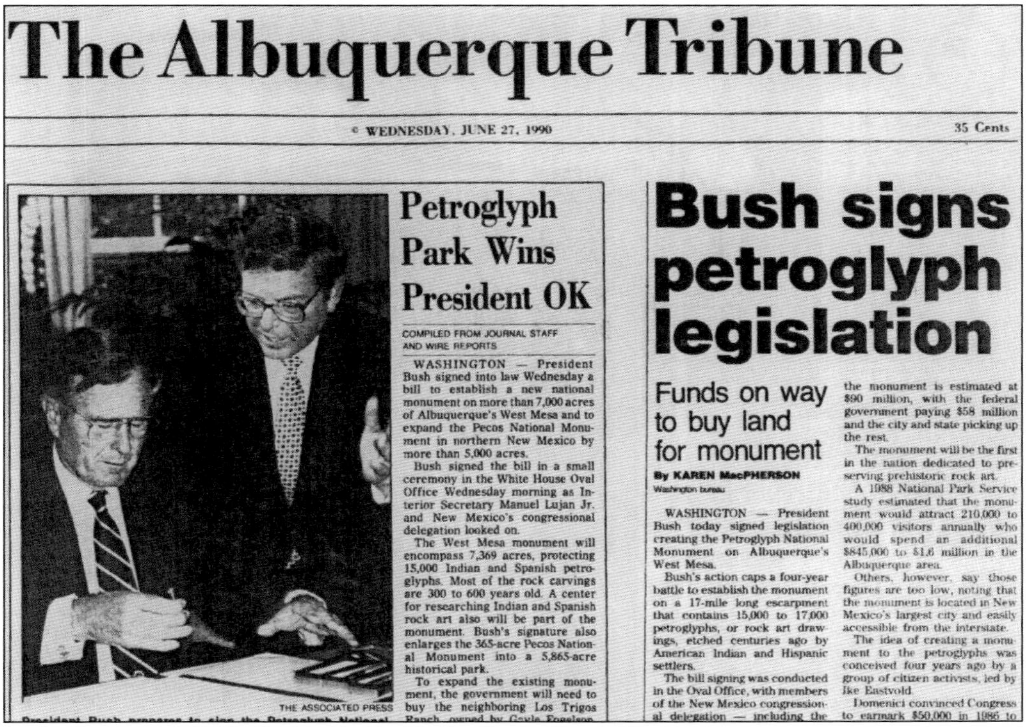

The Albuquerque Tribune

© WEDNESDAY, JUNE 27, 1990 35 Cents

THE ASSOCIATED PRESS

Petroglyph Park Wins President OK

COMPILED FROM JOURNAL STAFF AND WIRE REPORTS

WASHINGTON — President Bush signed into law Wednesday a bill to establish a new national monument on more than 7,000 acres of Albuquerque's West Mesa and to expand the Pecos National Monument in northern New Mexico by more than 5,000 acres.

Bush signed the bill in a small ceremony in the White House Oval Office Wednesday morning as Interior Secretary Manuel Lujan Jr. and New Mexico's congressional delegation looked on.

The West Mesa monument will encompass 7,369 acres, protecting 15,000 Indian and Spanish petroglyphs. Most of the rock carvings are 300 to 600 years old. A center for researching Indian and Spanish rock art also will be part of the monument. Bush's signature also enlarges the 365-acre Pecos National Monument into a 5,865-acre historical park.

To expand the existing monument, the government will need to buy the neighboring Los Trigos

Bush signs petroglyph legislation

Funds on way to buy land for monument

By KAREN MacPHERSON
Washington bureau

WASHINGTON — President Bush today signed legislation creating the Petroglyph National Monument on Albuquerque's West Mesa.

Bush's action caps a four-year battle to establish the monument on a 17-mile long escarpment that contains 15,000 to 17,000 petroglyphs, or rock art drawings, etched centuries ago by American Indian and Hispanic settlers.

The bill signing was conducted in the Oval Office, with members of the New Mexico congressional delegation — including the

the monument is estimated at $90 million, with the federal government paying $58 million and the city and state picking up the rest.

The monument will be the first in the nation dedicated to preserving prehistoric rock art.

A 1988 National Park Service study estimated that the monument would attract 210,000 to 400,000 visitors annually who would spend an additional $845,000 to $1.6 million in the Albuquerque area.

Others, however, say those figures are too low, noting that the monument is located in New Mexico's largest city and easily accessible from the interstate.

The idea of creating a monument to the petroglyphs was conceived four years ago by a group of citizen activists, led by Ike Eastvold.

Domenici convinced Congress to earmark $50,000 in 1986 to

On June 27, 1990, Pres. George H.W. Bush signed Petroglyph National Monument into law as New Mexico senior senator Pete Domenici looks on. Less than five years after the area was listed in the National Register of Historic Places, proponents such as the Friends of the Albuquerque Petroglyphs, the Sierra Club, and the League of Women Voters attained ultimate protection for 7,250 acres in the face of mounting threats and impacts. (*Albuquerque Journal*.)

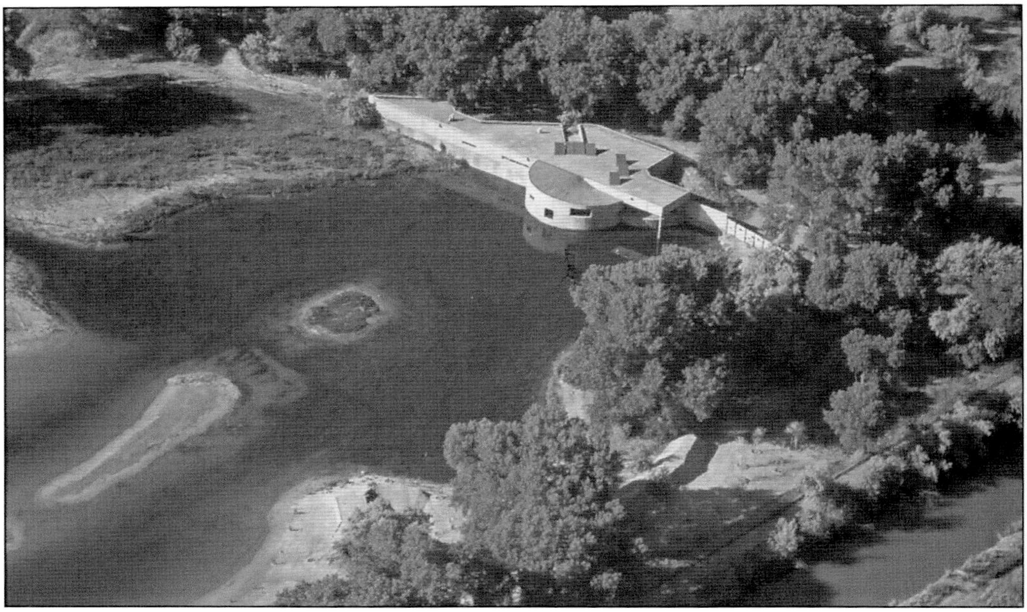

Growing interest in preservation for the Rio Grande's cottonwood forest spurred groups such as the Bosque Society to suggest a centralized base of activity. In summer 1982, the Rio Grande Nature Center was started on land owned by the City of Albuquerque. The center's innovative design was the work of architect Antione Predock. This spring 1985 aerial view shows the nature center's ponds just starting to establish. (OSD, Rex Funk.)

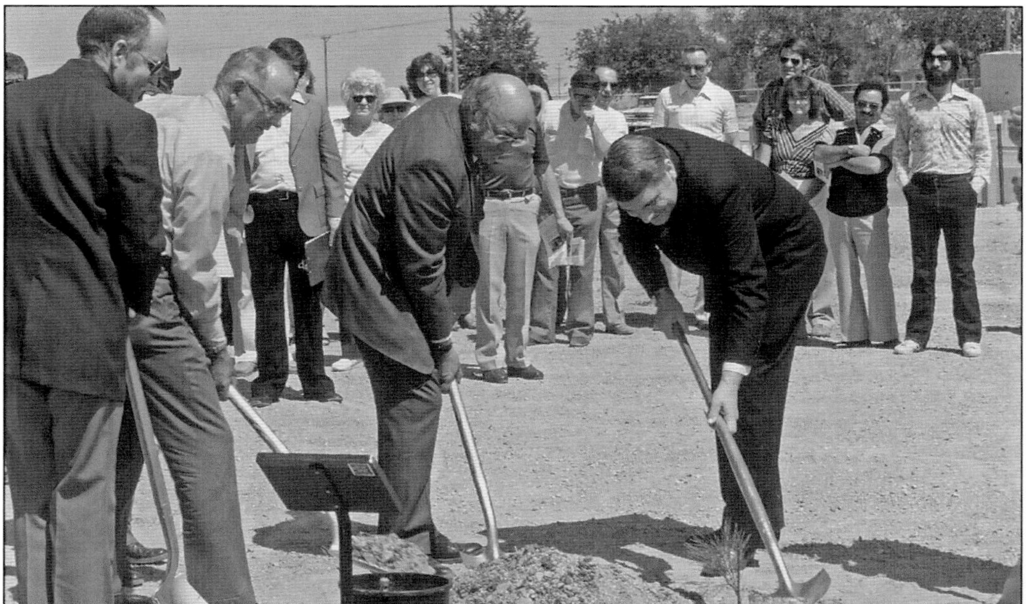

Gov. Bruce King and Mayor Harry Kinney plant trees at the Rio Grande Nature Center ribbon-cutting ceremony in the summer of 1982. Today, the Rio Grande Nature Center is the preeminent environmental education facility along the Rio Grande, hosting throngs of schoolchildren and 150,000 visitors annually. (OSD.)

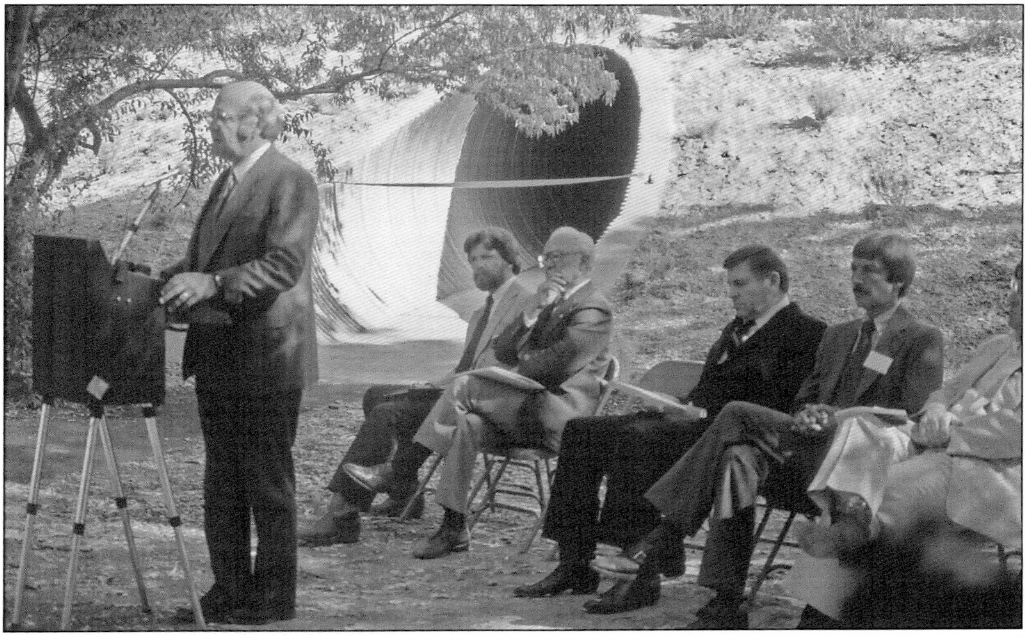

Ribbon-cutting ceremonies for the Rio Grande Nature Center included elected officials, state and local agencies, and a grateful public. Here, Mayor Harry Kinney delivers remarks as Gov. Bruce King (seated, third from left) awaits his turn at the podium. (OSD, Rex Funk.)

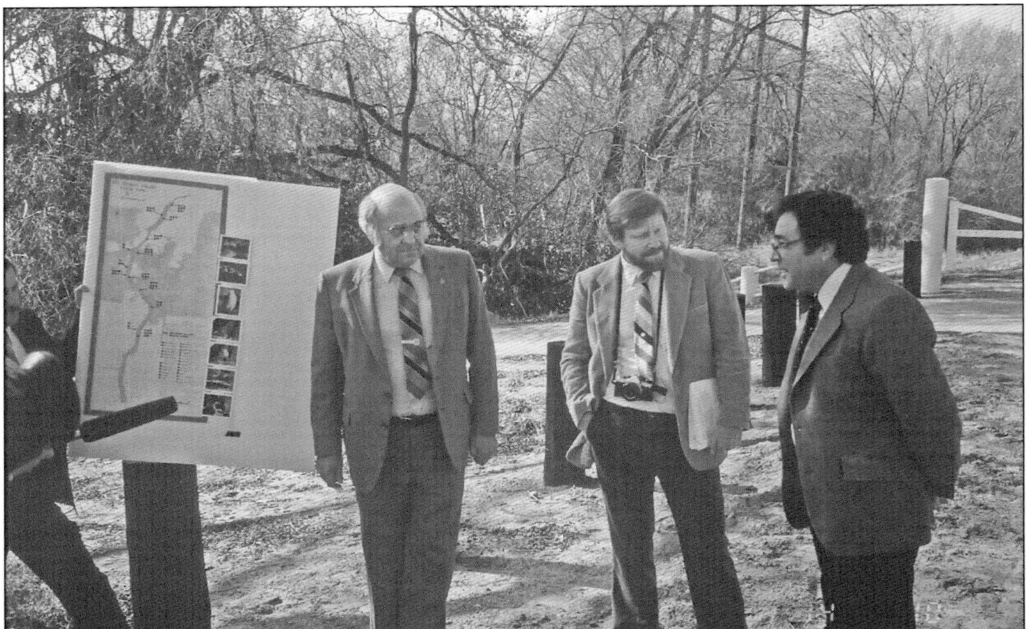

Mayor Harry Kinney (left), Open Space superintendent Rex Funk (center), and Parks Department director Orlie Sedillo discuss events of the day at the opening ceremony for the Rio Grande Nature Center in the summer of 1982. (OSD.)

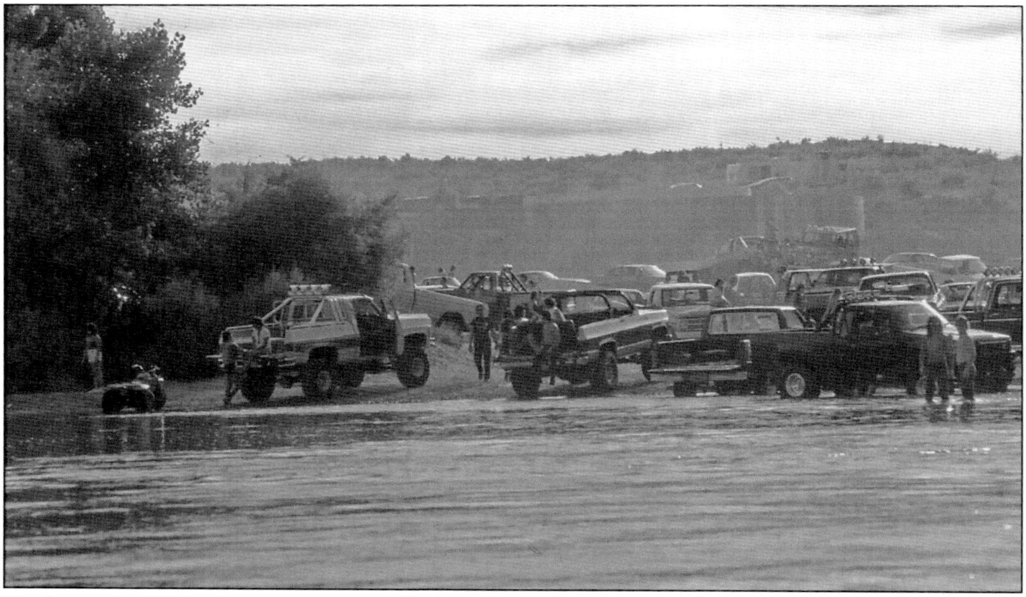

By the early 1980s, deteriorating conditions along the Rio Grande caused citizens to demand a change in management. Transient camps, woodcutting, trash dumping, and rampant vehicular access were so prevalent that the area was almost unusable for the average person. In response, the New Mexico State Legislature established Rio Grande Valley State Park in 1983 and designated Albuquerque's Open Space Division as the park's managing agency. (OSD.)

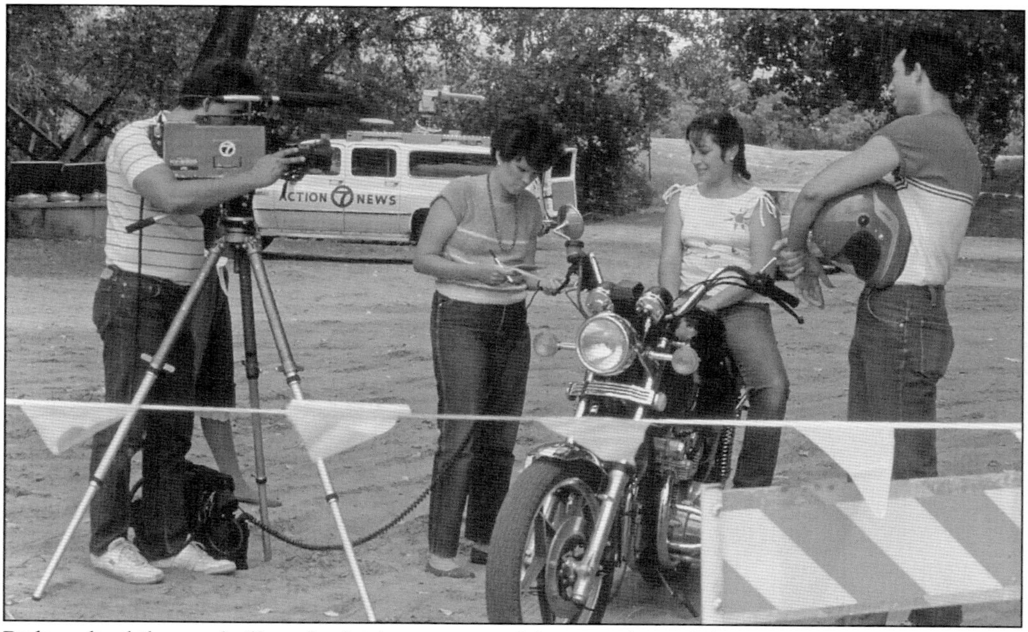

Riding dirt bikes and off-road vehicles was one of the more harmful activities taking place in the bosque. With over 30 miles of levee roads and multiple access points, closing off vehicle access was one of the greatest challenges facing the newly established state park. This move also proved to be unpopular with some members of the community, seen here in a summer 1985 interview with KOAT television. (OSD.)

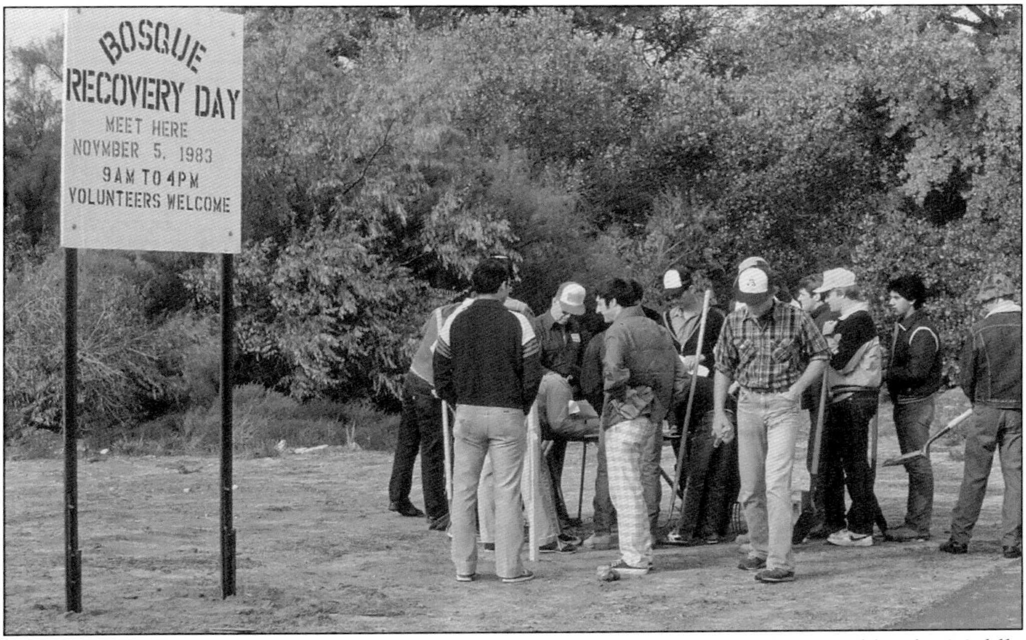

Soon after Rio Grande Valley State Park was established on lands mostly owned by the Middle Rio Grande Conservancy District, the hard work of changing destructive habits began. Public buy-in was a key tool in transforming the bosque from a dumping ground to a respected habitat. An image from one of the early Bosque Recovery Days is shown in this photograph from November 1983. (OSD, Rex Funk.)

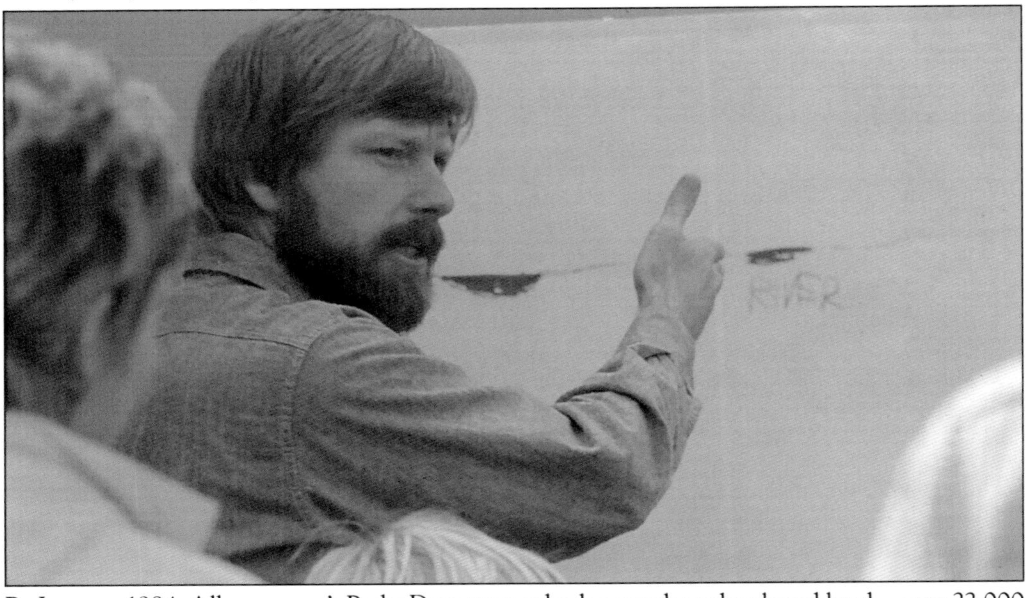

By January 1984, Albuquerque's Parks Department had so much undeveloped land—over 22,000 acres—and responsibility for newly established Rio Grande Valley State Park and the recently purchased Elena Gallegos grant lands, that a new division was needed. Former high school biology teacher turned planner and tireless preservationist Rex Funk was tapped to become the first Open Space Division superintendent. Funk served from 1984 until 1995. (OSD.)

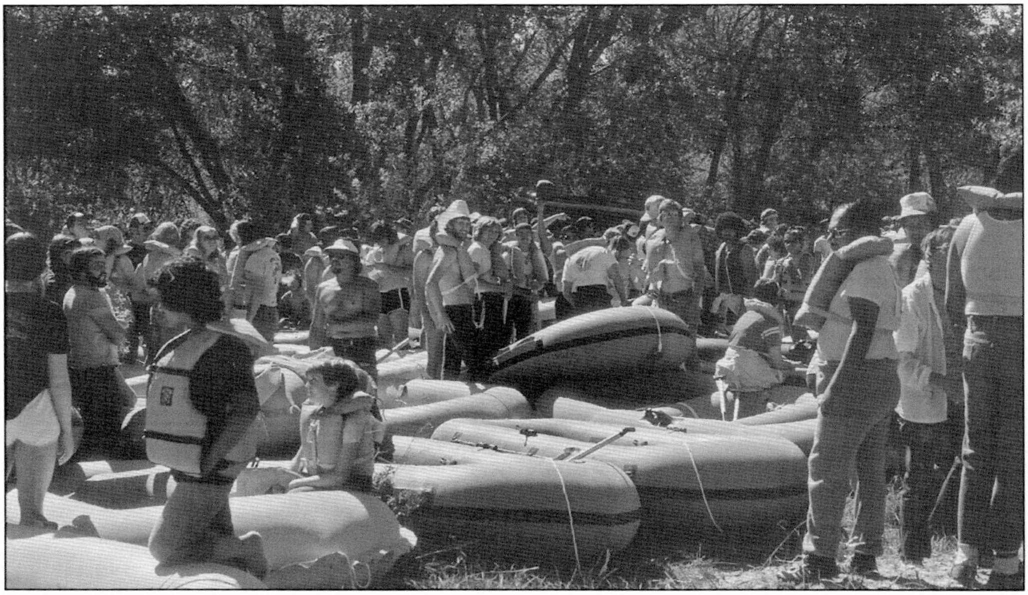

The annual Rio Grande raft race was popular in the 1980s before lower flows in the river, environmental concerns over endangered species, and deteriorating water quality cancelled many events. In this view of the 1980 race, dozens of revelers await the release of various waves of watercraft. (OSD.)

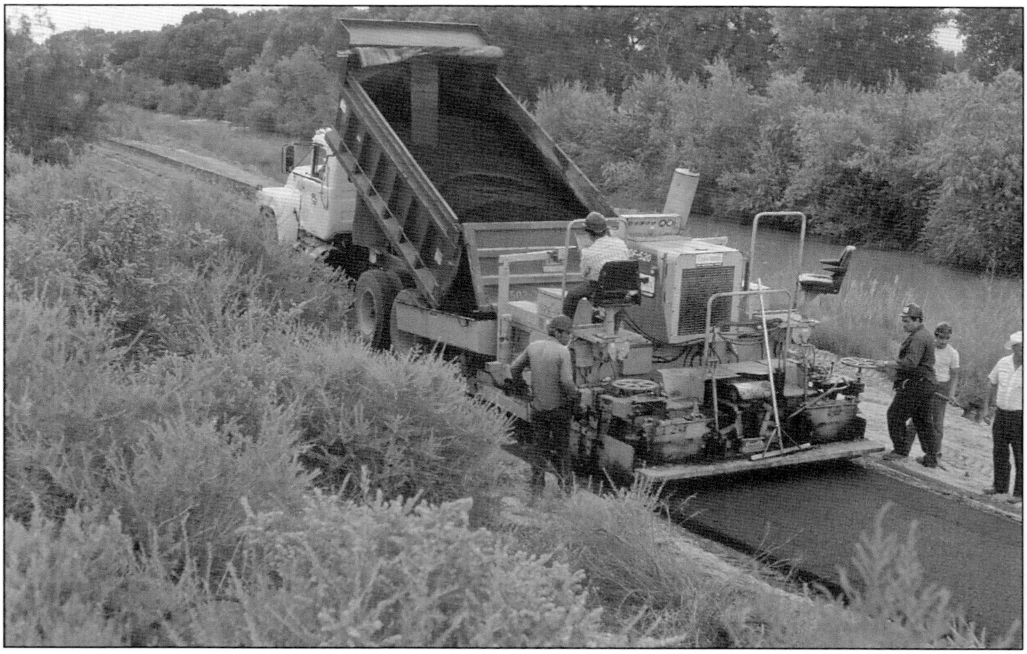

The Paseo del Bosque multiuse trail runs over 15 miles in length along the east side of the Rio Grande, from Alameda Boulevard on the north to the South Diversion Channel. The beloved trail was recognized by *Sunset Magazine* as one of the 10 best in the country. This August 1984 image shows asphalt lay-down machines at work building the trail north of the present-day Botanical Gardens. (OSD.)

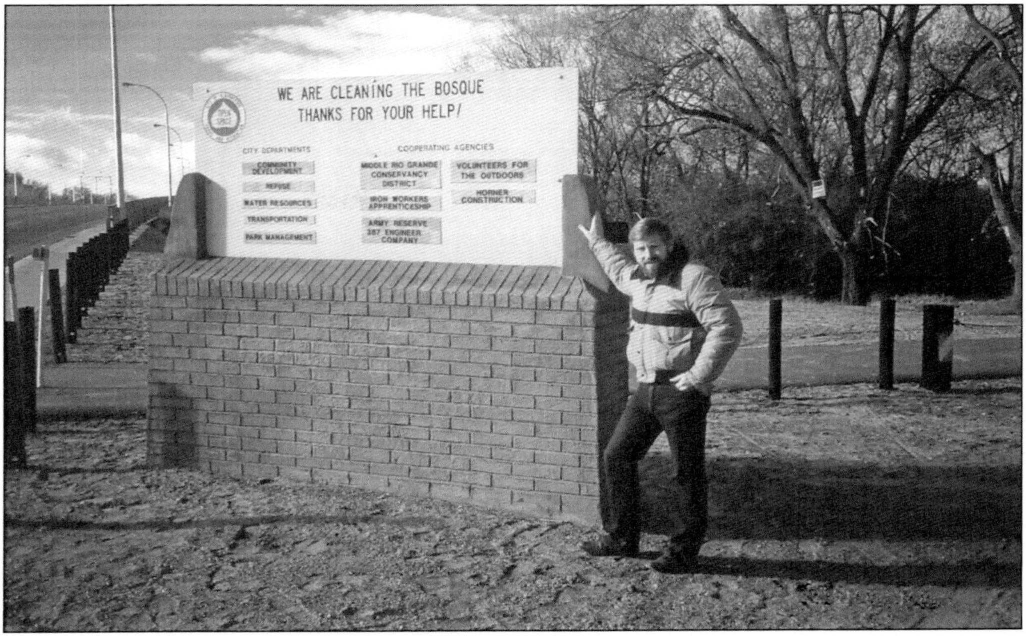

Soon after Rio Grande Valley State Park was established, among the first tasks were to restrict vehicle access, clean up the woods, and set up formal areas for visitors. Rex Funk poses in February 1985 at the public access at Central Avenue NE in front of a sign thanking agencies for help in cleaning up the bosque. (OSD.)

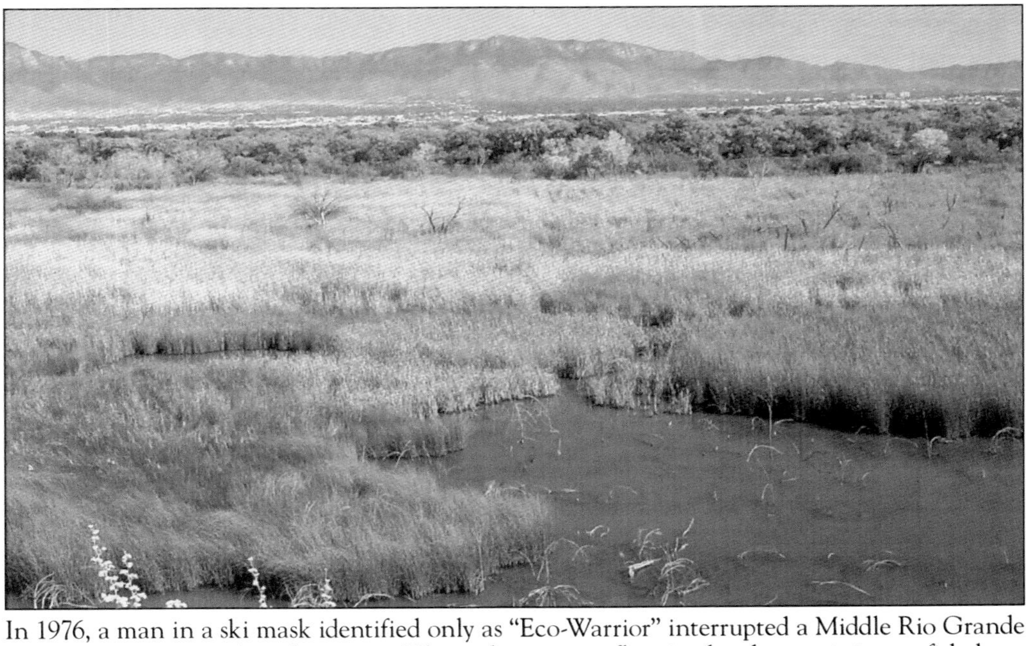

In 1976, a man in a ski mask identified only as "Eco-Warrior" interrupted a Middle Rio Grande Conservancy District board meeting. "Slopped upon your floor is a broth containing catfish, bass, carp, crayfish, muskrats, and ducks," he wrote. "This action informs you how the entire Oxbow area smells as a result of your arrogant decision to interrupt the life-waters of the last sweet-water marsh in the Albuquerque area." He was never seen again. (OSD.)

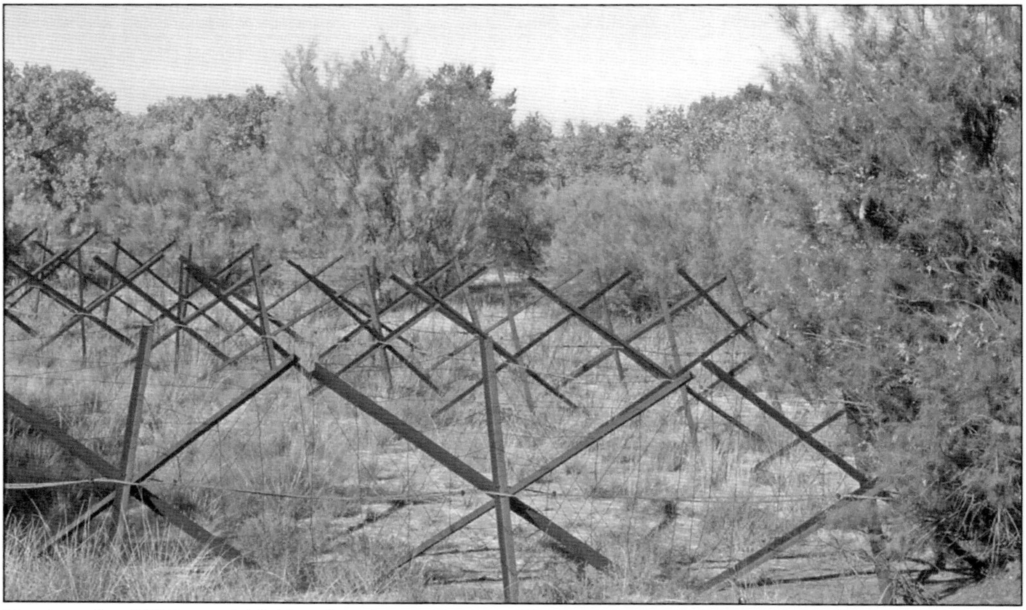

During the 1950s and 1960s, the Army Corps of Engineers and the Bureau of Reclamation put up over 30,000 "jetty jacks" throughout the Rio Grande valley near Albuquerque. The jetty jacks were designed to trap sediment and flood debris, thus armoring and protecting the erodible riverbanks. But dams and other flood controls caused the riverbed to drop, rendering most jacks obsolete. Many jacks are now being removed. (OSD.)

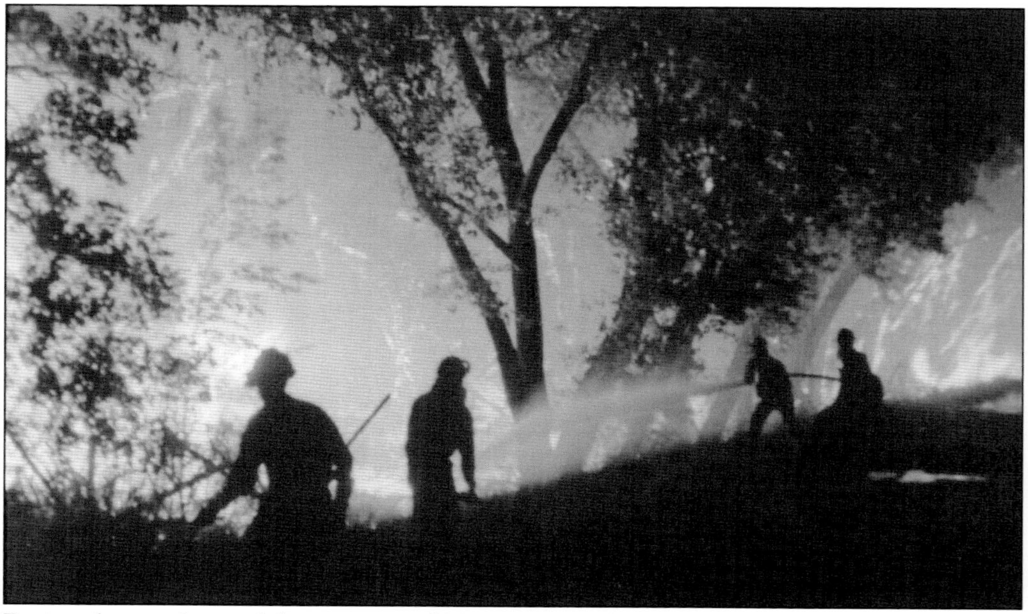

During the very hot and dry summers of 2002, 2003, and 2004, major wildfires broke out in the Rio Grande bosque. Dense underbrush created by invasive trees such as salt cedar, along with fuels left because the channelized river could no longer flood in spring, produced extreme fire hazards. The 2003 fires made national news, burning over 250 acres, and were only stopped by the valiant efforts of firefighters. (Albuquerque Fire Department.)

Pole planting is a tree-sprouting method that works especially well with cottonwoods and willows. Long, straight branches are cut during winter dormancy, and the resulting poles are planted in holes drilled into the water table. The branches rapidly sprout into trees as a way to recover fire-damaged areas. Open Space assistant superintendent Tony Barron (center foreground) has overseen 25,000 pole plantings and is pictured in 2005 beside some specimens. (OSD.)

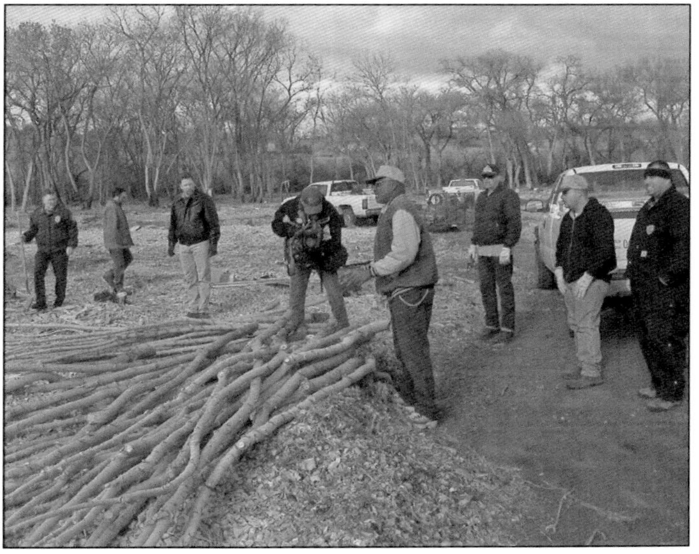

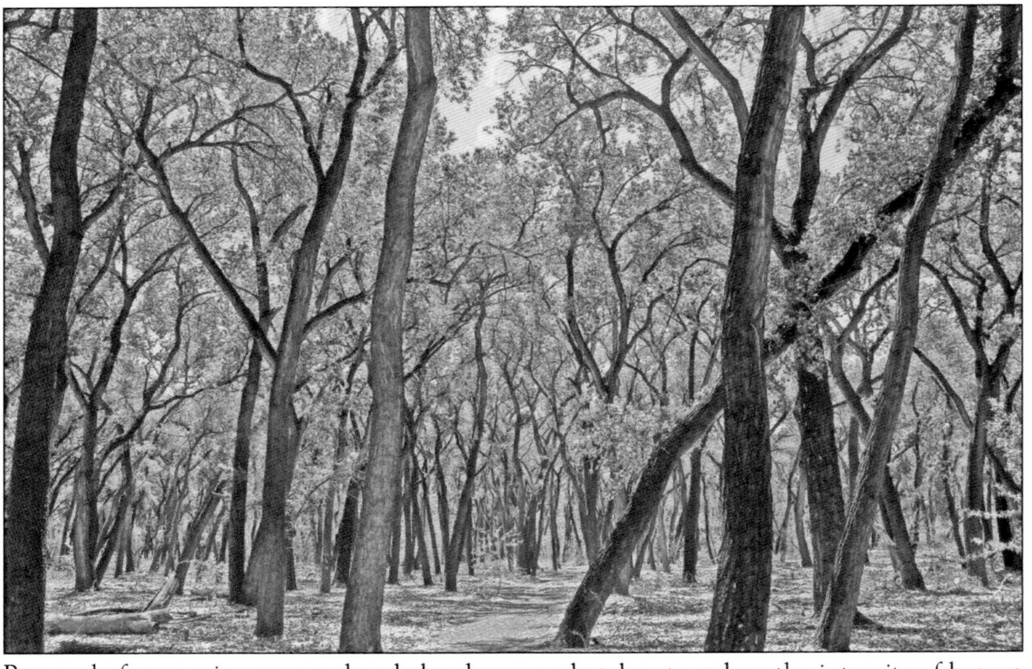

Removal of nonnative trees and underbrush was undertaken to reduce the intensity of bosque wildfires. Native trees such as cottonwood and willow are not adapted to fires, and their high mortality leads to invasion by salt cedars, elms, and Russian olive. This 2005 photograph on the west side of the river north of Montano Road shows a cleared bosque with a remaining stand of cottonwoods. (OSD.)

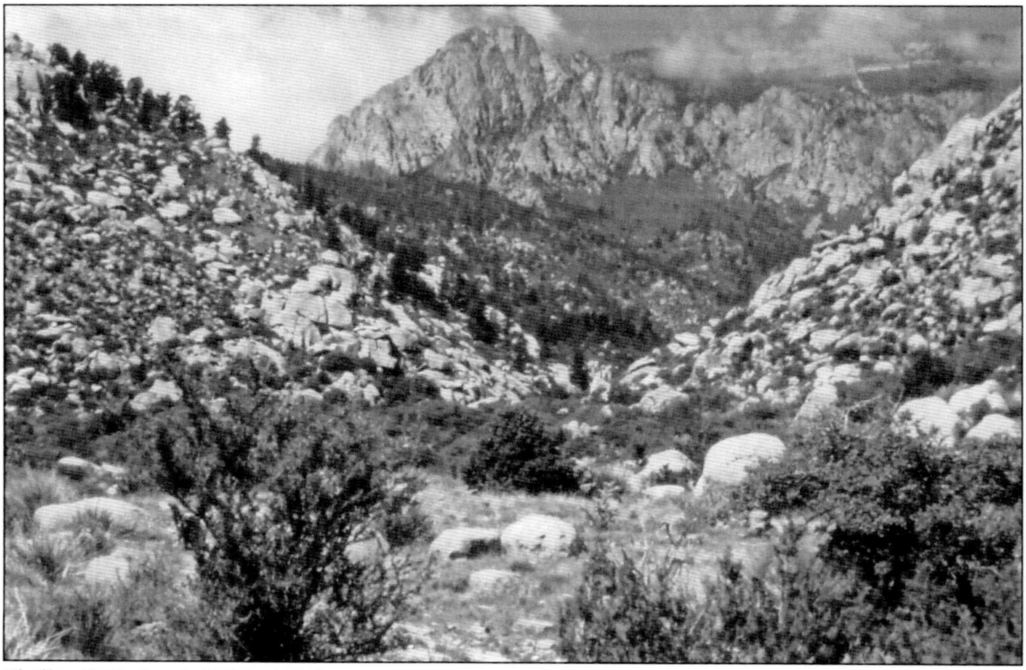

Phillip Tollefsrud (1938–1976) was a passionate advocate for the preservation of Albuquerque's wildlands. In the early 1970s, he urged groups interested in different areas such as the volcanoes, the Rio Grande, and the Sandia foothills to join together and create the Open Space Task Force. Tollefsrud coined the rallying cry, "The most beautiful backdrop a city could have." His own life was cut short at the age of 38 following a hunting accident. (OSD.)

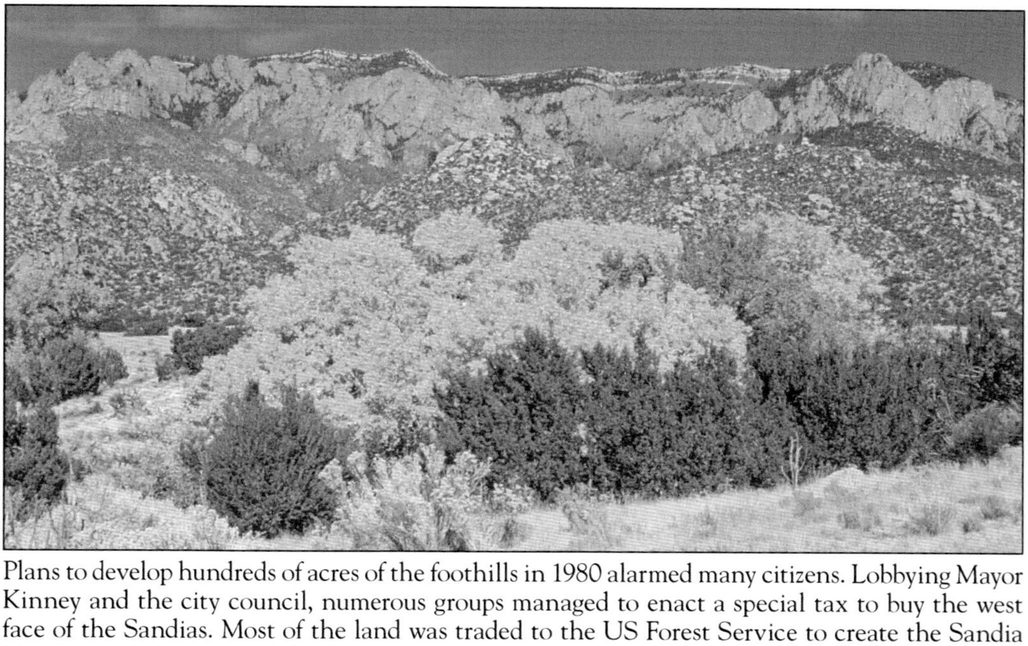

Plans to develop hundreds of acres of the foothills in 1980 alarmed many citizens. Lobbying Mayor Kinney and the city council, numerous groups managed to enact a special tax to buy the west face of the Sandias. Most of the land was traded to the US Forest Service to create the Sandia Mountain Wilderness, while the city retained 640 acres named Elena Gallegos Picnic Area to honor the original 1712 grant holder. (OSD.)

Harry Kinney, a native of Raton, New Mexico, came to Albuquerque to study engineering. He soon got involved in politics, serving as mayor of Albuquerque twice (1974–1977 and 1981–1984). Some of the greatest Open Space milestones were achieved under Kinney's administrations: purchase of the volcanoes, the Elena Gallegos grant, and Rio Grande Valley State Park. He is shown in 1982 touring the recently acquired Elena Gallegos land with Barbara Baca (center), now the Parks Department director, and Karen Baker (Volunteers for the Outdoors). (OSD.)

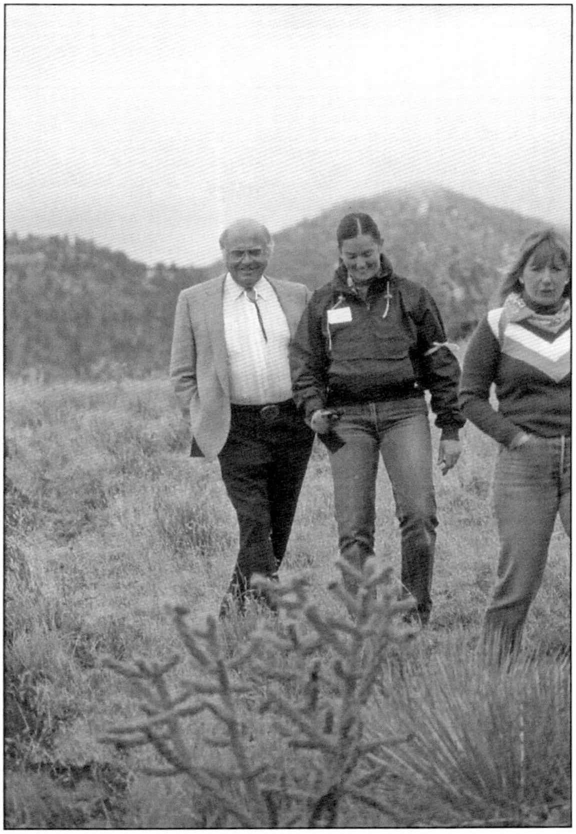

Orlando "Orlie" Sedillo took over from Bob Burgan as the third Parks Department director in 1979. Sedillo's professional experience at the state level and his vision for expanding both the parks programs and the Open Space system made him an ideal successor to Burgan. Sedillo loved horseback riding and kept a favorite horse at the Elena Gallegos Park, as shown in this November 1982 photograph. (OSD, Rex Funk.)

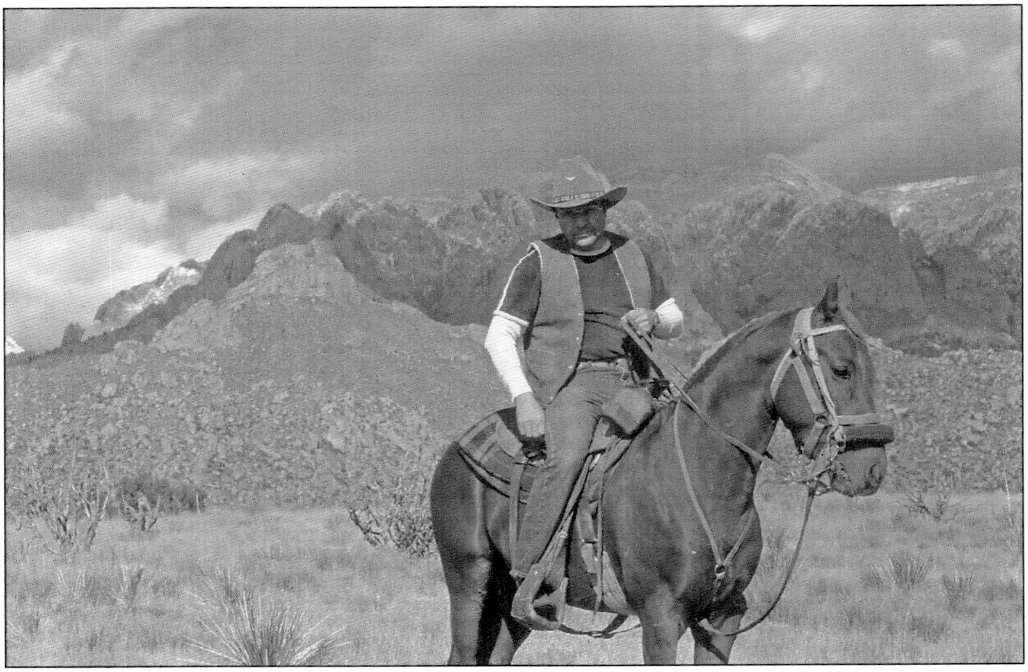

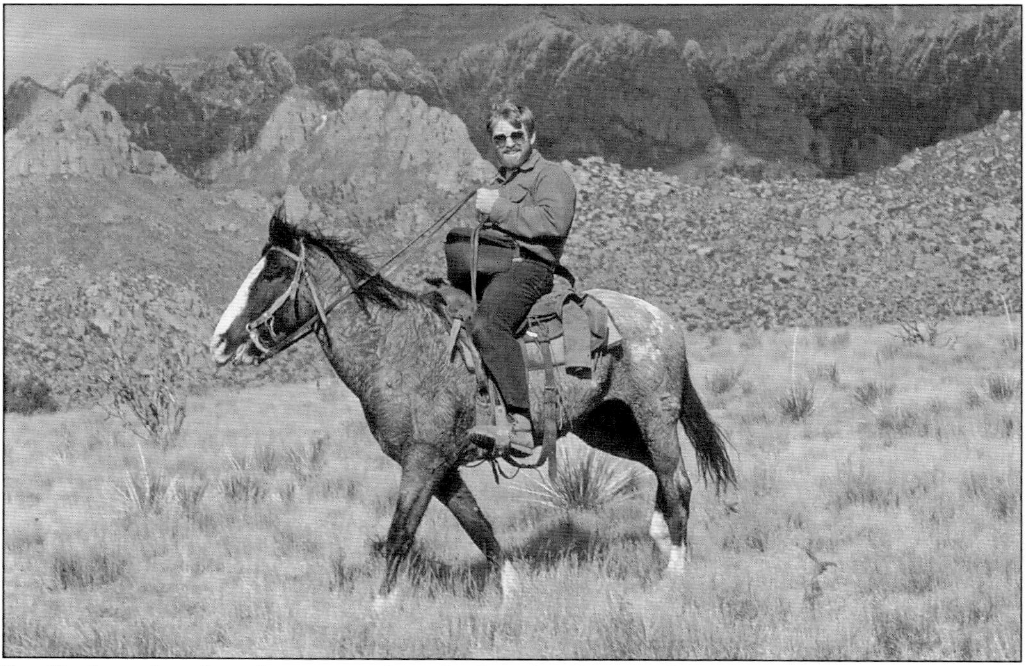

Rex Funk used to also take turns on horseback at the Elena Gallegos, as shown in this November 1982 photograph. (OSD.)

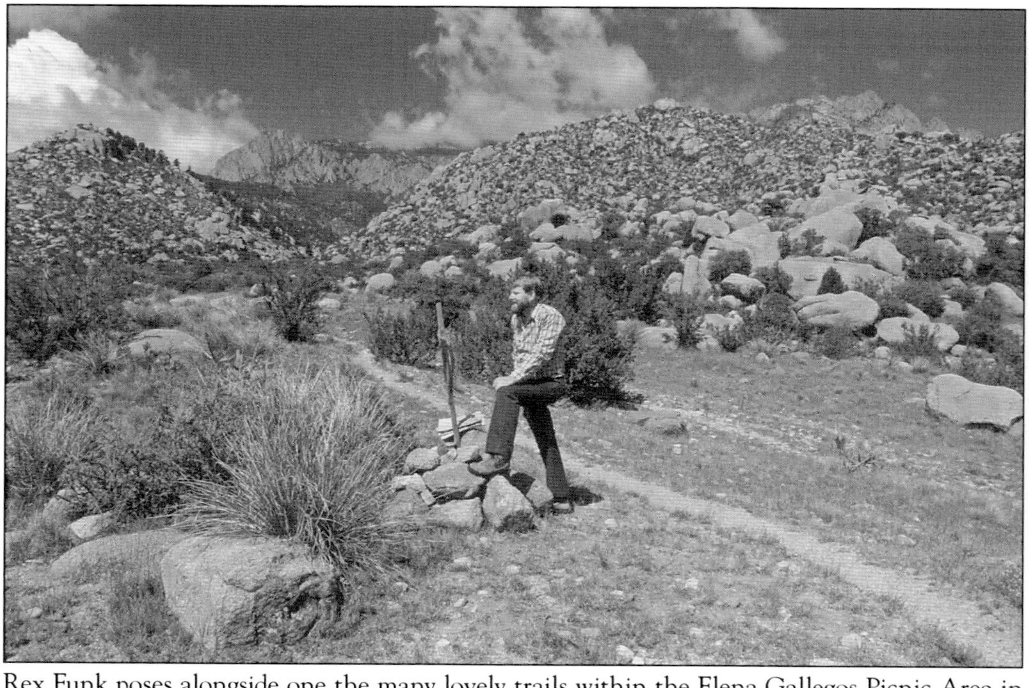

Rex Funk poses alongside one the many lovely trails within the Elena Gallegos Picnic Area in September 1982, soon after the property was purchased. Funk served as Open Space superintendent from 1984 until 1995 and set up environmental education programs and law enforcement patrols as mechanisms to protect the Open Space lands. (OSD.)

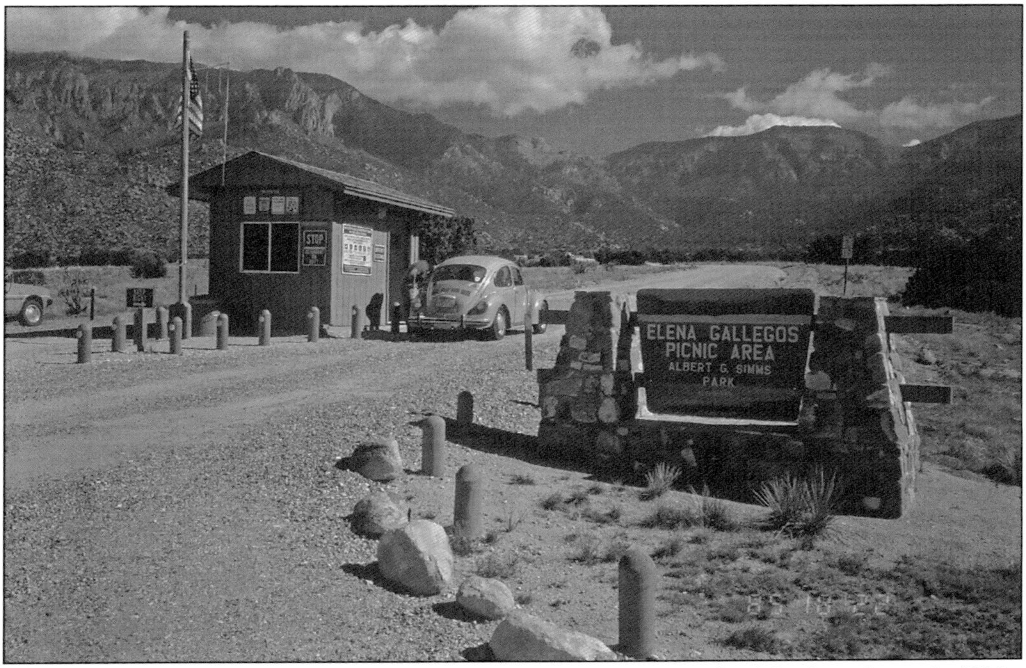

The old entry station to the Elena Gallegos Picnic Area was a tiny shack built in the early 1980s. Many thousands of visitors streamed by this simple booth every year until it was replaced by a modern visitor station in 1999. (OSD, Rex Funk.)

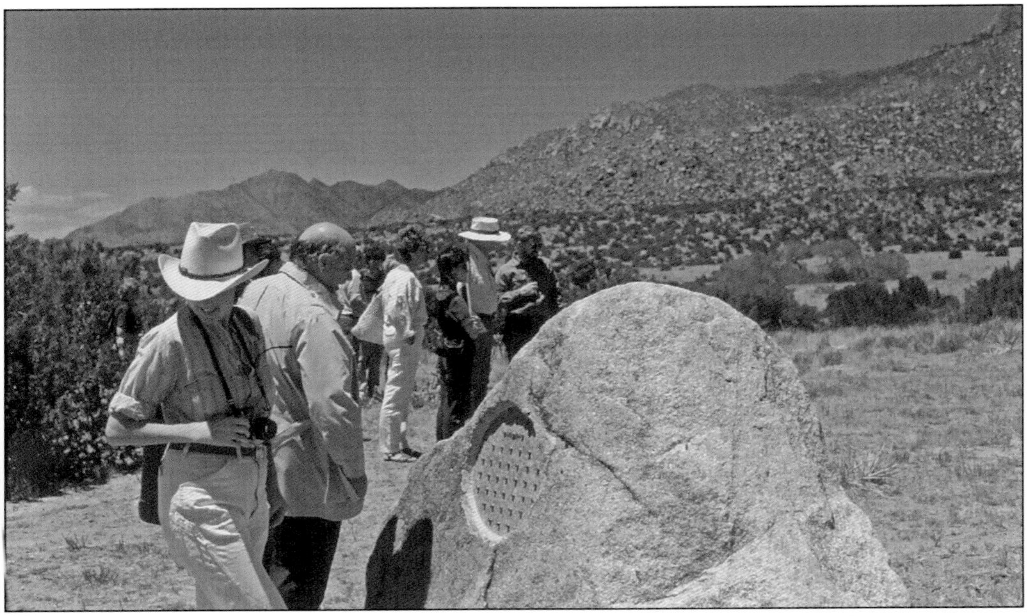

On August 6, 1983, a sculptural piece called *The Five Stones of Elena Gallegos* by Albuquerque artist Billie Walters was dedicated in memory of Phillip B. Tollefsrud. The sculpture was commissioned by the Albuquerque public arts program. The central piece of the sculpture was a granite boulder containing a polished inset circle with 38 copper pins, representing each year of Phillip Tollefsrud's inspired life. (OSD.)

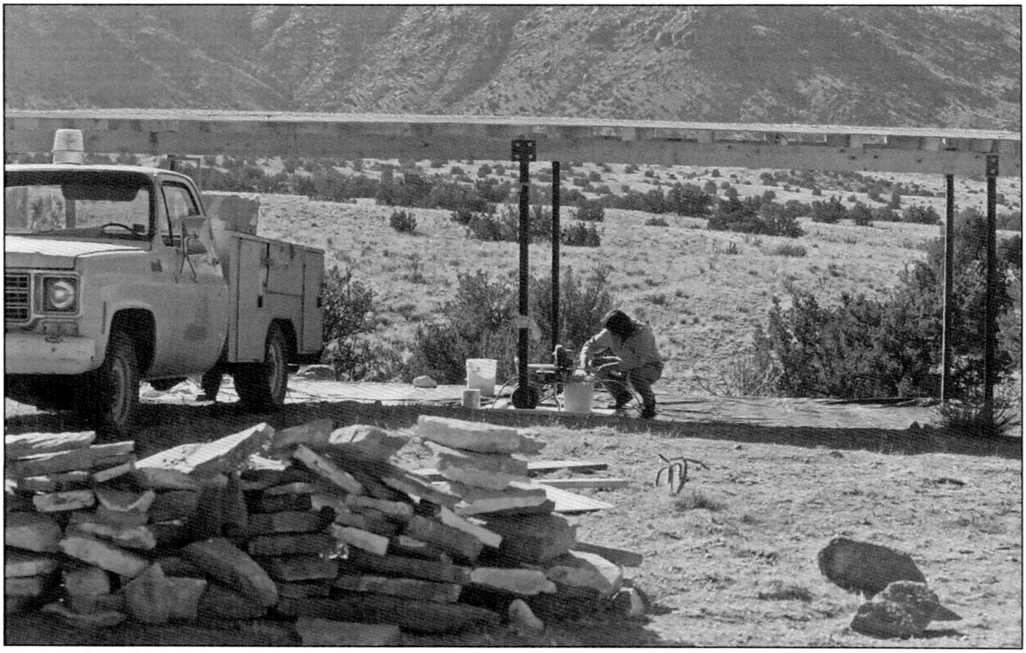

Soon after the successful acquisition of the Elena Gallegos grant, plans were put in place for recreation facilities at what would become the Open Space Division's flagship site for decades. In this March 1984 photograph, workers have poured the slab and put up the roof at the Double Shelter area. Piles of limestone are ready to be built into the ramada's pilasters and the pedestals for today's picnic tables. (OSD.)

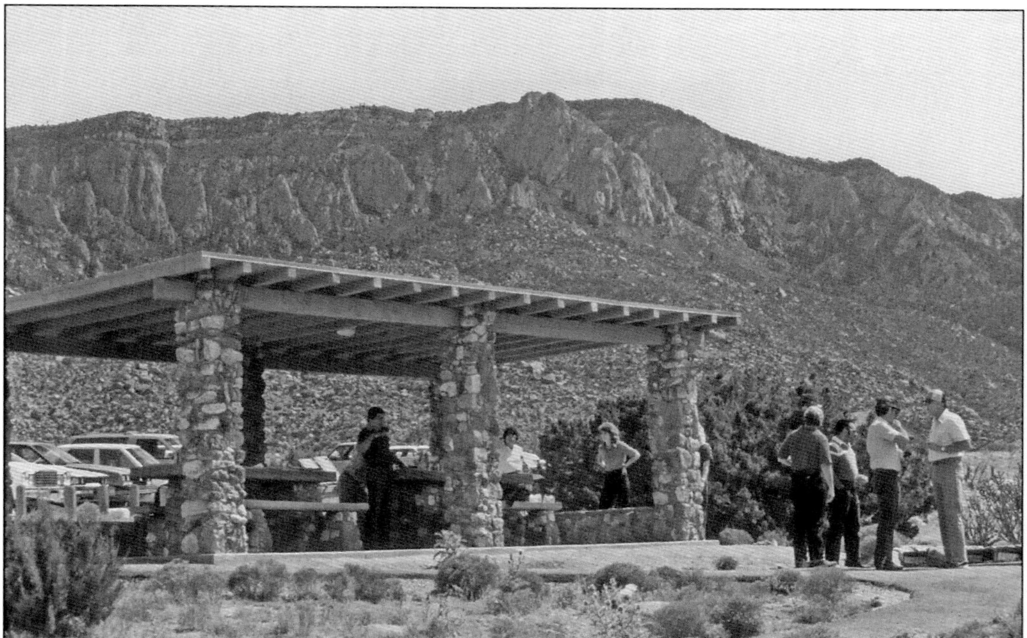

Another view towards the Double Shelter at the Elena Gallegos Picnic Area was taken about a year later in the summer of 1985 and shows the newly completed reservation area. (OSD.)

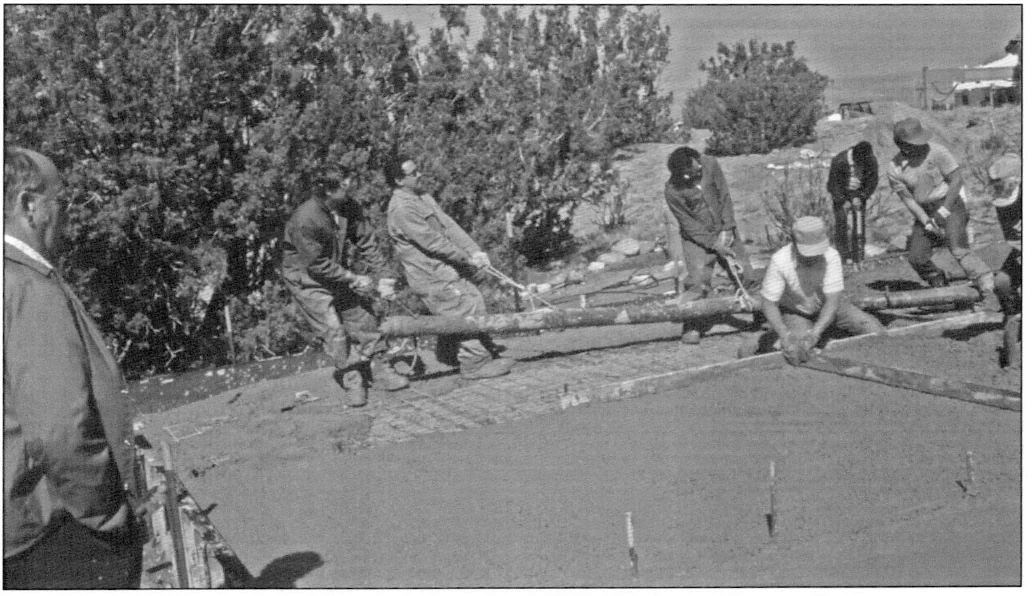

Open Space crews are hard at work pouring the slab for the future Kiwanis Reservation area in this June 1988 image. The Kiwanis Club had annual community service projects and decided to give a gift to the citizens of Albuquerque by building the premier facility at the Elena Gallegos Picnic Area. (OSD.)

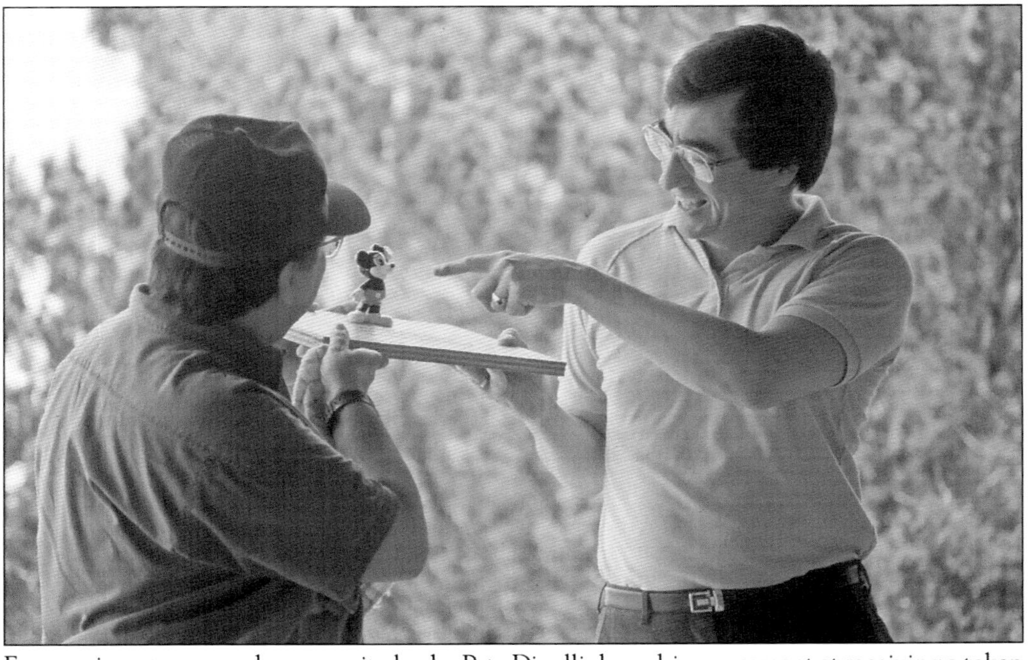

Former city attorney and community leader Pete Dinelli shows his amusement at receiving a token of appreciation for the completion of the Kiwanis Reservation Area. Dinelli helped spearhead the Kiwanis Club's fundraising and donation efforts to get a large group reservation area built at the Elena Gallegos Picnic Area. The reservation area was dedicated in July 1988 and has hosted innumerable family reunions, weddings, and celebrations. (OSD.)

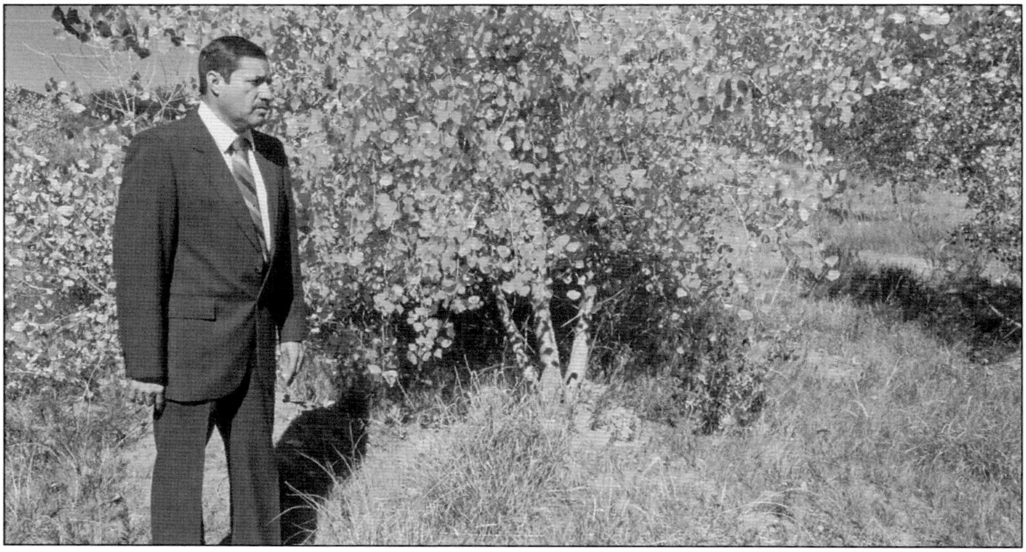

The Open Space concept, related programs, and critical lands needed not only the support of the mayor but also of strong city councilors. Among the staunchest council supporters over the years was Vince Griego, who represented the North Valley's District 2 from 1979 until 2003. Along the way, Griego successfully sponsored a 1996 mail-in election for a special sales tax set aside for Open Space lands and park development. (OSD.)

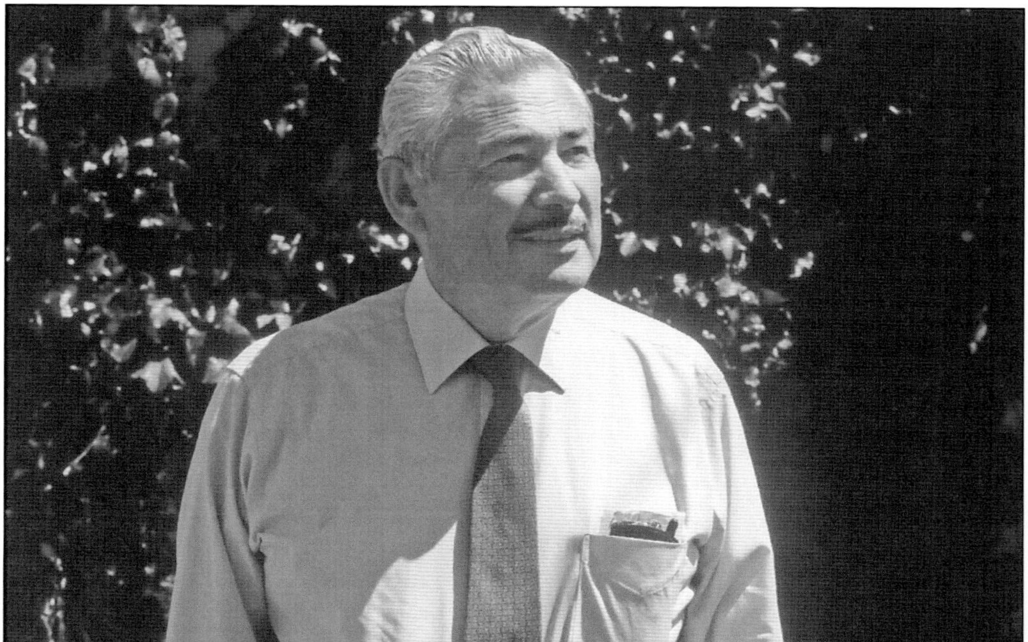

Another longtime city council supporter of Open Space was Patrick Baca, who represented the west side's District 1. Baca helped spearhead protection plans for the West Mesa and secure funds for land acquisition—actions that ultimately helped create Petroglyph National Monument. Patrick is the father of Barbara Baca, the Parks Department's current director. (OSD.)

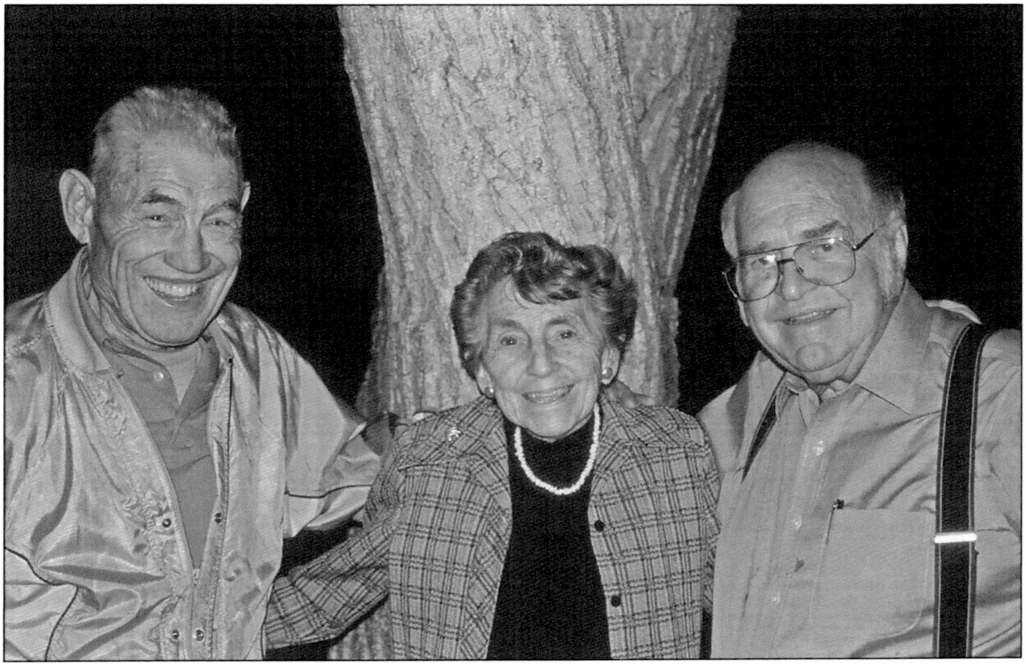

Three environmental heroes together for the last time in June 2001, Hy Rosner (87, left), Joan Rosner (82, center), and Harry Kinney (77, right) pose after a meeting of the Open Space Alliance. Mayor Kinney greatly advanced the Open Space cause during his two terms in office. The Rosners left for Florida after contributing so much to their community, most notably as authors and editors of *Albuquerque's Environmental Story*. (OSD, Jodi Hedderig.)

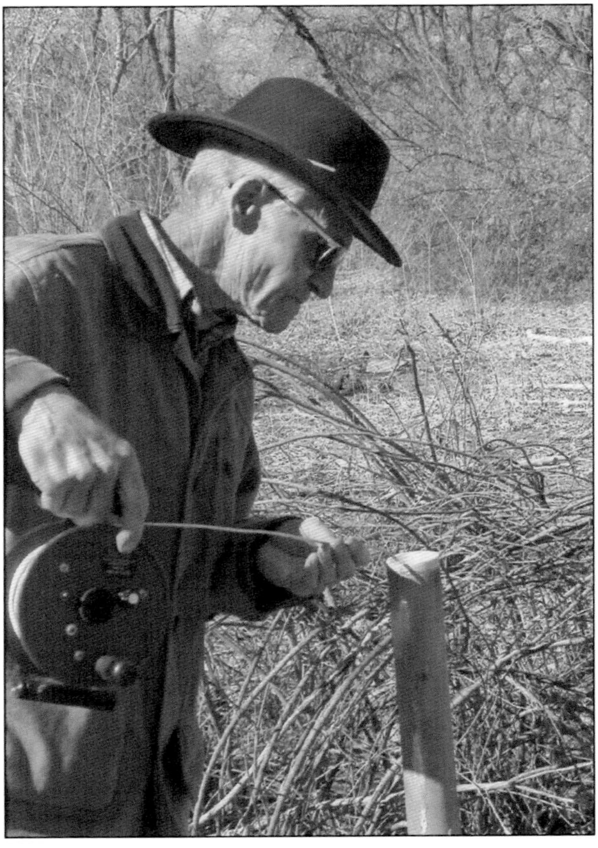

Cliff Crawford (1932–2010), professor emeritus of biology at the University of New Mexico, came to symbolize the bridge between the thirst to know and the means to investigate the natural world. The latter part of his career was devoted to the study of the Rio Grande bosque, and he started a program called the Bosque Ecological Monitoring Program, which has inspired thousands of students to get outside and learn scientific methods. (OSD.)

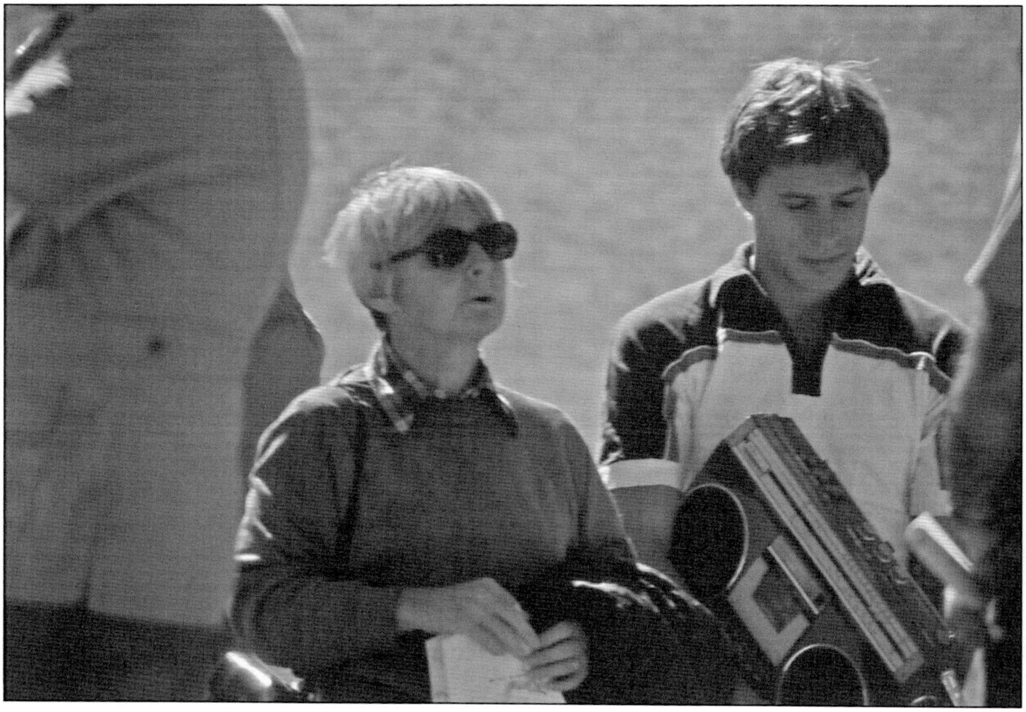

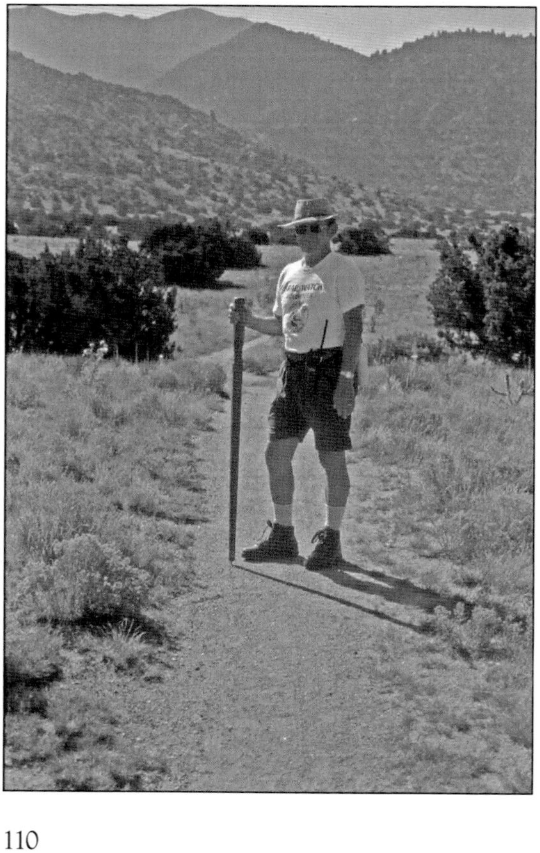

Kathryn "Kit" Sargeant was an early advocate of preserving the West Mesa and petroglyph areas. An archaeologist by training, Sargeant spent many hours giving tours to the public and bringing the past to life as a member of the Open Space Task Force. She is shown here on one such tour in October 1984. Kit was killed tragically on Christmas Eve 2001 at the age of 75. (OSD, Rex Funk.)

In April 1994, twelve active trainees called Trail Watch Volunteers were enlisted to assist Open Space programs. That group and others that followed have logged thousands of volunteer hours in the ensuing 16 years. In this August 1995 photograph, Paul Daily poses on the Pino Trail at Elena Gallegos Picnic Area. Daily contributed nearly 4,000 hours in education and mapping programs before he passed away July 2010. (OSD, Jim Sattler.)

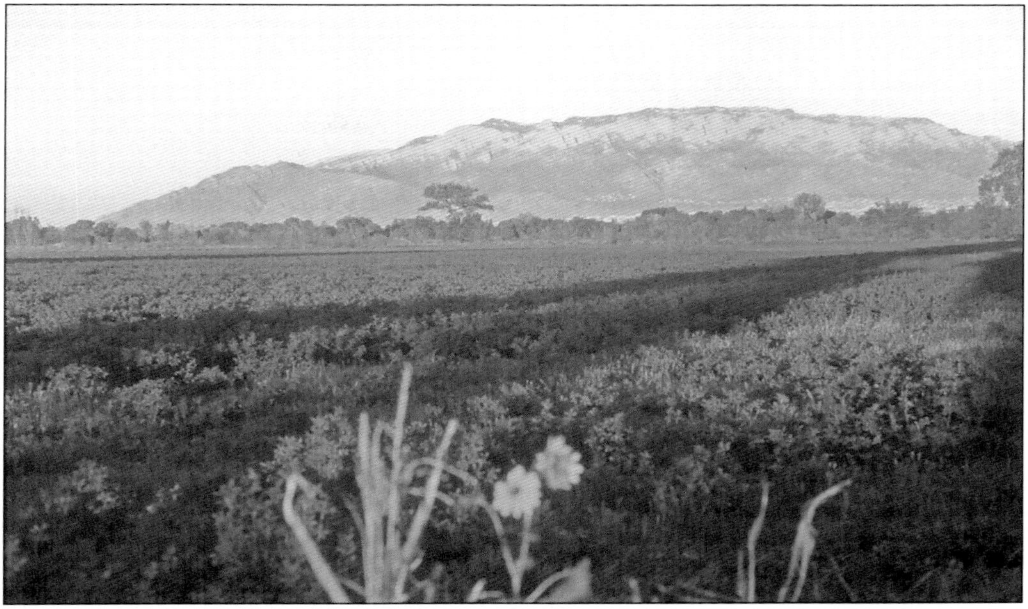

Development plans for 138 acres near Montano Road and Rio Grande Boulevard had proceeded to a stage by the summer of 1995 that north valley residents feared the Anderson Field they had grown to love would be gone forever. They persuaded Vince Griego, their city councilor, and Mayor Martin Chavez to institute a two-year gross receipts tax to buy open space and develop parks. (OSD archives, photograph by Anne Cooper.)

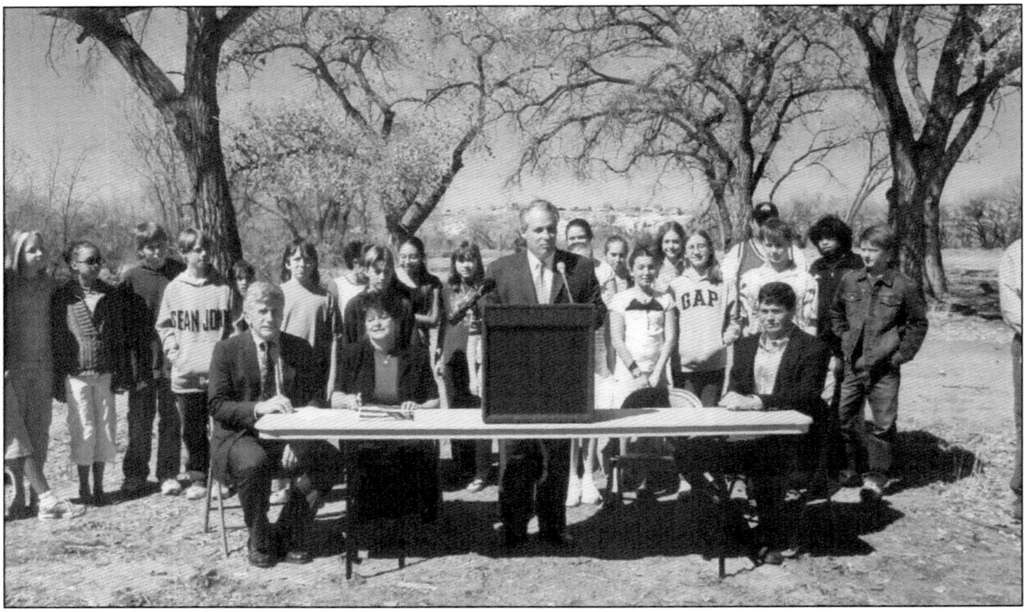

The one-quarter percent sales tax passed by a comfortable margin in a mail-in vote in the fall of 1996. The first parcel to be bought in April 1997 was Anderson Field, now called Poblanos Field in recognition of its traditional community place name. One of the most important purchases was 251 acres of cottonwood forest near Bosque School. This April 2004 photograph shows Mayor Martin Chavez announcing the acquisition. (OSD.)

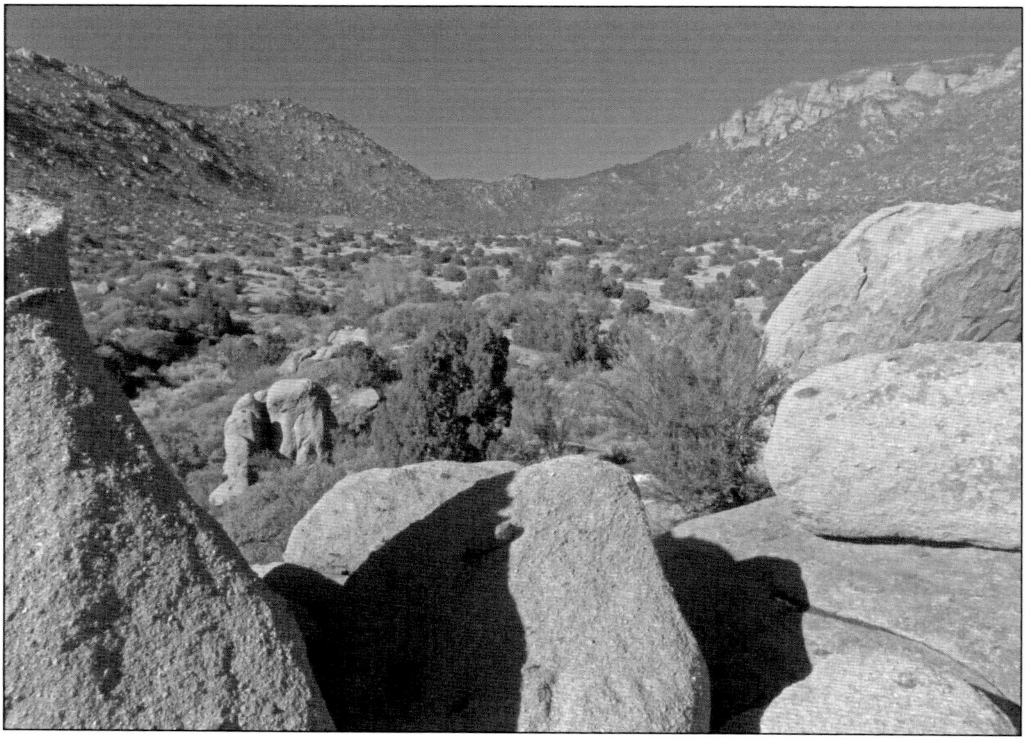

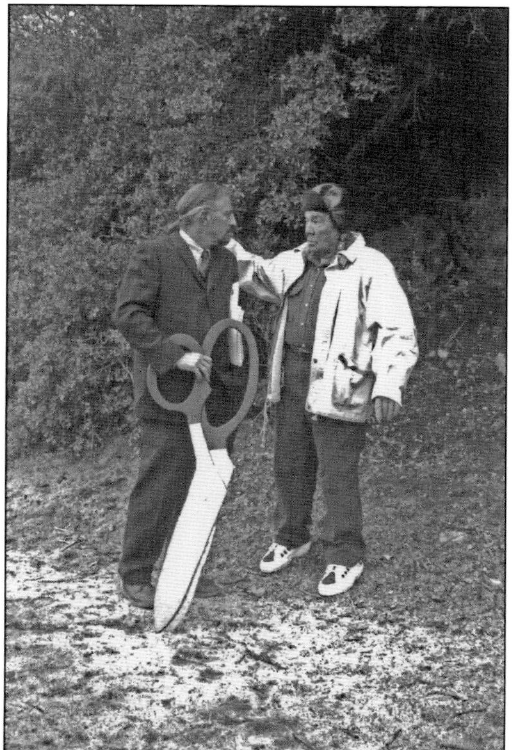

Another significant parcel acquired with quarter-cent funds was Tres Pistolas. This 106-acre tract on the north side of Tijeras Canyon was once part of the San Miguel de Laredo de Carnuel land grant of 1803. The Tres Pistolas name came from a wood log hollowed out as a livestock drinking trough, which had three pistols carved on it. The property backs onto wilderness areas in the Cibola National Forest.

The author (holding scissors) is pictured in June 1998 talking with longtime resident Tomás Herrera at the ribbon-cutting ceremony for Tres Pistolas. Herrera, then 81, had been a sheriff in the East Mountains for 40 years. His law-enforcement exploits were legendary, but his greatest claim to fame was as an extra in the 1963 movie *Lonely are the Brave*, starring Kirk Douglas. (Trust for Public Land.)

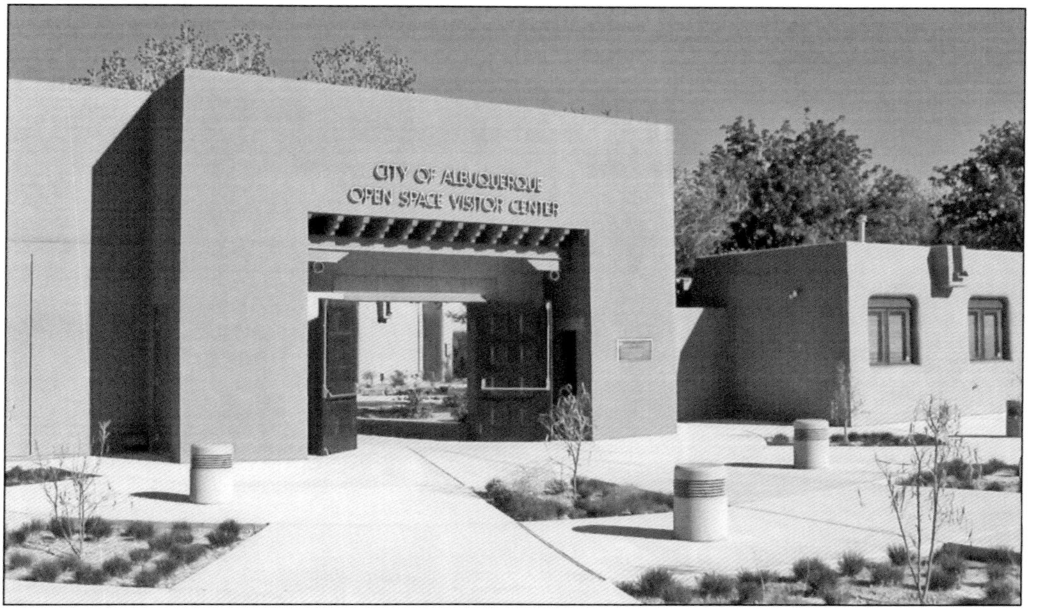

The centerpiece of Albuquerque's Open Space Program, its Visitor Center, was dedicated in October 2006. Renovated from an original residence purchased from Coda and Reba Roberson, the 8,000-square-foot center and surrounding 25 acres of farmland came in at a cost of just $3.5 million. The breathtaking Visitor Center has interpretive exhibits, art galleries, and native gardens and hosts numerous community events throughout the year. (OSD.)

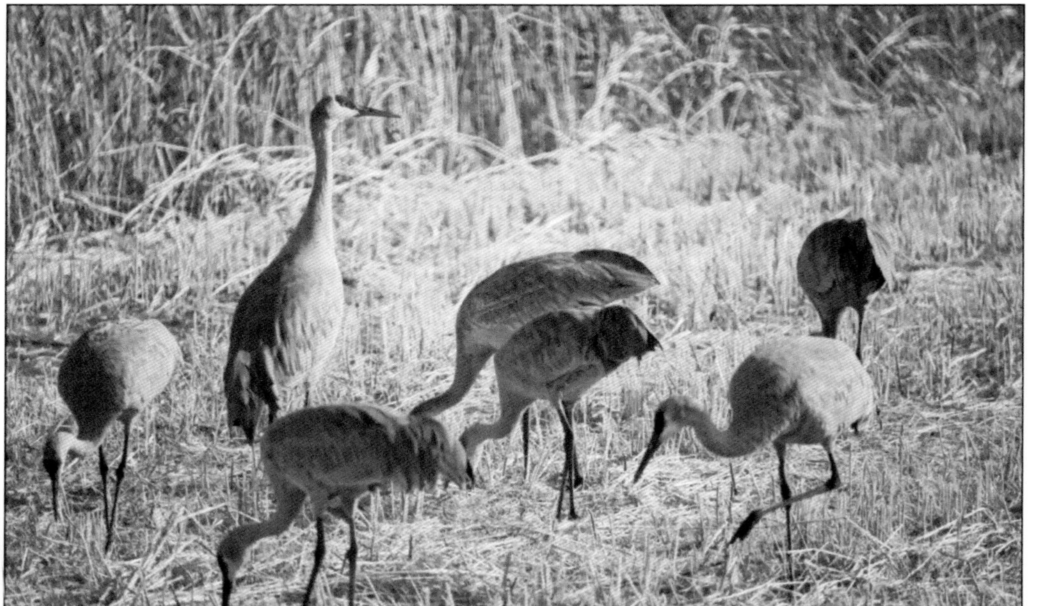

Each year from October until March, the Albuquerque area is blessed with the annual migration of sandhill cranes. The seasonal sounds of their unique calls and the view of these magnificent birds flying overhead is a cold-season treat. Hundred of cranes feed on crops grown for migratory birds on fields such as Poblanos or at the Visitor Center (pictured). (OSD.)

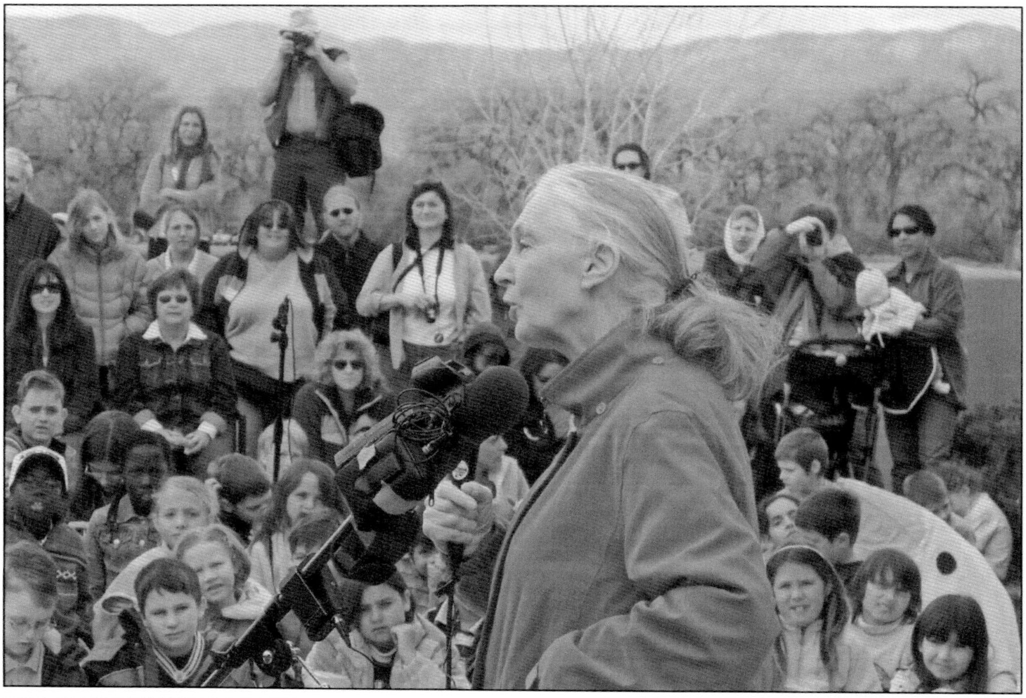

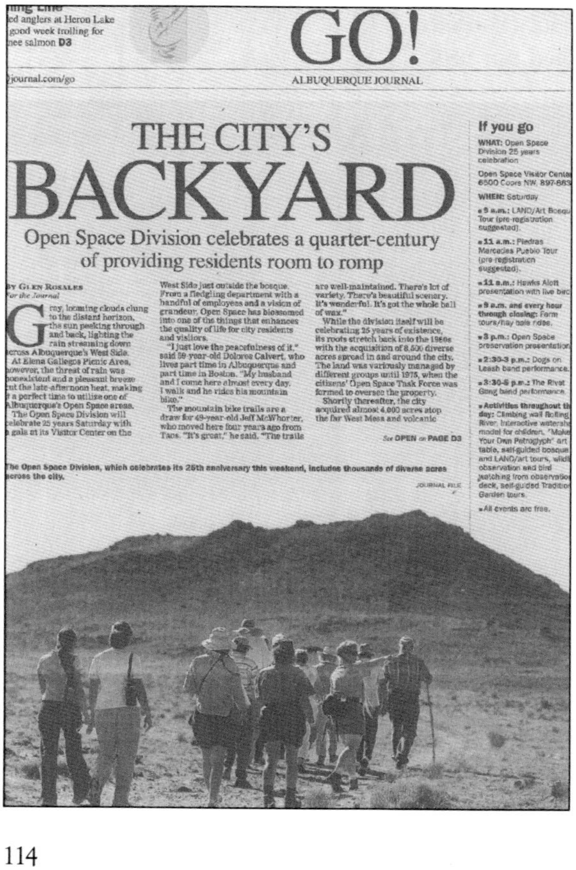

ed anglers at Heron Lake
good week trolling for
nee salmon **D3**

GO!

journal.com/go

ALBUQUERQUE JOURNAL

THE CITY'S BACKYARD

Open Space Division celebrates a quarter-century of providing residents room to romp

By Glen Rosales
For the Journal

Gray, looming clouds clung to the distant horizon, the sun peeking through and back, lighting the rain streaming down across Albuquerque's West Side.

At Elena Gallegos Picnic Area, however, the threat of rain was nonexistent and a pleasant breeze cut the late-afternoon heat, making it a perfect time to utilize one of Albuquerque's Open Space areas.

The Open Space Division will celebrate 25 years Saturday with a gala at its Visitor Center on the West Side just outside the bosque.

From a fledgling department with a handful of employees and a vision of grandeur, Open Space has blossomed into one of the things that enhances the quality of life for city residents and visitors.

"I just love the peacefulness of it," said 59-year-old Dolores Calvert, who lives part time in Albuquerque and part time in Boston. "My husband and I come here almost every day. I walk and he rides his mountain bike."

The mountain bike trails are a draw for 49-year-old Jeff McWhorter, who moved here four years ago from Taos. "It's great," he said. "The trails are well-maintained. There's lot of variety. There's beautiful scenery. It's wonderful. It's got the whole ball of wax."

While the division itself will be celebrating 25 years of existence, its roots stretch back into the 1960s with the acquisition of 8,500 diverse acres spread in and around the city. The land was variously managed by different groups until 1975, when the citizens' Open Space Task Force was formed to oversee the property.

Shortly thereafter, the city acquired almost 4,000 acres atop the far West Mesa and volcanic

See OPEN on PAGE D3

If you go

WHAT: Open Space Division 25 years celebration

Open Space Visitor Center
6500 Coors NW, 897-883

WHEN: Saturday

- **9 a.m.:** LAND/Art Bosque Tour (pre-registration suggested).
- **11 a.m.:** Piedras Marcadas Pueblo Tour (pre-registration suggested).
- **11 a.m.:** Hawks Aloft presentation with live birds
- **9 a.m. and every hour through closing:** Farm tours/hay bale rides.
- **3 p.m.:** Open Space preservation presentation
- **2:30-3 p.m.:** Dogs on Leash band performance.
- **3:30-5 p.m.:** The Rivet Gang band performance.
- **Activities throughout the day:** Climbing wall Rolling River, Interactive watershed model for children, "Make Your Own Petroglyph" art table, self-guided bosque and LAND/art tours, wildlife observation and bird watching from observation deck, self-guided Traditional Garden tours.
- All events are free.

The Open Space Division, which celebrates its 25th anniversary this weekend, includes thousands of diverse acres across the city.

JOURNAL FILE

In the spring of 2008, world-famous primatologist and ecologist Jane Goodall delivered a speech to an enthralled and overflow crowd at the Open Space Visitor Center. Goodall, then 74, was in New Mexico to announce a new regional environmental education initiative and graciously met with many adoring fans. She still keeps a rigorous speaking schedule while on the road 300 days a year. (OSD, Matt Schmader.)

In 2009, the Open Space Division celebrated its 25th anniversary with a year-long series of tours, lectures, displays, artwork, programs, and performances. The community's 50-year-long dream to preserve the wildlands in and around Albuquerque had paid off with a silver jubilee recognizing the accomplishments of the Open Space Division from its start as a new agency formed in January 1984 with three people working out of a salvaged trailer. (*Albuquerque Journal.*)

Six

After Shots

Albuquerque has gone through many changes in the three centuries since its formal founding as a villa of the Spanish empire in 1706. Its deeper history, thousands of years of long, of native peoples living along the Rio Grande is still preserved in some places such as the West Mesa and Petroglyph National Monument. Lands originally granted to traditional communities such as Alameda, Atrisco, Elena Gallegos, Carnuel, and San Pedro are still preserved in parts of the present-day Open Space holdings. The 125 years of photographic history contained in this book reminds readers that some things may change radically in but a few decades or generations, while other places are less affected by the sweep of time.

This final chapter shows some of the places previously introduced and gives a measure of relativity in terms of transformation in places that have seen dramatic changes in the past 75 years: Blueher's pond, the Rio Grande bosque, and Tingley Beach. The chapter revisits parks that have seen better days, such as Highland or McClellan Park, and witnesses the maturation of other spaces such as Roosevelt, Hyder, Bataan, and McDuffie Parks. And photographs reveal that Robinson Park, Albuquerque's oldest, continues to thrive much as it had when it was first created in the early 1880s.

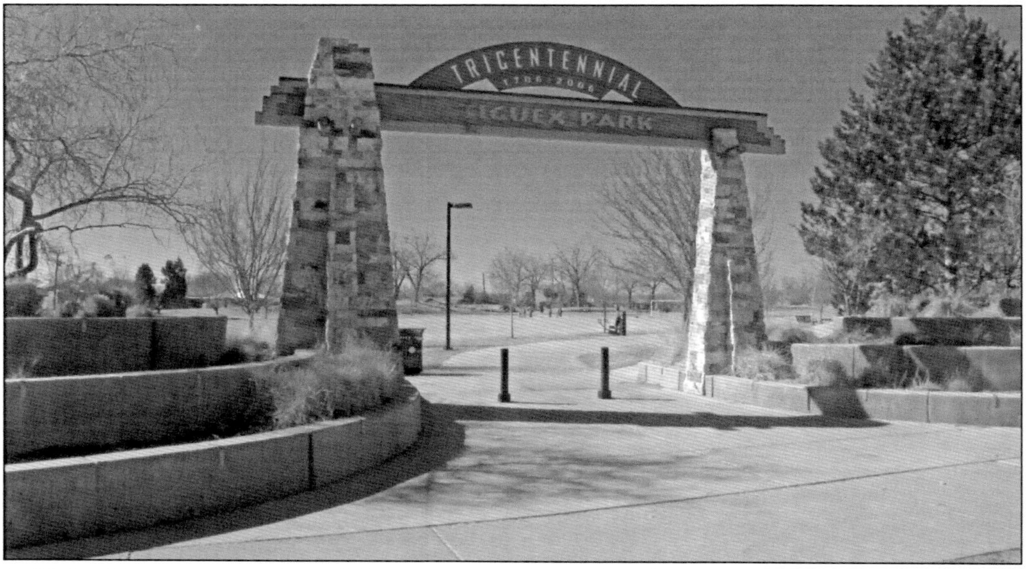

In 2006, Albuquerque celebrated the tricentennial of its founding as a Spanish villa with a year of commemorative events. A related project was the renovation of Tiguex Park, originally named for the pueblo peoples who have lived in Rio Grande Valley for many centuries. Tiguex TriCentennial Park was built on the spot of Blueher's Pond, a boating and swimming hole popular in the late 1800s. (Compare with page 20.)

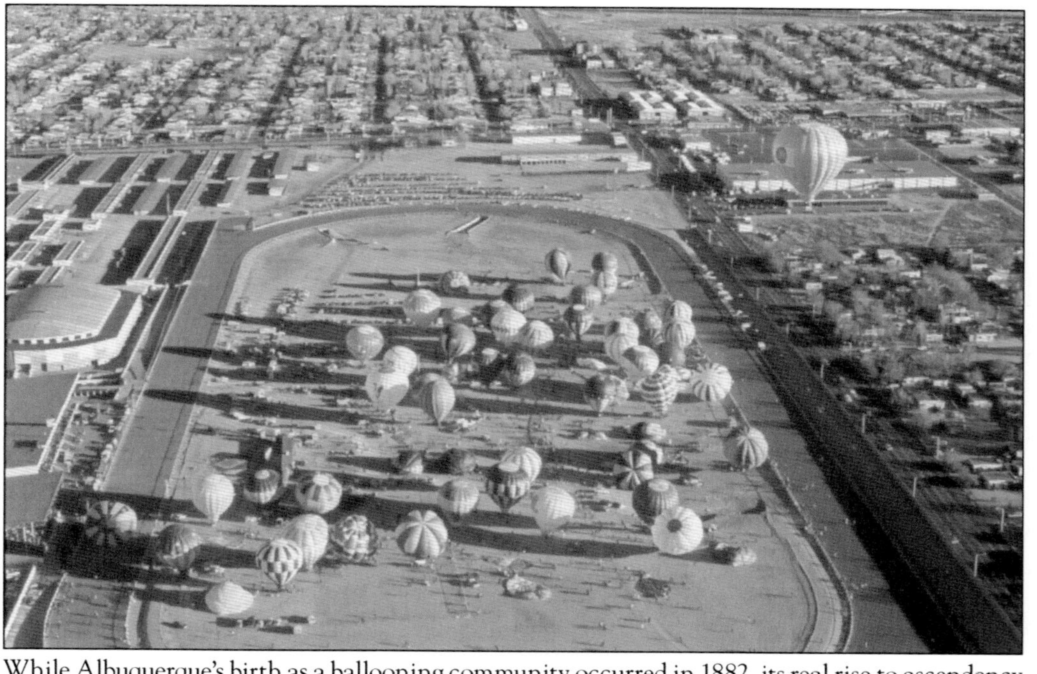

While Albuquerque's birth as a ballooning community occurred in 1882, its real rise to ascendency came with the creation of the International Balloon Fiesta. This 1974 image shows the event's second gathering in February being launched from the New Mexico State Fairgrounds at Louisiana and Lomas Boulevards. The Balloon Fiesta currently attracts over a million visitors each October and is sometimes called "the most photographed event in the world." (Tom McConnell.)

Aldo Leopold's early efforts to establish a park along the Rio Grande finally did come to pass 65 years after he first proposed the idea. It is no coincidence that his idea for a lake alongside the river also took shape as Tingley Beach: Clyde Tingley likely used Leopold's original idea. Today, trails and a cottonwood grove honor his contributions near the Rio Grande Nature Center. (Compare with page 32.)

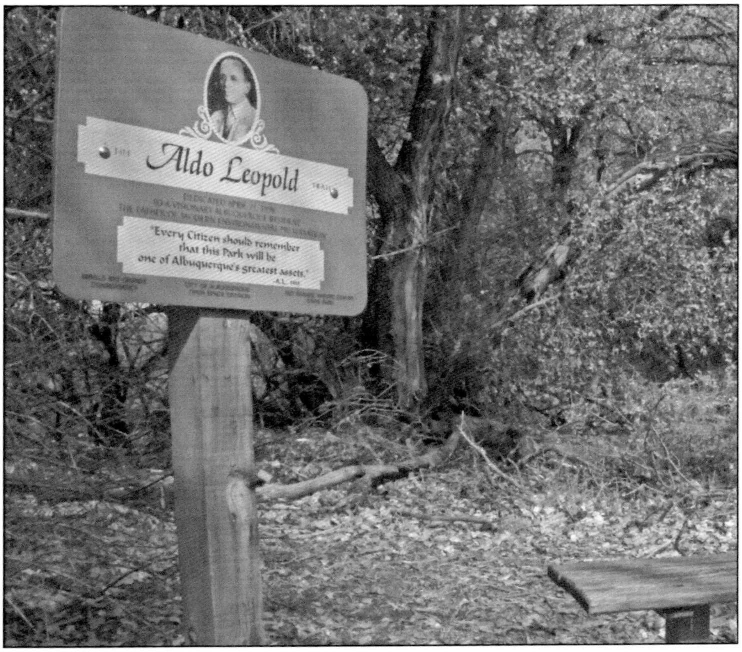

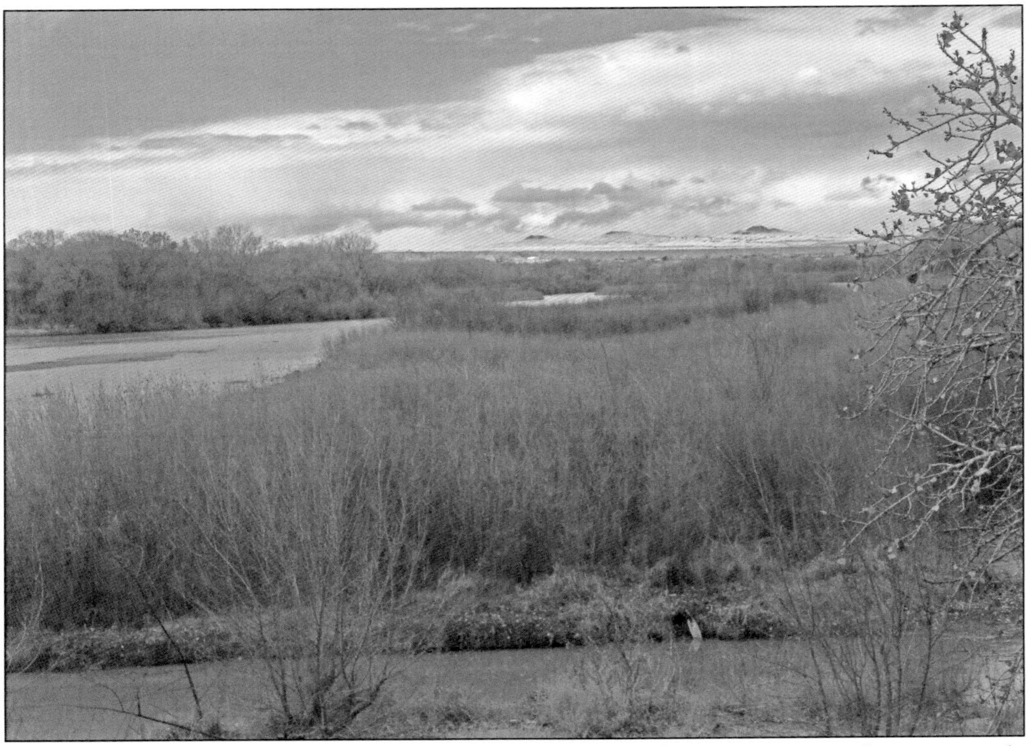

Leopold decried the abuse of the environment, and his goal in creating a park was not only recreational benefits for the public but also cleaning up and protecting the Rio Grande's woods. In this view looking to the northwest from Bridge Boulevard not far from the Hispanic Cultural Center, the "ten trainloads of tin cans" Leopold described are gone. (Compare with page 34.)

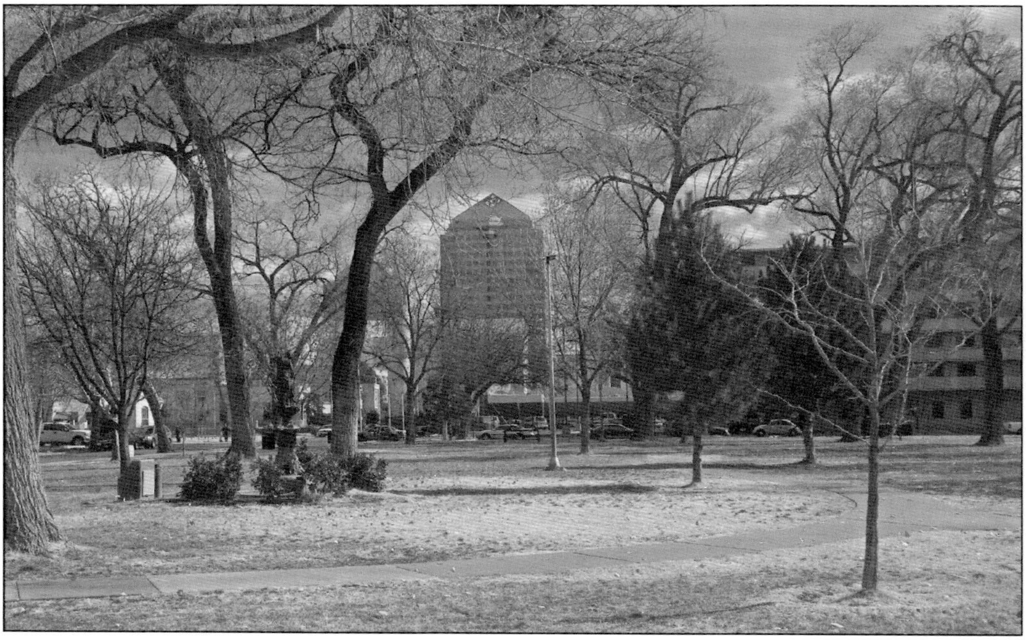

Robinson Park continues to thrive 125 years after becoming Albuquerque's first formal green space. Apart from the size of the trees and the distant skyline, the park retains its original feel. Now the location of a vibrant Saturday morning growers' market from spring through fall, the park has once again become a central point for a revitalizing area of the city. (Compare with page 30.)

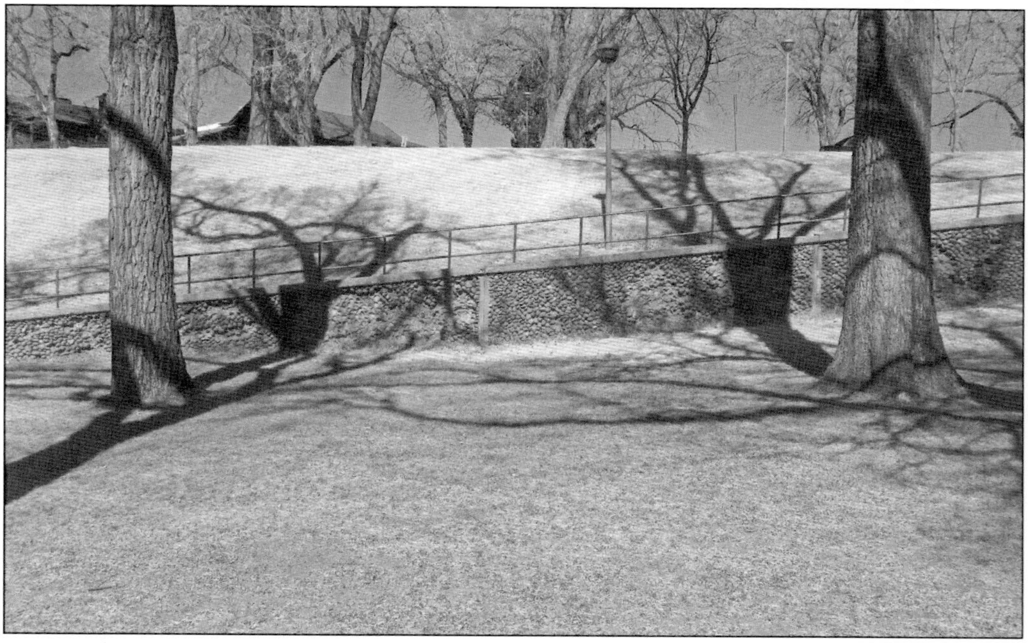

In 1959, the eastern half of Highland Park was lost to make way for the construction of Interstate 25. Many of the park's other major features, including the band shell and swimming pool, were also taken out by then. Highland Park is now experiencing a phase of revitalization as the surrounding neighborhoods rebuild, and renovation plans are being devised. (Compare with page 41.)

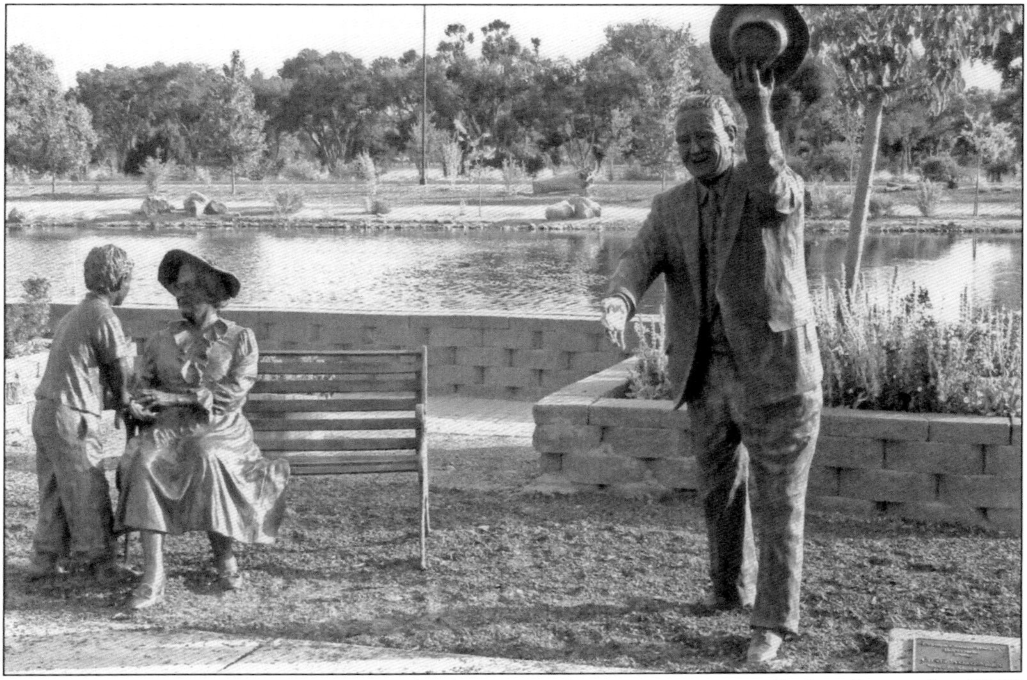

The memory of Clyde and Carrie Tingley lives on in bronze statues installed in September 2008 at the west edge of a restored Tingley Beach. Today, thousands come to fish, paddle in boats, and feed geese, but the heyday of outdoor swimming is long gone. (Compare with page 52.) (Rebecca Houtman.)

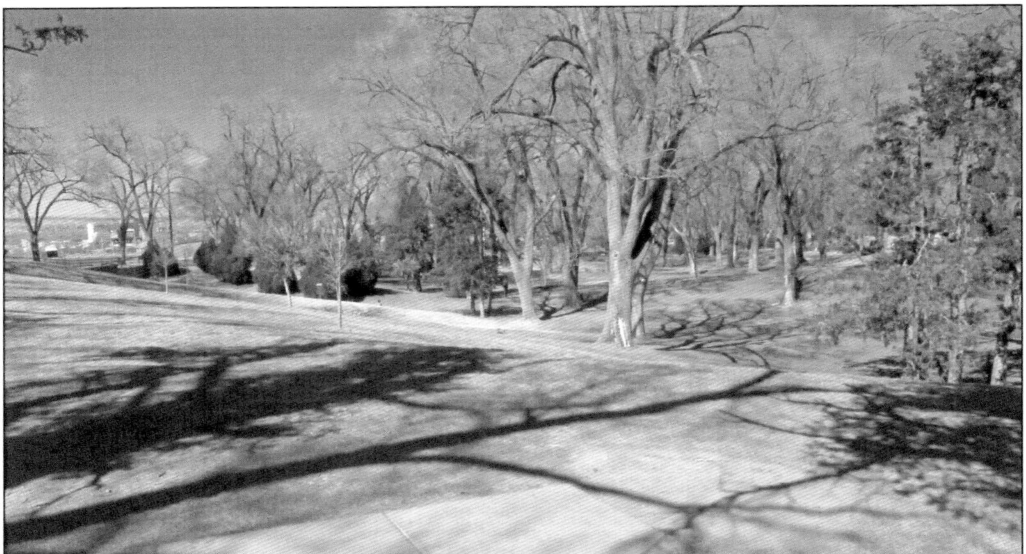

Clyde Tingley laid out Terrace Park in the early 1930s on the barrens of the East Mesa sandhills. At first lampooned for the idea, Tingley parlayed federal funds and workers to create one of Albuquerque's most venerated green spaces, which he named in honor of Franklin Roosevelt. Today, disc golfers and dog walkers continue to use the recently renovated park. (Compare with page 56.)

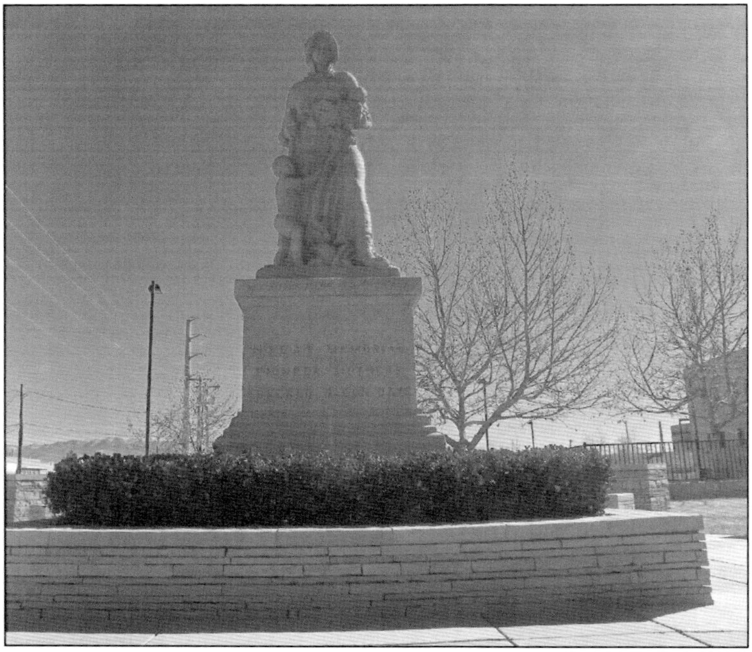

After a contentious battle over the fate of McClellan Park, forces behind building a large federal courthouse complex prevailed, and the park was demolished. One of its prominent features, the Madonna of the Trail statue installed in 1927, was kept on the site with the blessings of the Daughters of the American Revolution. (Compare with page 42.)

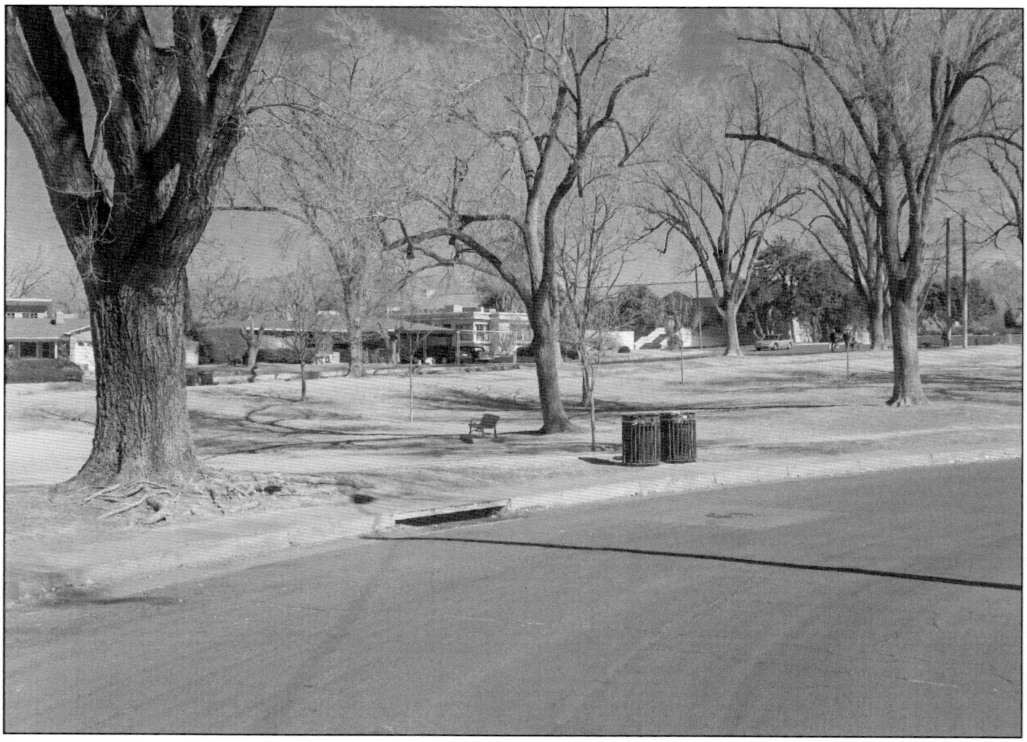

Surrounded by neighborhoods and quiet residential streets, Hyder Park is a well-used and loved park of late-1940s vintage. This view to the northeast with Bandelier Elementary School in the background shows trees, now over 60 years old, where tiny saplings were once planted. (Compare with page 67.)

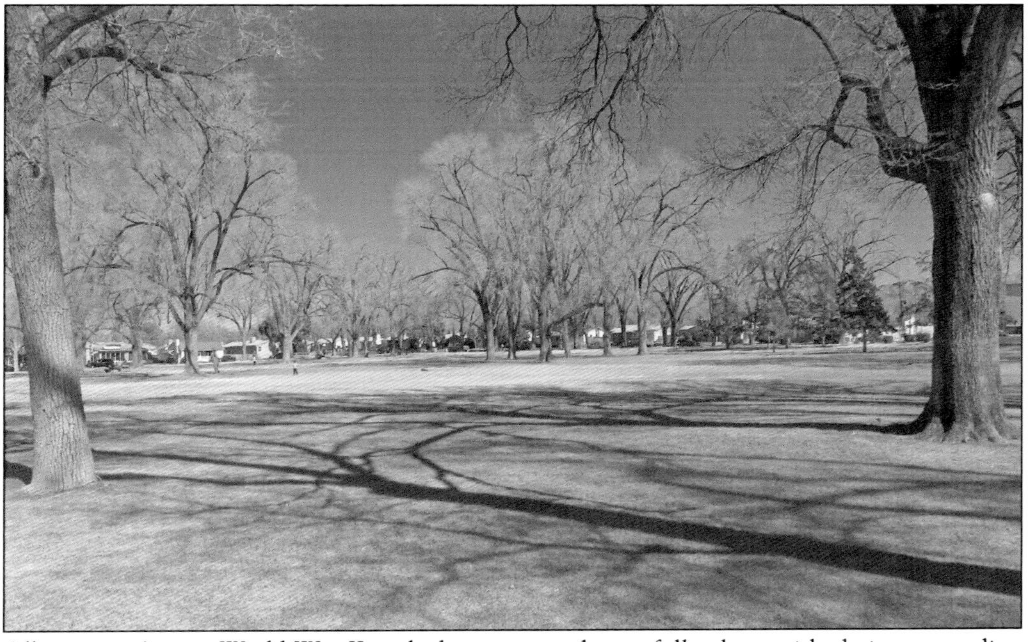

Albuquerque's post–World War II parks have matured gracefully along with their surrounding neighborhoods. This view looking northeast across Bataan Memorial Park shows how the trees and landscape contribute to the beauty and feel of the revered park. (Compare with page 67.)

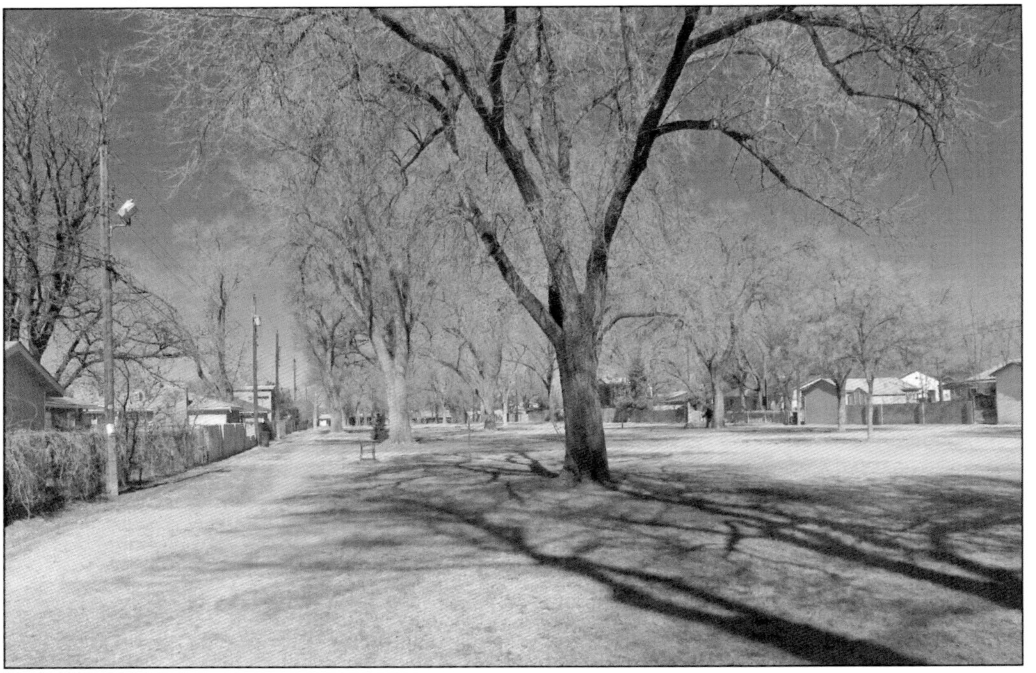

Perhaps the most dramatic transformation can be seen at McDuffie Park, named for the 1930s developer of the areas north of Lomas Boulevard near Carlisle Boulevard. A narrow strip sold to the city for $1 is now filled with large trees and surrounded by homes. McDuffie Park is sometimes called "Hidden Park" because it has no street-side access. (Compare with page 78.)

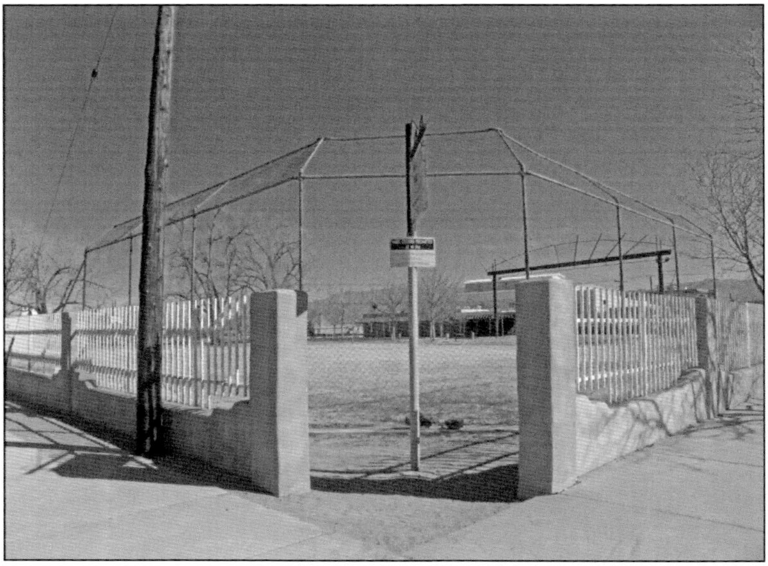

Looking northeast from the intersection of Sixth Street and Mountain Road towards the Wells Park Community Center, one can see what became of the 1940s walled horseshoe pit, now replaced by a backstop and fields next to the Wells Park Community Center. (Compare with page 70.)

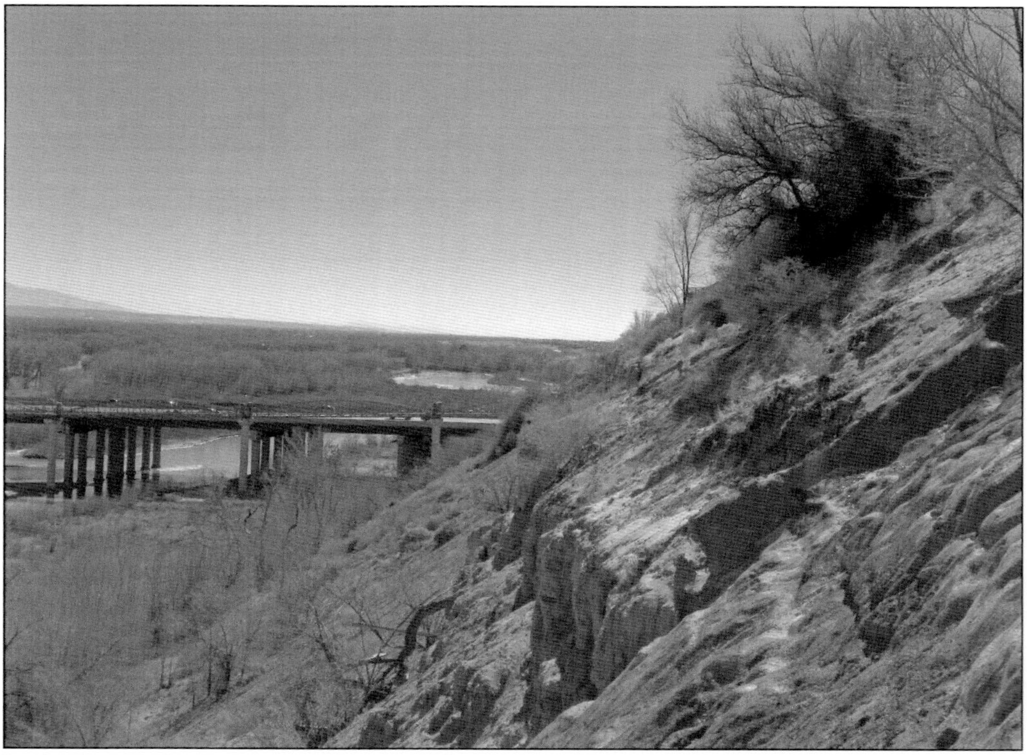

In the late 1960s, Interstate 40 continued westward across the Rio Grande and cut through an area known locally as the west bluff. In summer 2010, a multiuse bicycle and pedestrian bridge was built on the north side of the interstate to connect the west side of the river to the east side's Paseo del Bosque Trail. (Compare with page 79.)

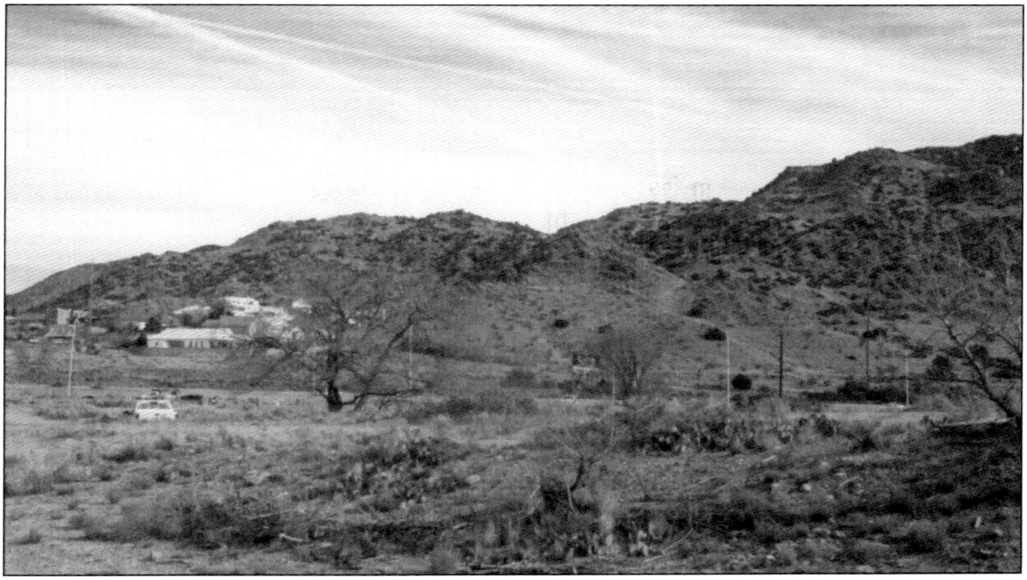

Plans for Little Beavertown to become the biggest draw on Route 66 and to rival Disneyland in popularity fizzled when Interstate 40 was built in the late 1960s. Various development plans for the property never came to pass, and in December 2010, the City of Albuquerque acquired 66 acres containing remnants of the amusement park plus a running stream along Tijeras Arroyo as its newest Open Space parcel. (Compare with page 80.)

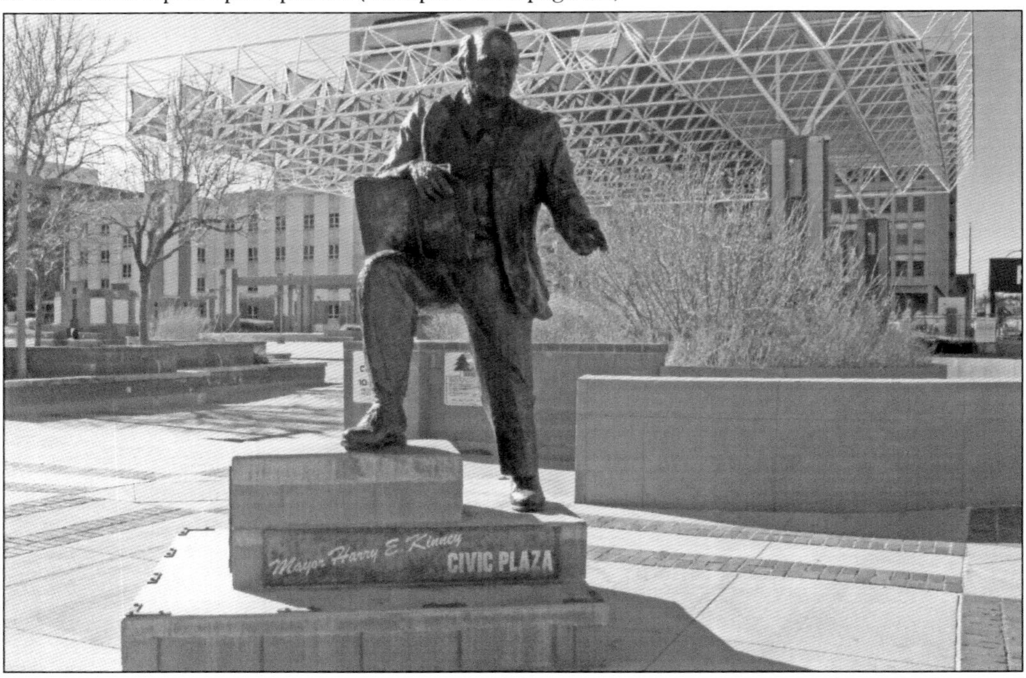

Harry Kinney's considerable contributions and lifetime of public service earned him the love and respect of generations. The two-time mayor of Albuquerque and Bernalillo County commissioner was also frequently seen driving a taxi and telling tales of his many exploits in later life. In his honor, the city's downtown civic plaza bears his name and a bronze statue. (Compare with page 103.)

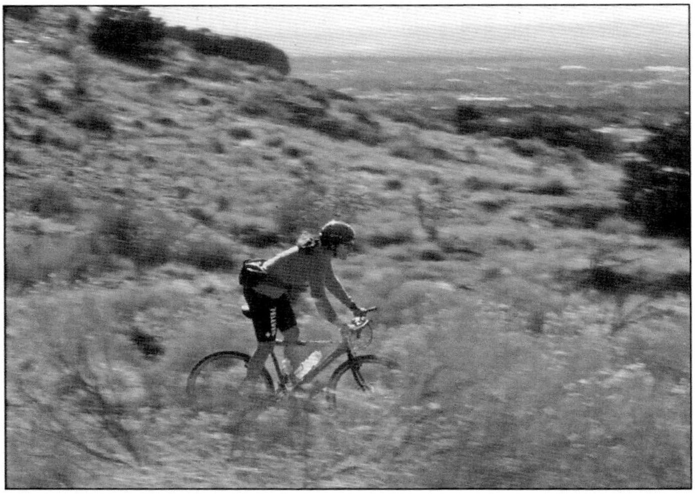

Albuquerque continues to be a premier bicycling town. With about 130 miles of paved trails and well over 100 miles of natural-surface trails in every part of the Open Space system, bicyclists have many choices for rides. While riders 100 years ago could not have imagined the changes in their sport—especially with mountain biking—they would have been thrilled at the prospect. (Compare with page 21.) (OSD.)

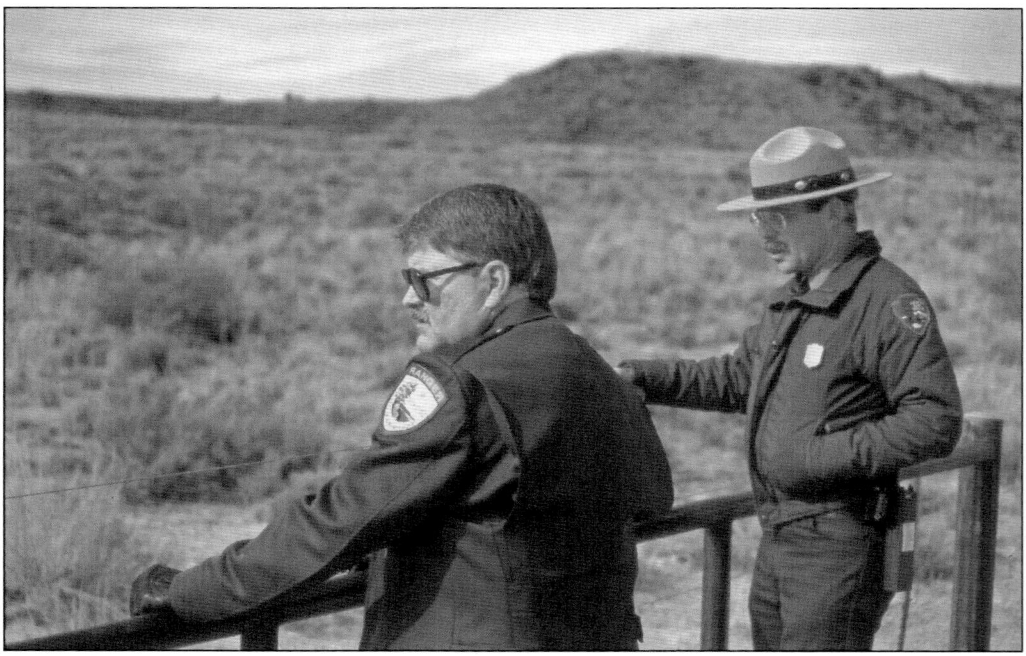

When Petroglyph National Monument was established in 1990, Congress decided on a bold new experiment in park management. Since the City of Albuquerque already owned over 4,000 acres in the new park, comanagement between the National Park Service and the city's Open Space Division was instituted. In this 1991 photograph, Open Space chief Stephen Thomas and NPS chief ranger Reed McCluskey embody that cooperative endeavor. (National Park Service.)

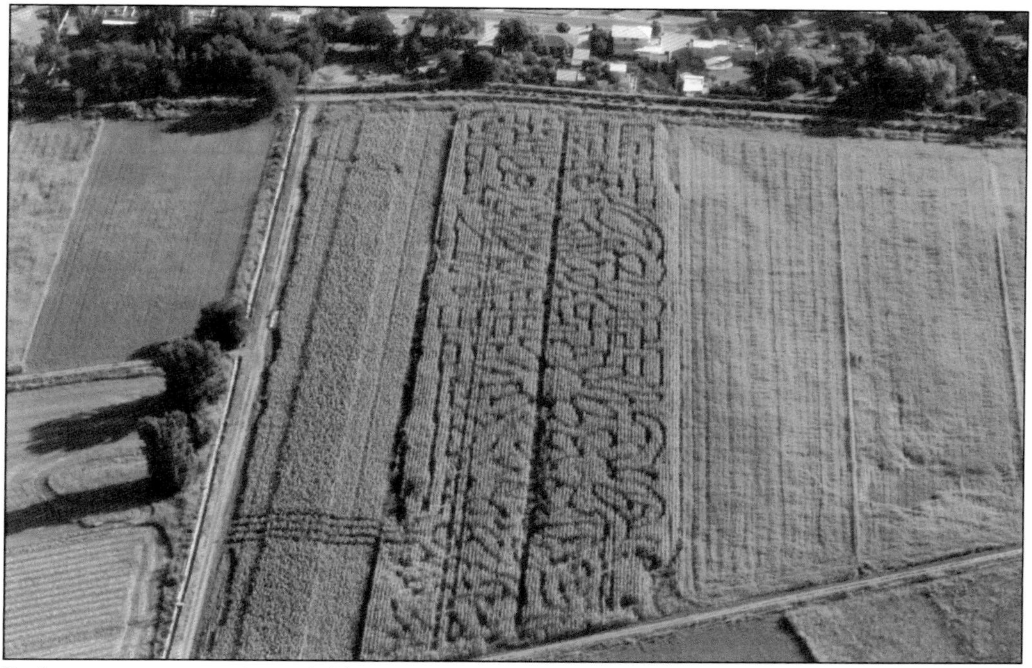

Each summer, acres of cornfields grown at Poblanos Fields by Rio Grande Community Farms transform into the annual maize maze. A collaborative effort between community farmers and the Open Space Division, the corn maze has now been a tradition for 13 years. (OSD.)

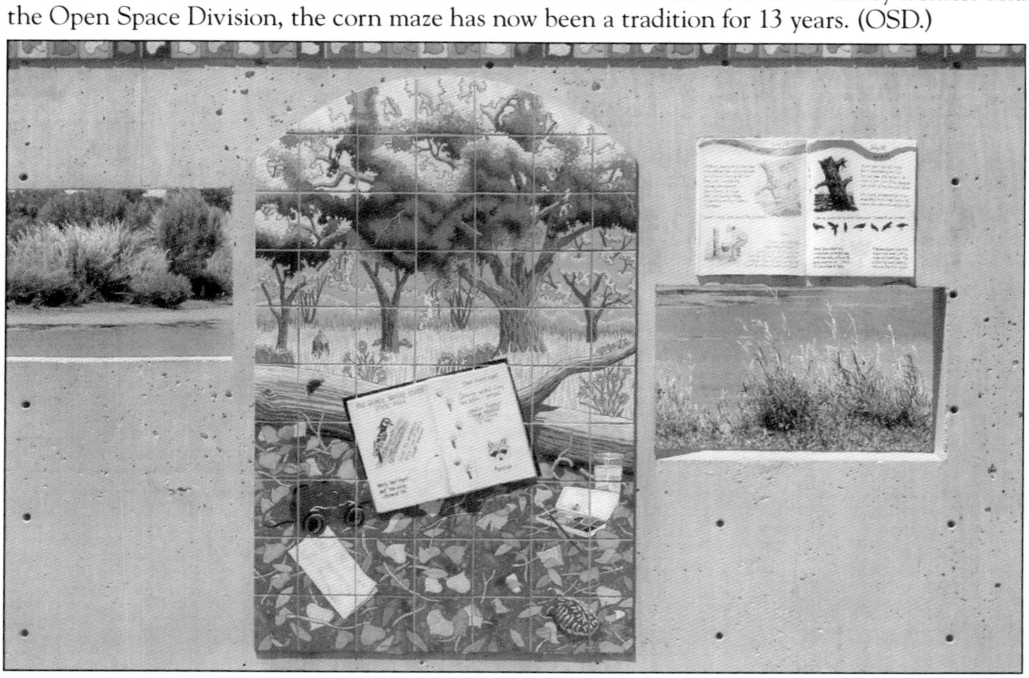

The Rio Grande Nature Center continues to thrive as a center for education and nature study. A wildlife viewing blind overlooking some of the center's wetlands has been beautified with a tile project by local artist extraordinaire Margy O'Brien, which was designed with Bonnie Schmader as pages from a nature journal.

Bibliography

Anella, Anthony and Mark Childs. *Never Say Goodbye: the Albuquerque Photographic Survey Project.* Albuquerque: Albuquerque Museum, 2000.

Balcomb, Kenneth C. *A Boy's Albuquerque, 1898–1912.* Albuquerque: University of New Mexico Press, 1980.

Biebel, Charles D. *Making the Most of It: Public Works in Albuquerque during the Great Depression, 1929–1942.* Albuquerque: Albuquerque Museum, 1986.

Fox, Nathan. *One When Step Matters.* Unpublished manuscript on file, City of Albuquerque Parks and Recreation Department, 2008.

Fye, Sandra. *Historic Photos of Albuquerque.* Nashville, TN: Turner Publishing, 2007.

Johnson, Byron A., ed., with Robert K. Dauner. *Early Albuquerque: A Photographic History.* Albuquerque: *Albuquerque Journal*, 1981.

Martin, Mary L. and Nathaniel Wolfgang-Price. *Greetings from Albuquerque.* Atglen, PA: Schiffer Publishing, 2007.

Palmer, Mo. *Albuquerque Then and Now.* San Diego: Thunder Bay Press, 2006.

Sargeant, Kathryn and Mary P. Davis. *Shining River, Precious Land: An Oral History of Albuquerque's North Valley.* Albuquerque: Albuquerque Museum, 1995.

INDEX